Exploring Institutional Logics in Technology-Mediated Higher Education

This book articulates the complexities inherent in higher education's multi-faceted response to the forces of mediatization—or how institutions change when their social communication gets mediated by technology—and introduces a novel perspective to comprehend them in a systematic way. By drawing on archival analysis and six organizational case studies, the author empirically traces the emergence of a cyber-cultural institution within higher education. As these case studies demonstrate, this new institutional logic requires creativity, individual recognition, and an underlying platform powered by cyber technologies and digitization of content. Using an analytical lens, this cyber-cultural perspective answers many questions about why faculty refuse to adopt online education, why students struggle with mediated teaching, and what possibly could be done to take online education to its next level.

Neelam Dwivedi is an Assistant Teaching Professor at Heinz College, Carnegie Mellon University, USA.

GW00569109

Routledge Research in Higher Education

For more information about this series, please visit: www.routledge.com/ Routledge-Research-in-Higher-Education/book-series/RRHE

Exploring Institutional Logics in Technology-Mediated Higher Education

Neelam Dwivedi

Routledge
Taylor & Francis Group

LONDON AND NEW YORK

First published 2019 by Routledge

2 Park Square, Milton Park, Abingdon, Oxfordshire OX14 4RN
52 Vanderbilt Avenue, New York, NY 10017

Routledge is an imprint of the Taylor & Francis Group, an informa business

First issued in paperback 2020

Library of Congress Cataloguing-in-Publication Data
A catalog record for this book has been requested

ISBN: 978-1-138-59880-5 (hbk)
ISBN: 978-0-367-66041-3 (pbk)

Typeset in Sabon
by Apex CoVantage, LLC

MIX
Paper from
responsible sources
FSC C013985

Printed in the United Kingdom
by Henry Ling Limited

To My Parents

Contents

Figures

Tables

Foreword

I am pleased and honored to write the foreword for this important book on technology-mediated changes coming to higher education. I first met the author, Dr. Neelam Dwivedi, in 2014 when she was a student in my qualitative research methods course. In her field study project for the course, she explored the effects of a new institution-wide administrative system in a large multi-campus university. Though it was *huge* in scope, I witnessed—through successive updates to our class—as she wrestled this complex topic into conceptual submission and produced an impressively coherent result. The next year I had another opportunity to witness her ability to address a large, complicated research problem in the field of higher education that balances theoretical insights and practical implications. I was invited to serve as a member of her dissertation committee. This time she was taking on a complex research problem on the academic side of higher education. She had decided to seek a theoretically coherent way to understand the impacts of technology mediation in higher education. It is that work that has resulted in this book. Through a combination of rigorous theoretical and field data analysis, Dr. Dwivedi has successfully captured the tensions that currently exist across the spectrum of higher education stakeholders. She characterizes this tension as resulting from a new cyber-cultural logic in higher education.

It is no exaggeration to say that there is, literally, a revolution underway in higher education. For thousands of years, the professor was the embodiment of the university: the focal point of knowledge—both its generation and its dissemination. But that is rapidly changing. As I read this book, I found myself continuously reflecting on my own career as a professor, which has been played out against the backdrop of the growth of technology-mediated education. When I was an undergraduate and graduate student in the 1970s, students still viewed the professor as the source of knowledge—and took notes in class. This was my image of higher education when I began my career in the 1980s. But very soon things began to change. And by the last year that I taught, 2017, half of my teaching assignments were conducted online. Over the past four decades, technology has been turning higher education inside out—with no end in sight.

Accompanying the increasingly dominant role of information technology in higher education has come a fundamental change in the professor's role. The job of the professor had been to generate, manage, and disseminate to students knowledge about a particular discipline. And the administration of higher education was originally about developing and nurturing the best professors as the means of enabling the best education for university students. In this model, information content was managed indirectly. As such, higher education administration was about people; the hiring and management of professors subsumed the management of the knowledge with which professors engaged. In that regard, a professor was like a priest or therapist: the person and the disciplinary information were inextricably linked. But now higher education, thanks to technology, is being deconstructed. Just as the invention of the printing press led to the separation of knowledge from the author, the roles that had previously been enacted by a single professor are now being assigned to a myriad of different types of higher education professionals: content developer, course manager, and instructional designer, to name a few. Consequently, the "professor" of another era is now one of many actors in the business of higher education. Dr. Dwivedi has made analogies between the professor, on the one hand, and the poet or playwright, on the other, and between the professor and the actor who performs the plays or poems.

To say whether all of this is for better or worse is not the goal of this book. The transformation of higher education is well underway with strong forces fueling its progression. Enabling technology, a desire to lower the cost of education, private sector interest in economic opportunities, consumer expectations, and the democratization of higher education are all factors.

As is so often the case with times of significant change, it is very challenging to step back and comprehend just what is going on. *This* is the contribution of Dr. Dwivedi's book. She employs a rigorous research approach and innovative theoretical insights to provide the reader with an accessible way of understanding what we are currently experiencing. She does so by articulating the current status of higher education as caught in a series of "tensions." A multiplicity of institutional identities, conflicting teaching schemas, content stratification, and cyber-cultural identity emerge as the key themes characterizing this era.

When considering audiences for this book, I conclude that anyone connected to or interested in higher education would want to read this book. It should be required reading for individuals who are currently in or considering a professorial career so that they can better understand their profession. The treatment of teaching schemas brings to mind the contribution this book would make to college teacher training courses as well as to those engaged in learning design. It will also enable university administrators to better understand the landscape they are navigating. In addition, those responsible for directing the future of higher education (both policy makers and investors influencing the not-for-profit and for-profit realms) would do well to read this book. As technology mediation moves to lower-level education, I see this book as valuable reading for those working in the K–12 domain as well. Technology professionals who are facilitating this revolution in higher education could benefit from understanding the impacts of their work on various stakeholders and, perhaps, become more sensitized to the sources of resistance they might encounter. And last but certainly not least, scholars engaged in higher education research need to have this book on their shelves to inspire further research into the tensions emanating from this new cyber-cultural logic in higher education that are identified and analyzed in this book.

December 10, 2018
Eileen Trauth, PhD
Professor Emeritus
College of Information Sciences & Technology
The Pennsylvania State University

Preface

The higher education field is perceived as an economic industry by some and a social entity by others. A related debate is whether higher education is a private or a social good. Amidst these conflicting viewpoints, education is increasingly getting mediated by technologies leading to changes in policies, procedures, and practices, often bringing challenges that need to be addressed. The traditional higher education organizations are responding to these challenges in complex and often contentious ways. The use of technology in teaching practice at the resident as well as online settings is being questioned, leading to another debate about whether technology is really helping or hurting student learning. While these debates provoke thought, they polarize constituents and are often biased. They create roadblocks in progressive transformations toward increasing access to education, improving quality, or reducing cost. Such tensions can be resolved by expanding our perspective that can allow better comprehension of the dynamics governing higher education. And for that, instead of casting higher education narrowly as a social or an economic entity, we need to understand the higher education's multi-dimensional role in our societies and how this role is perceived by its constituents.

The question then is twofold. First, are there perspectives other than those that view higher education as a social or an economic entity that could help resolve or transcend such differences? Second, are there other fields similar to higher education who traversed the path to mediated communication and could offer us some insights into how higher education should navigate its journey to digitization? For this purpose, I conducted a theory-driven multi-level qualitative field study and applied two theories—the theory of institutional logics and the mediatization theory—to come up with a comprehensive framework that addresses some of these questions. I first zoomed into the teaching practice as one of the core functions of higher education and analyzed how it is perceived by teachers, students, and administrators. This was done through a combination of organizational and field-level study. The former was done through 6 organizational case studies, and the latter involved a field-level analysis if archives spanning over 2 decades and covering over 20 field-level agencies that engage in policy advocacy. I engaged the theory of institutional logics to uncover institutional pluralism that captures higher education's multidimensionality and explains several dynamics summarized next:

1. Higher education in general and teaching practice, in particular, subscribe to a spectrum of institutional logics that extend beyond the bipolar views discussed earlier.
2. These institutional logics coexist in a complex institutional environment conflicting and cooperating with each other in various ways.
3. This institutional pluralism makes change contentious and therefore a challenge. It, in turn, leads to the impression that higher education is too slow and resistant to change.
4. It is this institutional pluralism that has given endurance to the higher education field and made it a highly esteemed sector.

I applied the theory of mediatization, which explains how institutions change when their social communication gets mediated by technology. Fields where communication is central to their function—e.g., performing arts, politics, and religion have undergone mediatization resulting in similar transformations and challenges. Such fields are called cultural institutions as they engage in the exchange of symbolic content. Viewing higher education as a cultural institution, I traced how the mediation of its content-exchange is leading to its mediatization, which in turn is not only changing its prevailing institutional logics but also leading to the emergence of a new cyber-cultural logic.

To reveal institutional pluralism prevailing in the higher education field and to identify changes and emergence of new logics are two important contributions of this study. I have integrated these findings into a framework that addresses as well as transcends the extant debate about why higher education is failing to improve on various fronts despite an urgent need as well as best of intentions and resources. The framework also points to the potential future directions that can be explored to bring sustainable change to the field of higher education.

The book is divided into seven chapters. In Chapter 1, I introduce the basic problem statement and present the gaps in extant research that my research tries to address. In Chapter 2, I elaborate the theories—institutional logics and mediatization—and then develop an integrated analytical framework as my research design to analyze teaching practice in the field of higher education. I also explain how I sampled and collected data from the field, organization, and individual levels. For readers who are interested in the details of my research methodology and techniques, I have further elaborated on the epistemology, the evaluation, and the analysis approach in Appendix B.

In Chapter 3, I discuss key findings at the macro level, focusing on broad patterns and emerging trends in the higher education field. In Chapter 4, I elaborate the findings at an organizational and an individual level, applying some of the theoretical constructs from the theory of institutional logics. I combine the two sets of findings from previous two chapters in Chapter 5 and use mediatization theory to analyze three core entities of teaching practice—teacher, student, and content to draw out how mediatization is impacting each one of them. I synthesize all these findings in Chapter 6 into an integrated view and develop a comprehensive framework that explains the set of prevailing and emerging institutional logics in higher education. Finally, in Chapter 7, I discuss the theoretical and practical implications of these findings and how they can chart a future course of inquiry.

There are two terms that need careful interpretation in this text. The first is distance education, which comprises all forms of education where the student and the teacher are separated in space and/or time. Based on the technology of the day, the distance education models have undergone many changes with the most recent model using Internet technologies generally referred to as 'online education.' However, the terms 'distance' and 'online' education are often used interchangeably. I too will use them interchangeably to avoid making the discussion too technology specific unless required by the context and to allow easier reference to other texts relevant to the topic.

The second term is 'institution.' In the higher education field, the organizations offering education are referred to as 'colleges and universities' or as 'higher education institutions.' Both pose a problem in this context. The former doesn't cover the upcoming forms of organizations, such as MOOCs and the latter conflicts with the term 'institution' in the theory of institutional logic. For these reasons, I will refer to all such entities offering higher education simply as higher education organizations, unless required otherwise by the context.

Acknowledgments

This book is about teaching, and through this book, I express my gratitude to all my teachers who have enriched my educational journey. First and foremost is my PhD advisor Dr. Sandeep Purao. He not only encouraged me to undertake such a project but also lent me free rein to discover what I truly wanted to do. He patiently listened to all the new research ideas that struck my fancy and never rejected them. Like a true coach, he offered his objective critique that sharpened my thinking and helped me focus. Thank you, Sandeep, for being my coach!

Another teacher who I would like to thank is Dr. Eileen Trauth who has been an inspiration and a mentor throughout my doctoral journey and beyond. I learned qualitative research methodology from her, and then she agreed to be my PhD committee member. She is a consummate scholar and a true teacher. She expects a lot from her students and she gives back a lot more in her honest and valuable feedback. Her responsiveness made me see her as a dependable guide that I could always reach out to. Her critiques and reviews have shaped my research in ways that I will always be grateful for.

As I navigated through my doctoral path, there were many individuals who inspired and supported me in unexpected ways and at unexpected times. I would always be thankful to late Dr. Donna Kuga who not only welcomed me into her campus as I entered academia but also fully supported me in my pursuit for a PhD. Ms. Dee Mooney, our academic assistant, was my go-to person to share my troubles and travails. Her simple but reassuring response, "You can do it," always worked wonders for my otherwise dwindling optimism. Dr. Mary Beth Rosson, our associate dean, trusted me that I could handle the rigor of a PhD program along with my other commitments. Dr. Luke Zhang, also my advisor, offered a new perceptive to assess my research findings by helping me zoom out and look at the forest, and not just count the trees. Dr. Rayne Sperling, my committee member, also helped me fine tune my findings to align with the research in the field of education. Dr. Lee Erickson, a fellow non-traditional student who had just graduated when I started, greatly inspired me by sharing her experiences and helpful do's and don'ts in the PhD pathways.

Conducting doctoral research and writing it up in one's first book are life-changing experiences and I am fortunate that I had so many well-wishers helping and encouraging me at every step. I was a non-traditional doctoral student working full time as an instructor, commuting 300 miles every week to attend classes with peers almost half my age. But as I started my research, a series of coincidences brought me close to a friend, Dr. Sushma Mishra, whose companionship helped me overcome whatever sense of alienation I felt because of my unusual profile. Without her wisdom and help at every critical juncture, I would not have been able to complete this research. Thank you, Sushma!

And then there are those individuals who I cannot name because of the anonymity needed in my research. They were vital in my research as they allowed me to interview them in their organizational settings and helped me understand their day-to-day work. They welcomed me into their worlds, shared their thoughts about their teaching and learning experiences, and introduced me to their colleagues and students. My research stands on their inputs and I am ever so thankful to them for their kind contribution.

Finally, while the research activities took me around, the actual 'research' happened at home through long hours of reading, writing, and staring into the void. During those times, I always had a friend and companion to bounce my thoughts off on. Ashu, my husband, helped me find my balance between the abstract and the real. His keen listening, quick assessments, and sharp questions helped me ground my research to the world around me. Thank you, Ashu, for being my anchor!

1 Undergraduate Education in the US

Projections and Gaps

There are two deeply contrasting views about the higher education sector in the US. The first view is that it is a highly esteemed sector that represents the most widely adopted Western model of education in the world (Scott 2010; Altbach, Gumport, and Berdahl 2011). The US is considered a world leader in the higher education domain as well as in research. This view is supported by the sector's rich history, its many successes, and worldwide reputation. It has close to 4,800 institutions granting postsecondary year degrees and generates over $500 billion of revenue per year (McFarland et al. 2017).

But the contrasting view is that the US higher education is ripe for disruption. This view is largely based on an economic outlook using which some have compared the higher education sector with sectors such as manufacturing, retail, and service industry while others have projected higher education's changing DNA to its complete annihilation (Economist 2014; Anson 2007; Martin 2011; Galloway 2017). Peter Drucker predicted in 1997 that the big university campuses would be relics in 30 years (as quoted in Lenzner and Johnson 1997). Christensen and Eyring (2011) applied the theory of disruptive innovation to predict higher education's fate as similar to that of technology industries who lost their strong foothold when low-cost innovators swept their established products out of the market in a few years. As quoted by Selingo (2016), Christensen projected in 2011 that "within 10 to 15 years, the bottom quarter of the market will either go out of business or merge" (5). The frenzied hype around online education led some to say that MOOC is to higher education what Napster was to the music industry (Shirky 2012). These perspectives apply the principles of markets to analyze higher education, comparing it with industries that were disrupted by online technologies. They do explain recent transformations to some extent but ignore higher education's challenge beyond economic sustainability, thus failing to guide future policy regarding higher education's broader role in our society.

A look at the statistics also doesn't offer much help. From 2000 to 2014, the number of postsecondary institutions that participate in the Title IV federal student financial aid programs increased by 10%, the higher education sector's revenue went up from $300 billion to $567 billion, and the total undergraduate enrollments increased by 32%. But the cost of undergraduate education more than doubled, and its four-year graduation rate stagnates at around 55%. Although online education has grown since the government's Title IV funding approval in 1998, only 12.3% of undergraduate students are enrolled exclusively in distance education (IES-NCES 2017b, 2017a; McFarland et al. 2017). Universities are asking the faculty to teach online courses, but the faculty acceptance to online teaching is not moving beyond 30% since 2002 (Allen and Seaman 2015).

These gaps between the projections and the reality beg the question: Are we missing something? Is there an alternate point of view that could explain some of these anomalies? To find such a way, I conducted this research to capture the perspectives held by constituents in the field that directly and indirectly influence the inner workings of the higher education field. The motivation was to step beyond the economic viewpoint to analyze the contemporary forces at play. As the picture of these perspectives developed, the gaps announced themselves, much like in a jigsaw puzzle, revealing a distinctly unique face of higher education in general and teaching practice in particular. While these gaps were visible to some extent at an intuitive level, I bring them forth empirically and synthesize my findings with what the research in the field of higher education has already noted.

Prevailing Perspectives

The evolution of the higher education sector in the US has shifted approximately every 30 years since its foundation in the 17th century, thereby having lived through about ten generations (Geiger 2011). Starting with the generations of colonial colleges followed by republican education, and the classical denominational colleges of the late 19th century, the role of higher education continued to be

> cloaked with a public purpose, with a responsibility to the past and the present and the future. The college was expected to give more than it received from the particular young men who were being prepared to do society's work.
>
> (Rudolph 1962, 177)

The higher education sector in the US reached its golden era of academic revolution in the mid-20th century but its transformations since the latter half of the 20th century are viewed as shifting from a "civilizing agency" serving the society (Clark and Trow 1966, 19) to an industry competing in a marketplace (Slaughter and Rhoades 2011). Its foundational role as a social institution, where a social institution is "an organized activity that maintains, reproduces or adapts itself to implement values that have been widely held and firmly structured by the society," is being overshadowed by other more pressing economic priorities (Gumport 2000, 73).

Following World War I, massification and vocationalism began to change the intellectual fabric of higher education, which in turn led to its shift from a social to an industry outlook (Clark and Trow 1966). The function of higher education dramatically diversified from simply educating the elite to "educating the masses, advancing knowledge through research, contributing to economic development by employing and producing workers, and developing industry applications" (Gumport 2000, 74). In the 1970s, enrollments slowed down, the Higher Education Act got amended to make federal loans available directly to students, academic research started getting privatized and thus academic capitalism emerged in the field of higher education (Geiger 2011; Slaughter and Rhoades 2004). The metaphor of higher education changed from being a social institution to that of an industry, and the vocabulary changed from trust and prestige to market competition, accountability, customer service, and profit. The focus of higher education shifted from the quality of learning to access and then cost, changing higher education's focus to efficient administration and management of services (Scott 2010). The challenge of balancing the social versus industrial identity led researchers to offer higher education's critical assessments (Gumport 2000), normative prescriptions (Zemsky, Wegner, and Massy 2005; Hendrickson et al. 2013), and analytical explanations (Slaughter and Rhoades 2004).

The post-World War II period from 1945–75 also witnessed what Geiger (2011) termed as the phase of academic revolution. In this era, the college-student population grew several folds, and the federal largesse boosted scientific research that "produced an ephemeral golden age in American higher education" (61). The academic role acquired a scholarly status, making research, teaching, and service integral to its definition. The perspective that aligns with this image was termed by Clark and Trow (1966) as an academic culture, which identifies with faculty members' intellectual concerns and students' passion for pursuing knowledge. Such a mindset was encouraged in research universities as well as liberal arts colleges that valued scholarly pursuits. And teaching was

> based primarily in the arts and sciences, sought to engage students in a broad range of human thought and achievement and to foster the habits of inquiry that lead to both heightened understanding and the creation and refinement of knowledge.
>
> (Zemsky, Wegner, and Massy 2005, 128)

While this mindset still governs some aspects of higher education, it is getting diluted with capitalism taking over academic priorities (Slaughter and Rhoades 2011).

Apart from these three perspectives—social, industry, and academic—there are finer variations that reflect a spectrum of contradicting missions in the field. For example, liberal arts versus practical and vocational training; prestige versus profits; and quality versus access versus efficiency (Scott 2010). Small liberal arts colleges have been traditionally associated with the mission of citizen building, representing social institution more closely. However, large private and public universities are portrayed as closer to capitalistic institutions following the industry, especially private ones (Slaughter and Rhoades 2004; Altbach 1999).

The turn of the 21st century introduced a new dimension to this mix as information and communication technologies started altering the mechanisms adopted by higher education to achieve the variety of its missions. The online education phenomenon is just one in the series of attempts made by the sector to promote distance education. The distance education started as being paper-based, and as technologies evolved, it adopted radio, television, and now the Internet. According to a report published by the Institute of Education Sciences—National Center of Education Statistics (IES-NCES), the percentage of students enrolled in undergraduate degree programs in the non-profit sector (public or private) is over 90%. From within this population, the percentage of students enrolled exclusively in four-year distance education courses is 14%. In comparison, the percentage of the student population enrolled in online education in the for-profit sector is 61%. These statistics may lead one to think that online education is driven by profit motivation, much like an industry. But there are many non-profit organizations such as the University of People and Saylor Academy that have adopted online mechanisms to pursue their social motivations. The mediation of instructional content manifests on both sides of the social vs. industry spectrum, irrespective of profit motivations or lack thereof. However, when viewed through an academic perspective, online education is failing to gain acceptance because many teachers are resisting the mediation of their teaching. Different stakeholders in the field of higher education interpret this resistance differently. Some attribute this resistance to the observation that faculty members perceive online education to be of lower quality because of the loss of face-to-face interaction and lack of student engagement. Others think that most academics view online education as a purely economic venture that deviates from the loftier academic mission. Some also think that teachers view online education as a threat to job security, or simply do not want to change their old ways of doing things. Whatever may be the reasons behind this resistance, it is evident that there are factors other than profit or social welfare that contribute to the success or failure of online education. This means that the cost of higher education or its social motivations may be necessary indicators but not sufficient to comprehend higher education's present or project its future.

Zooming into the academia's resistance to online education brings an unexplored dimension into focus, and that dimension is the digitized instructional content. Shifting our focus from the higher education's cost to its content opens up new perspectives. It allows higher education to be viewed as a cultural institution, as has been previously characterized (Williams 1981; Thompson 1995) but has not yet been empirically explored. Cultural institutions engage in the "activity of producing, transmitting and receiving meaningful symbolic forms" (Thompson 1995, 16). They "involve some form of creativity in their production [. . .] are concerned with the generation and communication of symbolic meaning, and [. . .] their output embodies, at least potentially, some form of intellectual property" (Throsby 2001, 4). However, the creativity underlying this symbolic content, especially in teaching, has remained hidden or dormant within four walls of a classroom in resident education models, and loosely coupled with rest of the organization (Weick 1976). With technology now capturing and mediating the teaching function, this symbolic content has been exposed to the outside world, much like any other cultural good, thereby forcing higher education's cultural characteristics to come to the fore.

Viewing higher education as a cultural institution is based on two foundational premises. The first is that higher education creates and disseminates knowledge as symbolic content, putting it in the category of cultural institutions as explained earlier (Thompson 1995; Williams 1981). Second, a historical comparison of other cultural institutions, especially performing arts, with transformations currently unfolding in higher education reveals many parallels, indicating how higher education is forging a path similar to the one traced by institutions of music and theater when technology mediated the creation and distribution of their art. They too had their traditional model of delivery in a face-to-face setting disrupted by the emergence of recording technologies. The content could be captured in media, separated from the creator, transformed in many ways, and distributed widely for consumption. This research posits that any intellectual or creative content, once captured, affords similar opportunities.

To explore this line of thought, I needed a theoretical framework that can help capture all perspectives, delineate their boundaries, identify conflicts within and among them, and explain how technology is influencing them. I present such a framework in the next chapter that integrates two theories—the theory of institutional logics and the theory of mediatization. Institutional logics represent various perspectives, and mediatization represents how these perspectives change when technology mediates social communication. These conceptualizations seek to capture prevailing institutional logics concerning teaching in higher education and explain how mediation of teaching is mediatizing these logics. They also try to uncover emerging logics that could not only explain contemporary transformations underway in the higher education sector but also help develop a comprehensive view of teaching practice in higher education.

Emerging Picture

When I shifted the focus of analysis to symbolic content and applied the aforementioned integrated theoretical framework to the field of higher education in the US, a spectrum of seven institutional logics emerged. Six of them are prevailing logics while the seventh is a new rising logic as education is getting mediatized. The prevailing logics are academic, community, corporation, market, state, and social. The emerging logic is what I termed as cyber-cultural because it is rooted in the cultural component of symbolic content as well as in the cyber component of mediated education. These seven logics coexist, collaborating with some while conflicting with the others. Their boundaries are defined by their contradictions and the resulting tensions. A brief preview is provided here to help the reader contextualize the chapters that follow.

The academic logic pertains to the profession that the college and university teachers have traditionally belonged to. They view higher education as a frontier for human inquiry and a platform for developing and sharing subject matter expertise. They perceive themselves as free thinkers who pursue educational goals based on the tenets of academic freedom, tenure, and shared governance. But these tenets are increasingly being challenged since the emergence of corporation logic within higher education organizations and the forces of market logic in the field. Corporations seek efficiency and standardization through an elaborate bureaucratic structure that views academicians as employees. Markets take a transactional approach where they view the student as a customer and education as a product to be sold within a highly competitive landscape. With the corporation and the market logics gaining their foothold, the state logic has emerged as a regulating entity trying to ensure that the higher education organizations do not deviate from providing education in a responsible manner.

As the administrators of higher education organizations are trying to ensure economic viability by advancing corporation and market logic, they often come in conflict with the academic logic reflecting the historic academic versus administrative tussle. But despite their differences, they are part of a community that represents the internal facing logic of a college or a university to which the students, staff, and teachers feel connected to. This community manifests internally through group associations, clubs, sports, cultural activities, and interpersonal relationships that contribute toward students' overall growth as a person. When this community tries to fulfill its role as a citizen of its larger society, it reveals its external face and represents the social logic that tries to bring social equity and development through teaching, research, and service.

Amidst these logics, the emergence of technology-mediated education, especially its most recent form of online education, is giving rise to the new cyber-cultural logic. It is bringing out the education's cultural logic to the forefront. While academic logic is finding this phenomenon to be against its traditional values, the corporation and the market logics are looking at it as a harbinger of a much-needed disruption. The state logic is supporting cyber-cultural logic because of the technology's potential to make higher education more accountable by tracking and reporting quality metrics. The community logic is finding itself challenged as the sense of community is severely compromised in the virtual world. The social logic, on the one hand, is supporting cyber-cultural logic as it is making education more accessible, but on the other, it is discouraged by the fact that the virtual student body no longer belongs to a common society to which it could contribute.

This push and pull among seven institutional logics answer many questions such as why faculty members are resisting online education, or why students still seek classroom-based teaching despite the conveniences offered by online education. The emerging picture also showcases the multiple roles played by teachers as knowledge experts (gurus), learning facilitators (coaches), and attention engagers (artists). With instructional content getting digitized, these transformations are demanding a teacher's role to be redefined. Viewing education as a cultural activity positions instructional content to be treated like a work of art that needs to be designed, developed, packaged, and presented in a manner in which other cultural institutions, especially performing arts, have historically been doing since they underwent mediatization. I describe the path and the methodology I took to arrive at the emerging picture described earlier in the following chapters.

2 Finding Perspectives

Institutional Logics

Founded on the heritage of philosophers such as Durkheim, Weber, Marx, Veblen, and Commons, institutionalism in general and the institutional theory, in particular, have a rich and complex history (Scott 2005; DiMaggio 1991). While acknowledging the theory's history and its multiple variants, my research focuses on the aspects derived from neo-institutionalism and orients toward organizational sociology. It draws largely from the frameworks proposed by Friedland and Alford (1991) and Thornton, Ocasio, and Lounsbury (2012). The underpinning thesis of these frameworks is that the institutional logics offer the rationale behind day-to-day activities conducted by various social entities. Friedland and Alford (1991) conceptualized society as an inter-institutional system of logics—mainly capitalist market, bureaucratic state, democracy, nuclear family, and Christian religion in Western societies—that are available to individuals and organizations to shape their preferences and practices. Each of these logics influences social entities in different ways—e.g., capitalism brings commoditization, the bureaucratic state brings regulation, democracy brings voting practice, and religion brings prayer. Fields, organizations, and individuals draw from these logics variedly to guide their actions and decisions.

Thornton and Ocasio (2008) defined institutional logics as "socially constructed, historical patterns of material practices, assumptions, values, beliefs, and rules by which individuals produce and reproduce their material subsistence, organize time and space, and provide meaning to their social reality" (107). Building on the inter-institutional framework of logics as proposed by Friedland and Alford (1991), Thornton, Ocasio, and Lounsbury (2012) further conceptualized society as a nearly decomposable system of institutional orders comprising seven ideal types—family, community, religion, state, market, profession, and corporation (refer to Appendix D: Inter-institutional System Ideal Types). They used the concept of ideal types that are logically pure forms that reflect the exaggeration of certain aspects of their respective logics. They are analytic categories developed as typologies (Doty and Glick 1994).

The institutional logics identified by researchers in various contexts are essentially ideal types—e.g., editorial logic and market logic were two ideal types identified in an empirical study focusing on the changes in the educational publishing industry in the US (Thornton and Ocasio 1999). Organizations and individuals draw selectively from these pure forms based on their cultural and social preferences. Ideal types provide "an abstract model used to gauge the relative distance of the observations from the pure form" (Thornton, Ocasio, and Lounsbury 2012, 51). Prior empirical research using this theory in the higher education domain has shown some of these logics, although manifesting differently in different contexts. For example, Townley (1997) analyzed performance appraisals in the context of Canadian higher education and found ideal liberal academy and market-rationality influencing the phenomenon of interest. Lounsbury and Pollack (2001) analyzed the institutionalization of service-learning practice in higher education in the US and found open-system vs. closed-system logics coexisting in that context. Dunn and Jones (2010) traced how science logic is replacing the care logic in medical education. Scott (2010) argued that over a period, the institutional logics that have emerged in the higher education sector had favored education quality, cost, or access. Their importance has varied with the role of institutional actors. More recently, Gonzales and Ayers (2018) analyzed various empirical studies conducted in community colleges and found that institutional logics of family, democracy, religion, state, and neoliberalism as a form of capitalism are deployed to form labor expectations set forth for the faculty.

While all these studies exemplify the variety of ways in which the theory of institutional logics has been applied to analyze different phenomenon, there are two aspects pertinent to the phenomenon of interest at hand. First is the notion of institutional pluralism which signifies that more than one logic informs a field. If the number of logics informing a field is high, it means higher plurality which then means that "the degree of variation across organizations will be greater; that is, organizational identities and practices are more likely to be distinctive" (Thornton, Ocasio, and Lounsbury 2012, 136). The second related aspect is that amidst this plurality, there exists one dominant logic which becomes the lens used by most social actors to elaborate and analyze a phenomenon. For example, according to Gumport (2000), the market logic has acquired dominance in the field of higher education that has led the scholars to use economic theories to analyze online education. The drawback of adopting the dominant institutional logic to elaborate and analyze a phenomenon is that "these elaborations subsequently become factors in the reproduction of these institutions and thus contribute to their hegemony, whether through socialization of institutional personnel or formulation of public policy" (Friedland and Alford 1991, 260). While the industry logic provides useful insights, it perceives individuals imparting education as with little or no creative agency. It ignores the value of teaching as a creative act and converts it into an industrial process to be efficiently delivered as per prescribed instructions. However, research shows that teaching as a profession is taken up by highly creative intellectuals who cannot be viewed as automatons (Sawyer 2004; Horng et al. 2005; Bramwell et al. 2011). The analogy of manufacturing or service industry fails to view teachers and students engaged in the intellectual and creative act of knowledge exchange, thereby ignoring a critical perspective.

This failure of extant research to view higher education as playing a role beyond selling products or offering services motivates this research. While remaining neutral to the higher education's role to fulfill social or economic goals, it strives to reveal an alternative view that engages the creative side of the field. It brings forth the creativity of teaching practice into the discussion, which the social vs. industry debate has largely ignored. Through this repositioning, it strives to surface the underlying principles that guide teachers in their day-to-day jobs; principles that have not been considered in understanding the institutional logics governing the field of higher education.

There are several aspects of this framework that require systematic application and analysis. For this purpose, the following sections elaborate three characteristics critical to comprehend the framework: building blocks of institutional logics, dimensions of their manifestations, and forms of their manifestations.

Building Blocks

In the framework of the inter-institutional system of institutional logics shown in Appendix D, there are seven ideal types representing seven institutional orders. Each ideal type is further decomposed into elemental categories that uniquely identify each ideal type. These elemental categories are drawn from the "established social science concepts" and capture "analytical interpretation that should highlight key concepts and foreshadow testable hypotheses" (Thornton, Ocasio, and Lounsbury 2012, 59). Each elemental category is "a mutually exclusive alternative to the elemental categories of the other institutional orders" (72). In this manner, the content of each cell of this matrix captures the unique characteristic of each institutional order. This matrix with columns as institutional orders and rows as categories represents the building blocks of society. The framework presents nine such categories, but their selection can vary with the research context. While I draw their interpretations from empirical findings in my study, the following descriptions articulate their use within the framework discussed earlier:

The first elemental category—root metaphor—is the association of the institution with an analogy to the natural world that "obscures its purely human origins" to be sustainable (DiMaggio and Powell 1991, 25). Individuals and organizations use these metaphors to "perceive and categorize their activity and infuse it with meaning and value" (Thornton, Ocasio, and Lounsbury 2012, 54). For example, the root metaphor for the market is a transaction, for the state—a redistribution mechanism, for the corporation—a hierarchy, and for the community—a common boundary.

The second elemental category is the source of identity from where the social actors draw their identities, either in terms of group or category memberships or identification with particular social roles. The sources for category identities may be from entities such as an actor's industry, profession, organization, or nation. The role identities are in terms of relations with other social actors, such as a parent or a professor. Identities often become the centers around which communities coalesce, for example, communities of practice. Thornton (2004) proposed the source of identity for markets as being faceless, whereas those for corporations as bureaucratic roles. Thornton, Ocasio, and Lounsbury (2012) identified the source of identities for market logic to be a business model and for corporation logic to the management or the administration.

The third category is the source of legitimacy. Meyer and Rowan (1977) defined it as a source of formal organization structure that may not be related to how technical work activity is coordinated and controlled. It is an external means of establishing that an organization is "acting on collectively valued purposes in a proper and adequate manner" (349). Scott (2008) defined legitimacy as "a condition reflecting perceived consonance with relevant rules and laws, normative support, or alignment with cultural-cognitive frameworks." It is a "symbolic value to be displayed in a manner such that it is visible to outsiders" (59–60). Thornton (2004) empirically traced the change in the source of legitimacy in the higher education publishing field in terms of how the editorial logic that derived its legitimacy from personal reputation was being replaced by the market logic whose source of legitimacy is the firm's market position. Thornton, Ocasio, and Lounsbury (2012) proposed the sources of legitimacy for a family as unconditional loyalty and for the market as the share price.

The fourth category is the source of authority that represents the positional, relational, and economic determinants of leadership power and privilege (Thornton, Ocasio, and Lounsbury 2012). Positional power is inherent in the actor's role or position, whereas the relational power is drawn from the structure of relationships among actors. The economic sources of power are those issues that influence the position of a firm in the market. While there are these three variants of the sources of power and authority, the prevailing institutional logics legitimize one or more of these sources of power. Institutional logics "define the rules of the game by which executive power is gained, maintained, and lost in organizations" (Thornton 2004, 72). Tracing the history of changes in the higher education publishing industry, Thornton (2004) found the importance of economic determinants increasing and the effect of positional or relational determinants on leadership succession decreasing. The theoretical framework at a societal level shows the source of authority for profession as professional association, which is relational, and for the state, it is bureaucratic domination that is positional (Thornton, Ocasio, and Lounsbury 2012).

The fifth category is the basis of norms which represents the criteria for establishing what is appropriate or not. For a family, it is household membership, for a market it is self-interest, and for a corporation, it is firm employment. These norms shape the day-to-day actions and decisions taken by the actors within a social setting. This construct builds upon the normative pillar of institutional logic, which is one of three, the other two being regulative and cognitive (Scott 2008). According to this three-pillar framework that supports institutional logics, regulative pillar signifies rules and policies governed by external agencies whereas normative pillar comprises values and norms that are morally governed, internalized by social actors based on the roles they play. The cognitive pillar refers to the meanings and interpretations that actors derive from the nature of reality. Thornton, Ocasio, and Lounsbury (2012) argue that norms are variable attributes that vary across institutional orders.

The sixth category is the basis of attention which establishes the criteria for allocation of limited cognitive resource for information processing. This category addresses the question of "how actors organize their attention and what causes actors to change their focus of attention from one set of problems to another" (Thornton 2004, 37). This construct draws from the argument that individuals use their limited attention, whether automatically or willingly, for what is considered important by the prevailing institutional logics. So in the case of the higher education publishing industry, Thornton (2004) found how the focus of attention shifted from prestige to competition as the dominant logic changed from editorial to market.

The seventh category is the basis of strategy that defines how individuals and organizations make sense of their environment. Making profits makes sense to the markets whereas enhancing personal reputation is what seems meaningful to professions. This sense-making then serves as a springboard for action, thereby becoming the basis for strategy. Taking the example of higher education publishing industry again, as the institutional logic shifted from editorial to market, its strategy changed from pursuing organic growth to growth by acquisitions. The former considered the quality of craft to be more meaningful while efficiency made more sense to the latter.

The eighth category is informal control mechanisms that comprise mechanisms other than formal structures that exercise control on an individual's or an organization's actions and decisions. Markets are informally controlled by industry analysts, corporations by their culture, and professions by their celebrity professionals.

The ninth category is the economic system that focuses on financing, workforce, customer demands, physical capital, and supplies, as well as external competition and cooperation. Markets leverage market capitalism, corporations exercise managerial capitalism, and professions use personal capitalism in terms of professional knowledge and expertise.

Dimensions

Institutional logics manifest along two dimensions—horizontal and hierarchical. The horizontal dimension demonstrates the form of institutional pluralism that allows multiple institutional logics to coexist at the same societal or a field level. These logics often contradict each other, and these contradictions are the tell-tale signs of boundaries between institutional logics. For example, conflicts between the state and the religion demonstrate that these two logics coexist in our society and showcase how these two logics differ from each other.

The second dimension is hierarchical that generates cross-level effects and through which societal-level logics permeate into lower levels of fields, organizations, and individuals, and manifest as material practices and symbolic interpretations. These manifestations are partially autonomous indicating that while the upper-level logics constrain or enable the constituents below, the lower-level elements have the means to change the upper-level logics by selectively drawing from one or more of the supra-institutional logics and exploiting their contradictions. For example, capitalist societies may influence a field such as higher education to adopt market-principles in its policies, making higher education organizations as sellers and students as consumers of education. But in reverse, students and faculty may resist such efforts and try to infuse their academic and social priorities through their agencies.

Manifestations

At a field level, institutional logics are expressed symbolically as theories and frames that manifest as material structures and practice. Theories explain how and why structures and practices are shaped the way they are, and accordingly direct the vocabularies of practice. For example, economic theory explains the structures and practices of the market logic. Gumport (2000) argued that microeconomic theory provides market metaphor as the "legitimating idea that is used to make sense of, and ultimately to redefine the parameters of, public higher education" (73). The microeconomic concepts, such as demand, supply, commodity, and profitability, were adopted as a vocabulary of practice thereby leading to the emergence of 'industry' logic in higher education. Frames are less systematic rhetorical interpretations adopted by different parties to mobilize or resist change. For example, the projections around how online education will destroy traditional higher education as we know it has generated calls to "critically examine the rhetoric of online education" (Werry 2002, 12), thereby questioning the vocabulary of practice and its underlying theories and frames.

These logics are dynamic and always changing, often due to influences coming from multiple directions, triggered by one or more of the following three sources:

- Supra-logic: This influence comes from a level above in the hierarchical dimension. For example, the emergence of industry logic in higher education field draws from a supra-institutional market logic reflecting capitalism and competition that operates at the societal level (Gumport 2000).
- External logic: This logic originates from another field at the same horizontal level. For example, the emergence of science logic in contradiction to the care logic in the field of medical education came as an influence from the parallel, external field of science (Dunn and Jones 2010).
- Resource environment: The third source is the change in the resource environment that directly impacts the material structures and practices within a field. For example, the stock market as a resource altered the market practices of investing and capital exchange (Thornton, Ocasio, and Lounsbury 2012).

While theories and frames permeate societal and field levels, institutional logics at the organizational and individual levels manifest in the narratives that are more specific to their immediate context. Organizations and individuals express the institutional logics that they draw from through their identities, goals, schema, and attention that shape and give meaning to their day-to-day actions and decisions. Identities define who they are, goals define the rationale of their actions, schemas enable cognitive processing of their situated actions and events, and their attention points to what they direct their actions and decisions. In simpler terms, identity, goal, schema, and attention answer the questions about who, why, how, and what within a narrative. They influence the upper levels of institutional logic through cross-level effects. Each of these four constructs is briefly described next:

- Identity (who): "Individuals have multiple social identities, defined both in terms of group or category membership . . . and in terms of identification with particular social roles. . . . Relevant category identities include a social actor's industry, occupation or profession, employer, department, voluntary-organization affiliations, race, gender, ethnicity, nationality, and geography. Role identities are defined relationally, in terms of a social actor's relationships with other social actors" (Thornton, Ocasio, and Lounsbury 2012, 85–86). As individuals draw from multiple logics, they also have multiple identities. And much like logics, these identities also often conflict with each other.
- Goal (why): "Multiple and often discrepant goals guide cognition and action in diverse situations and domains." And these discrepant goals are tightly linked to an entity's multiple identities. "Goals, like social identities, are culturally embedded" (86–87) and therefore capturing goals linked to social identities helps us arrive at the logics that an entity draws from.
- Schema (how): The construct of cognitive schema originates in the field of social cognition (Fiske and Taylor 2013) and is defined as an individual's own organized knowledge in the form of an "abstract representation, including the concept's attributes and the relations among them" (104). It enables individuals to guide their expectations, resolve ambiguities, and draw inferences, which in turn influences their decision making. Schemas are "like mental short-cuts that we use to simplify reality" (Augoustinos, Walker, and Donaghue 2014, 68). Schema as a concept has been named differently, such as 'givens,' 'interpretive schemes,' and 'mental-models' in various streams of research (Walsh 1995). It is classified into four types—person schemas, self-schemas, event schemas, and role schemas (Augoustinos, Walker, and Donaghue 2014). Person schemas focus on dominant personality traits, such as 'extrovert' or 'neurotic,' that help individuals make inferences when interacting with others. Self-schemas are about how individuals view themselves based on their past experiences. Event schemas are cognitive scripts that guide individual actions based on their goals and how to achieve them. And role schemas are the "knowledge structures people have of the norms and expected behaviors of specific role-positions in society" (70). It is the last one that I apply in my study to understand the role of a teacher as viewed by individuals.

Attention (what): "What problems and issues get attended to and what solutions are likely to be considered in decision making?" (90).

This construct expresses the final stage before a symbolic interpretation translates into a material decision and action. We attend to what we consider as important or urgent which in turn is guided by our identities, goals, and schemas.

Mediatization

Mediatization is the phenomenon of changes in institutional logic resulting from technology mediation of communication processes in social and cultural institutions (Hjarvard 2013). The theory of mediatization originated in cultural and media studies and has been applied to analyze institutions, such as politics (Strömbäck 2011), religion (Hjarvard 2008), and performing arts (Auslander 2008). As an example, when musical and theatrical performances were captured and separated from their performers by recording technologies, the "evanescent experience" became an "economic product" (Chanan 1995). Technology mediation created a new culture industry that redefined cost, quality, and access to art and entertainment. Although threatened, live entertainment survived; however, its traditional ways were altered in response "to the oppression and economic superiority of mediatized forms" that forced it to "become as much like them as possible" (Auslander 2008, 7). Mediation led to mediatization of art, which not only transformed artists' creativity and audiences' tastes, but also the art's surrounding ecosystem. As Chanan (1995) explained the impact of technologies from phonographs to compact discs on music:

> The machine that turned the intangible sound of music into a material object was also to register huge changes in interpretation and performance styles, for which it is largely itself responsible. The difference between a compact disc of Beethoven's Fifth by the latest prize-winner of an international conductors' competition and the original 78s of the recording by Nikisch in 1913, let alone between Moreschi and, say, Michael Jackson—these differences are more than technological, but encompass a stark sea-change in the musical climate, and a profound transformation of musical consciousness. . . . The effects of this innovation were both economic and aesthetic, and emerged in stages, revealing different aspects in the process.
>
> (6–7)

This phenomenon, termed as "mediatization" is now unfolding in the realm of higher education as instructional technologies are mediating teaching and learning (Friesen and Hug 2009; Miège 2008). Broadly, there are two approaches to analyze the phenomenon of mediatization— one that applies the concept of media logic becoming central to institutional logic (Altheide and Snow 1979), and the other through the study of change in institutional practices (Couldry 2004; Driessens et al. 2010). Media logic as an analytical construct represents the "form" of communication regarding the grammar of the medium and norms used to define the content. For instance, news on television follows a certain format with its grammar and norms, whereas news on radio follows another. Television content needs good visuals whereas radio needs to avoid long pauses (Strömbäck and Esser 2009; Altheide and Snow 1979). The need to tailor the content based on its delivery channel shows that in most contexts, media logic is employed to capture people's attention. The medium that carries the content, therefore, constrains the media logic. However, some researchers have found media logic as too linear and elusively defined to study mediatization, and have therefore called for an alternative concept of "practice" to be engaged (Couldry 2004; Lundby 2009).

Studying practice as an ontological construct has emerged as a new paradigm not only in media research (Couldry 2004), but also in political science (Driessens et al. 2010), organization science (Feldman and Orlikowski 2011), professional education (Lee and Dunston 2011), education policy (Rawolle 2010), and sociology (Schatzki, Knorr-Cetina, and von Savigny 2001). The meta-theoretical framework of institutions logic adopted in this research transcends the debate between media logic vs. practice approach by operationalizing media logic within a new institutional logic and establishing its relationship with underlying practice. In other words, the variety of content used for teaching and learning captures the concept of media logic, which in turn offers a range of models for teaching practice in higher education.

With media logic and practice as two potential focal points of analysis, the outcomes of mediatization manifest in two ways—phases of mediatization and their impact on the institutions. The former focuses on "how" mediatization unfolds over a period and the latter analyzes "what" is its impact on various aspects of the institutions. There are varied terms and definitions for the phases of mediatization (e.g., see Schulz 2004; Mazzoleni and Schulz 1999) that can be summarized broadly into four phases:

1. Mediation: A technology begins to mediate a social or institutional communication process
2. Adoption: The use of mediation technology widens
3. Reciprocation: The institutional and media logic influence each other
4. Domination: Media logic governs or controls institutional logic

Among these four phases, while the initial mediation and adoption are largely sequential, the reciprocation phase is dialectical with the media and institutional logic intersecting and trying to transform each other. This interactive dynamic is also called the "double logic of remediation" in the theory of mediatization (Couldry 2008). The performing arts showcase an instance of this dynamic where the live vs. the recorded performances continue to influence each other, modeling themselves after one another. For example, "television originally modeled itself on the live-form" that later turned into "the more recent phenomenon of live events modeling themselves on mediatized representations, in a reversal of the previous historical pattern" (Auslander 2008, 7). The outcome of this reciprocal process as witnessed in these fields is domination where the new dominates the old. For example, live performing art tries to emulate recorded performances as much as possible, thereby indicating that recorded media now dominates.

The second impact of mediatization is regarding the changes in internal routines or external perception. The impact on routines translates into how certain activities get done—e.g., decision making in politics (Reunanen, Kunelius, and Noppari 2010), narrative structure in the theater (Auslander 2008), or "practices" adopted by politicians (Driessens et al. 2010). Rödder and Schäfer (2010) analyzed the impact of mediatization regarding the visibility of scientific research in news media and concluded that the scientific institution's resistance to media is high because, unlike politics or sports, media logic does not dominate science.

Mediatization doesn't view media as a separate entity that could influence or be influenced. Instead, it perceives media as permeating into the institutions and making long-term structural changes, while becoming their integral part (Hjarvard 2013). For example, mediatization of politics explains how "political institutions increasingly are dependent on and shaped by mass media" (Mazzoleni and Schulz 1999, 247). This phenomenon of mediatization results from media acquiring a greater authority in defining norms and practices of social institutions, such as culture and politics, and moving from being an external entity to the center of a social process (Blumler and Kavanagh 1999).

To ensure appropriate applicability of the theory of mediatization to the context of higher education, I make two important considerations. First, the definition of media, and second, the epistemological stance. A large part of the literature on the theory of mediatization focuses on mass media, thereby restricting the definition of media to the content produced by companies and disseminated through channels such as radio, television, and newspapers (Krotz and Hepp 2012). Rawolle and Lingard (2014) identified three different kinds of mediatization of education: first, the development, use, and effects of computer technologies in education; second, the politics and the effects of journalism on education and its practices; and third, the impact of image and representations on the practices of education.

My research pertains to the first of these three kinds, and for that purpose, I adopt an alternate definition of media to extend the theory of mediatization to the educational context. It is the content developed and disseminated from within the educational organizations for instructional purposes. In other words, it is instructional media. This duality of interpretation, as pointed out by researchers (Friesen and Hug 2009; Miège 2008) is important to note as it emphasizes the shift in perspective required to analyze the mediatization of higher education. Figure 2.1 articulates this duality explicitly. On the left, it shows mass media mediatizing social and cultural institutions, while on the right it shows instructional media mediatizing educational institutions. Media qualifies as mass media when published through channels such as radio, TV, or press, and as instructional media when produced and disseminated through instructional media platforms.

The second consideration is about epistemological stance regarding how it is different from the prevalent applications or interpretations of the theory of mediatization. The differences most relevant to this research are value neutrality, the academic authority of educational institutions, and the analytical epistemology of this research.

- Value neutrality: Most applications of the theory of mediatization view mass media as governed by social, political, and cultural ideologies, which the media institutional promote as their agendas (Lull 2000). But the educational institutions serve a higher purpose of providing a value-neutral education to help students interpret the world around them, including the ones created by media institutions (Friesen and Hug 2009). In this way, I analyze mediatization of higher education without imposing ideological biases in any way.
- Academic authority: Mass media platforms, such as radio, try to legitimize the content created or presented by them (Altheide and Snow 1979; Durham and Kellner 2009). Education platforms, such as colleges and universities, also do that but they also confer an enhanced social status to their students by virtue of their academic authority (Kamens 1977; Anson 2007). This authority influences the relationship between teachers and students that is different from the relationships between, say, radio-jockeys and their audiences.

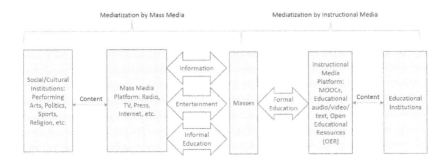

Figure 2.1 Mediatization of cultural vs. educational institutions

- Analytical epistemology: Research on mediatization has traditionally adopted a critical lens, focusing on the negative influences of mass media on society. Addressing the calls made for a non-normative analytical approach (Hjarvard 2013; Schulz 2004), this research adopts a value-free and analytical stance.

In this manner, I use the theoretical lens of mediatization with the term "media" redefined to exclude any prevalent biases about mass media and take an analytical instead of a critical stance. Articulating institutional pluralism in the field of higher education and analyzing their transformation through the lens of mediatization are the two core objectives of my endeavor.

Teaching Practice

Viewing practice as a material manifestation of institutional logics establishes a theoretical connection between the two. This connection can be seen in the practice of voting concretizing democracy and prayer concretizing God, as argued by Friedland and Alford (1991). It is also important to note that the relationship between institutional logic and practice is dynamic and bidirectional as a change in one influences the other. This bidirectional relationship allows inferring a change in governing institutional logics by analyzing the changes in teaching practice and vice versa. Although practice theory by itself is an independent corpus of theories ranging from Marxian Activity Theory and Latour's Actor-Network Theory to Gidden's structuration and Bordieu's praxeology (Nicolini 2012), its integration with institutional logic allows the articulation of individual and organizational behavior, thereby allowing multiple levels of analysis (Thornton, Ocasio, and Lounsbury 2012). This bidirectional and multi-level relationship affords a strong theoretical as well as an empirical foundation on which to base the findings of this research.

The ontology of practice theory is that

> social reality is fundamentally made up of practices; that is, rather than seeing the social world as external to human agents or as socially constructed by them, this approach sees the social world as brought into being through everyday activity.
> (Feldman and Orlikowski 2011, 1241)

Drawing from this ontology, I adopt the definition of practice as "embodied, materially mediated arrays of human activity centrally organized around shared practical understanding" (Schatzki 2001, 11). This definition engages the physical presence of individuals engaged in activities, any material resources that they use, and the contextual meaning of the domain in which they conduct their practice.

The practice of teaching is an interaction between three core entities— the provider, the peruser, and the content—where the provider is the teaching individual or the organization, the peruser is the student as an individual or a group, and the content is knowledge delivered live as a lecture or recorded as instructional media. The pedagogic research often uses this triadic teacher-student-content model, especially in the research on online education (Amundsen 1993; Anderson 2003). The activities underlying this practice are the creation and dissemination of content by the teacher, perusal of content by the student, and the resulting interaction between them. To effectively analyze a practice, one needs "zooming in on the accomplishments of practice, and zooming out of their relationships in space and time" (Nicolini 2012), and the teacher-student-content triad offers such a model that represents the micro as well as the macro perspective of teaching in the larger context of the higher education field.

An Integrated Framework

In summary, three concepts—institutional logic, practice, and mediatization—provide a comprehensive analytical framework that shapes the ontological viewpoint for this research (see Figure 2.2). These concepts are related to each other in the following way. The field of higher education has multiple institutional logics embedded in it. These logics provide organizing principles for individuals and organizations to define, conduct, and rationalize their behavior and activities. These activities and behaviors become socially meaningful and get established as practices through which individuals and organizations draw their identities, beliefs, values, and assumptions. However, these logics often have contradictions that provide opportunities for individuals and organizations to change their practices, thereby changing prevailing logics. The emergence of, or changes to, existing logics is also brought about by changes in external resource environments that materially impact existing practices, which in turn change institutional logics. In the context of higher education, online education has provided a new resource environment, impacting the teaching practice, and thereby leading to changes in, or the emergence of, institutional logics.

Figure 2.2 presents the integrated theoretical framework contextualized to the field of higher education. The field spans multiple organizations that offer higher education, agencies that govern or regulate these organizations, and constituents such as professors, administrators, and students who carry out the day-to-day teaching and learning activities. The changes in prevailing logics and the emergence of new logics on the left can be observed by capturing changes in its elements on the right. The teaching structures and practices are changing due to the changes in the resource environment of online education, for example, accreditation of online education programs, emergence of MOOC platforms, freely

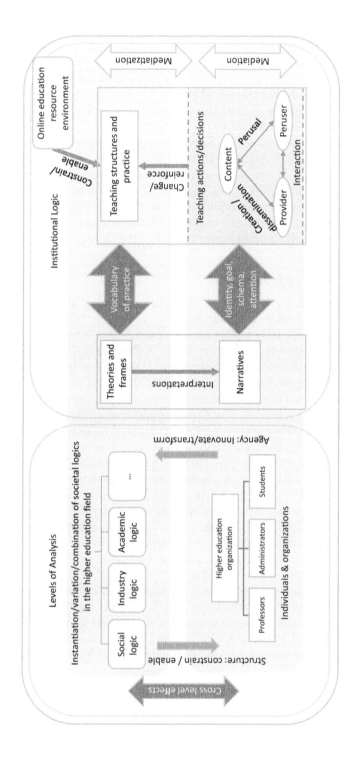

Figure 2.2 An integrated theoretical framework for higher education

available online content, and various technologies to impart education. As the teaching structure and practice are changing, a new vocabulary of practice is beginning to emerge, which can then help capture the institutional changes. Using this theoretical framework articulated earlier, the rephrased research questions are as follows:

1. What are the prevailing institutional logics that influence the practice of teaching in the context of higher education in the US?
2. How is the adoption of online education mediatizing these prevailing institutional logics?

In the following sections, I describe the entities identified at all three levels of analysis for data collection.

Levels of Analysis

> All three levels of analysis are necessary to adequately understand society. Each level of analysis is equally an abstraction and a reification; each is implicated in the other; none is more "real" than the other. Individual action can only be explained in a societal context, but that context can only be understood through individual consciousness and behavior. We conceive of these levels of analysis as "nested," where organization and institution specify progressively higher levels of constraint and opportunity for individual action. The relevant temporal frame in which it makes sense to study variation is longest for institutions and shortest for individuals. The relevant spatial extent over which activities can be organized is greatest for institutions and least for individuals. The symbolic world can only be constructed theoretically at the institutional level.
>
> (Friedland and Alford 1991, 242)

The quote above explains three key goals set for my research design. First is the epistemological principle of capturing multi-level as well as temporal dimensions of institutional logics at a field level. It points toward having a multi-method strategy covering the field, organization, and individual levels, and including historical analysis to cover temporal dimension, as also proposed by Thornton, Ocasio, and Lounsbury (2012). To address these two requirements, I adopted a research design that comprises the field-archival analysis spanning the period from 1997 to 2017, six organizational case studies, and individual interviews within those organizations.

Applying the concept of ideal types to identify, explicate, or validate the prevailing institutional logics in a particular field helps achieve the second goal of aligning with the perspective of institutional logics. The approach follows the concept of developing ideal types that are "a method of interpretive analysis for understanding the meaning that actors invest their actions with" (Thornton and Ocasio 2008, 110). The ideal-type approach starts with a typology which is then fleshed out with ideal types as second-level constructs and relationships among them (Doty and Glick 1994). Starting with building typologies has also been used in other sociological research outside of institutional research (Layder 1993). An interpretive epistemology to capture symbolic interpretations of institutional logics that form the basis of their emergence and change helps develop such a typology. Therefore, this research adopts qualitative techniques for data collection and analysis to arrive at contextually rich explanations of the phenomenon of interest (Mason 2002; Trauth 2001).

The third goal is to build upon theories that explain the phenomenon of changes in institutional logics when the social communication processes get mediated by technologies. The theory of mediatization has been instrumental in explaining such changes in other cultural institutions such as politics, religion, and performing arts (Hjarvard 2013; Auslander 2008; Strömbäck 2011) and, therefore, can be extended to explain the changes caused by the mediation of teaching practice unfolding in contemporary higher education. Mediatization as a concept reflects theoretical coherence with the meta-theoretical framework of institutional logics discussed earlier in the following ways:

1. Mediatization is a meso-level phenomenon (Hjarvard 2013) and therefore at the same field level as institutional logic perspective.
2. Mediatization is a phenomenon of change, similar to the concept of institutional logic, necessitating the inclusion of the temporal dimension in the study.
3. Mediatization focuses on the change in institutional logic either by the emergence of new institutional logic as media logic or change in practices (Strömbäck 2008; Couldry 2004), both of which are central to the institutional logic perspective.

Therefore, applying the theory of mediatization to the context of higher education using the institutional logics perspective offers a coherent strategy to map the higher education's landscape. I provide a short discussion in Appendix A on some other contending theories that I had explored prior to settling on to the framework discussed earlier.

3   Macro Contradictions

In this chapter, I discuss key patterns found in the field-level data. Numerous agencies and associations at regional, state, or national level govern or regulate teaching in the higher education field. Depending on their level and their nature, these agencies and associations influence teaching practice in different ways. For example, the US Department of Education (USDE) and Council for Higher Education Accreditation (CHEA) are national-level agencies that accredit programs, a process that also involves assessment of teaching practices in these programs (CHEA 2002). As stated by Hendrickson et al. (2013), "The vast number of colleges and universities in the US pales in comparison to the number of organizations that exist to support, represent, and evaluate them" (199). To overcome this challenge, I started with two resources that cover a broad landscape of higher education field— Harcleroad and Eaton (2005) and Hendrickson et al. (2013)—to develop an initial list, and then continuously revised as more documents were reviewed and analyzed. Table 3.1. summarizes the final list.

Zooming in further into the sector, the undergraduate education represents over 85% of the postsecondary student population in the US, with 17 million enrollments in undergraduate programs versus 2.9 million in graduate programs in 2015 (McFarland et al. 2017). While online has transformed both the undergraduate as well as the graduate education, the undergraduate education represents a much larger population, and therefore the focus of my study. Within the purview of undergraduate education, I studied the phenomenon of online education's growth by analyzing archival documents related to teaching practice in the 20-year period from 1997 to 2017. To develop a deeper historical and contextual understanding, I also analyzed some documents dating before this period, wherever required.

For each of the agencies listed in Table 3.1, I started collecting its data by first visiting its website and understanding the organization, its history, and its overall mission. Then I zoomed in to see if any of its web pages, articles, or other publications referred to the teaching practice in the field of higher education. This included distance education, policies related to

Table 3.1 Field-level data sources

Source
1.   US Department of Education (USDE)
2.   American Association of University Professors (AAUP)
3.   American Council on Education (ACE)
4.   Association of Public and Land-grant Universities (APLU)
5.   Association of Governing Boards of Colleges and Universities (AGB)
6.   Trade publications (*Chronicle, Inside HigherEd, Forbes*)
7.   American Federation of Teachers (AFT)
8.   American Association of Community Colleges (AACC)
9.   Council for Higher Education Accreditation (CHEA)
10.   Association of American Colleges and Universities (AACU)
11.   Trust Foundations (Gates Foundation, Pew Trust, Lumina)
12.   National College Credit Recommendation Service (NCCRS)
13.   American Educational Research Association (AERA)
14.   Council of Independent Colleges (CIC)
15.   American Association of State Colleges and Universities (AASCU)
16.   Alternate education providers (Pearson, StraighterLine, Coursera)
17.   Miscellaneous (Stanford University, DEAC, Babson Survey Research Group)

students or faculty members, or any other factors that impacted teaching and learning. The documents that satisfied this criterion were added to my archival for further analysis. This continued till I reached a point of saturation where I could not find any new information about the agency.

Then in the second round of analysis, I found three sets of themes emerging. The first set represents the overarching problem in the field, summarized as the iron triangle by Immerwahr, Johnson, and Gasbarra (2008). This iron triangle has the cost, the access, and the quality of higher education as its three corners, posing a challenge of how to improve one without negatively impacting the other two. The second set of themes pertains to the field's key constituents as listed in Table 3.1 that have collectively been called the "hidden hand" by Harcleroad and Eaton (2005, 195). These constituents participate in field-level discourse captured in document archival analyzed in this study. They represent the agencies engaged in policy advocacy and therefore shaping the field of higher education in significant ways. And the third set represents the emergence of an alternate world of education that encompasses several transformations unfolding in the field. In all these three themes, the emergence of online education has had a role to play.

Finally, in the third round of analysis, I then used my theoretical framework to interpret these three sets of themes. These theoretical interpretations are discussed in Chapters 5 and 6. In the following sections, I provide a detailed elaboration of the three themes. I also cite two types of sources—one that refers to the archival document used as data in my study, and two that refers to extant research related to my findings as appropriate.

The Iron Triangle

Although the problem of cost, access, and quality has historical roots spanning several centuries in the US, I discuss the key findings from longitudinal data from a more recent past, thereby focusing on the problem's contemporary manifestations relevant to this study. These three problems were found to underlie all critical decisions and discourses about higher education in general and teaching in particular at the field level.

Cost

The cost of higher education has escalated more than twofold over the last 30 years (IES-NCES 2017a; McFarland et al. 2017). This incessant increase has raised questions about higher education's value and its provider's accountability. It is viewed as a contributor to student consumerism and competition among providers, turning higher education field into a marketplace (Slaughter and Rhoades 2011). Although the severity of this problem reached its current stage over centuries, a trace of recent history shows that the roots of contemporary cost issues took hold when the federal government got involved in trying to make college education affordable through grants and loans in the 1970s. Since then the concerns about an unabated increase in cost have been on the rise.

Economists have tried to explain the problem through theories, such as the revenue theory of cost (Bowen 1980) and the theory of cost disease (Archibald and Feldman 2011). The first theory says, among other things, that higher education raises all the money it can and spends all that it raises in the quest for educational excellence, prestige, and influence. The second theory is premised on the economics of performing arts (Baumol and Bowen 1967), according to which the costs in industries that rely heavily on highly skilled professionals with advanced expertise "habitually outpace the annual inflation rate" (Thelin 2013, 84). Examples of such industries are those employing performing artists, lawyers, medical doctors, professional athletes, and higher education professors. As Archibald and Feldman (2011) argued, a faculty member remains the primary vehicle to deliver education and any attempts to scale by increasing class size or hiring less expensive adjunct teachers are perceived as a compromise in quality. Another proposed solution is to get rid of faculty tenure, but that is also rejected by many with the argument that it negatively impacts student learning (Trower 2012; AERA 2013a). Trying to reduce cost by changing student financial aid policies may not only negatively impact quality or access but is also complex, contentious, and, therefore untenable.

Two solutions proposed by experts are relevant to this research. First is to increase teaching focus on faculty performance thereby addressing quality and accountability issue, and second is to use distance learning technology to bring down the cost (Thelin 2013). I discuss the first solution later in this chapter under the section on the faculty. The second solution of using distance learning technology to reduce cost has been viewed with cautious optimism. The argument is that the realization of cost savings is not immediate, is only marginal, and requires an upfront investment in technology infrastructure, personnel, and course development (Hitt and Hartman 2002; Kellogg Commission 1998; Immerwahr, Johnson, and Gasbarra 2008). This outlook is coupled with the perception that "as colleges and universities—including traditional, residential campuses with a full-time student body—add the option of distance learning courses on the internet, the result will be to lower institutional expenses without lowering tuition charges" (Thelin 2013, 89). These findings indicate that while many attempts have been made to address cost issues, the search for a feasible solution continues with no immediate answer.

Access

Student diversity in terms of race, ethnicity, and age has been increasing over the years. In 1976, the percentage of white, black, Hispanic, and Asian/Pacific Islander undergraduate students was 82%, 10%, 4%, and 2%, respectively. In about 40 years, this percentage has changed to 55%, 14%, 18%, and 6% (IES-NCES 2016a), indicating a significant shift in student demographics as well increased access to higher education across minority races and ethnicities. However this may be more a reflection of the increased diversity in the US population at large, where the percentages of white, black, and other races as reported by the US Census Bureau changed from 87.5%, 11%, and 1.4% in 1970s to 72%, 13%, and 15% percent, respectively, in 2010 (Hobbs and Stoops 2002; Humes, Jones, and Ramirez 2011).

Similarly, regarding age, the ratio of traditional-age students (18–24 years) versus non-traditional (25 or greater) has changed since the 1970s from about 70:30 to 60:40 (IES-NCES 2017b). The efforts to reform higher education to allow broader access have been around for some time. Access to non-traditional student population has been the focus for agencies such as ACE (since 1945) and NCCRS (since 1974) that have advocated for alternate credit recommendations for working adults who acquire learning either on the job or through non-traditional education providers. The need to extend access to non-traditional education seekers was formally recognized in 1971 when the Commission on Non-traditional Study funded by the Carnegie Commission on Non-traditional Study was created to assess higher education's response to societal changes (Gould 1973).

As access and diversity in higher education have been broadening, online education is helping increase access to education across race and ethnicities. The percentage of students taking distance courses or programs close to or more than doubled since 2003 for all four races mentioned earlier. Similarly, online education has also helped increase age diversity with the percentage of students in traditional as well as non-traditional group increasing about twofold in the period from 2003 to 2012 (IES-NCES 2014). These findings indicate that as higher education is becoming more accessible to minority races, ethnicities, and non-traditional age groups, online education is also expanding in its adoption across all segments of the student population.

Quality

The quality concerns in higher education date back to mid-1980s (Ewell 2001) and much of the issue relates to the fact that quality is an elusive concept to measure. There are three ways in which the quality of education has been measured in the field. The first is by counting the number of students moving through the system of higher education regarding graduation and retention rates. As cost escalated, higher education's accountability came under scrutiny. The USDE decided to track graduation and retention rates at a national level in 1996. As per Kena et al. (2016), graduation rate is the "percentage of students who complete their program within 150 percent of the normal time for completion (e.g., within 6 years for students pursuing a bachelor's degree)" and the retention rate is "the percentage of students returning the following fall" (234–235). Not only have both these metrics been lower than the expectation, but they also have not changed much since their tracking began. Graduation rates in four-year colleges moved from 55% to 59%, while in two-year colleges they hover around 30% since 1996 (IES-NCES 2016c). Similarly, retention rates in the 10-year period from 2006 to 2015 have barely inched from 70% to 73% (IES-NCES 2016d). Another problem with these metrics is that they are seen as representing less about the quality and more about the quantity of what the higher education system is producing (CHEA 2012).

The second way to measure quality has been to look at the process of education in terms of how the students are taught and how much do they learn. The accreditation agencies have been trying to capture these aspects since 1952 as they qualify higher education organizations to participate in the Title IV program for government-funded student financial aid. However, their accreditation approach is often criticized for focusing less on learning and more on internal processes as a gatekeeper to receive federal and state grants and loans (Spellings 2006). To address this concern, the federal government took an active stance to establish "student learning outcome" as an important indicator of a higher education organization's effectiveness in 1989, which has now become one of the critical areas in accreditation assessments across the nation. But as discussed later in this chapter, this measure has attracted much opposition from agencies representing faculty members who view it as a threat to their academic freedom.

The third approach, although relatively informal, is to measure the incoming students' readiness to undertake college-level education. Reports by Levine (1997) and Bailey et al. (2016) indicate that nearly one-third of all undergraduates entering college have had to take remedial courses since 1997. Another report published by NCES shows the number improved to 20% in 2007–08 (Sparks and Malkus 2013). This perception about students' lack of readiness for college-level education often surfaces in the context of quality, indicating that the quality problem exists at the input as well as the output ends of the higher-education process. As evident from the aforementioned, quality's elusiveness coupled with less than satisfactory levels in all its measurements continues to be a challenge.

The Hidden Hand

Different constituents of the field view the problems of iron triangle in different ways, best summarized as "where you sit affects what you see" (Archibald and Feldman 2011, 7). There is a multitude of agencies representing these constituents that influence higher education through means such as policy advocacy, funding, and quasi-governmental functions. They range from accreditation bodies to regional compacts, consortia, institutional member organizations, professional member organizations, and foundations (Hendrickson et al. 2013), also known as meta-organizations in higher education (Scott 2010). Their powerful, yet invisible influence on academia has been named "the hidden hand" by Harcleroad and Eaton (2005). While their influence may seem hidden, their mission and agenda are fairly explicit on their websites and in the articles or reports published by them. To structure the findings from the data collected from these agencies, I grouped them into the following categories based on a rough approximation of who they represent:

1. Faculty members: e.g., AAUP, AFT, AERA, AACU
2. Administration: e.g., ACE, APLU, AASCU, AACC
3. Accreditation: e.g., USDE, CHEA, NCCRS, ACE (CREDIT)
4. Alternate/emerging education organizations: e.g., MOOC providers, StraighterLine, Saylor Academy, Pearson Education

This categorization emerged from interpreting the constitution of these agencies and statements expressed in their documents, especially those related to teaching practice. It is likely that these agencies represent more than what this categorization shows, but the motivation is to reveal the logics that they predominantly draw from. This also means that one agency may draw from more than one logic or may represent more than one constituency. For example, ACE largely represents the administrators of higher education organizations, but may also represent faculty members in certain contexts. A brief overview of two agencies from each of the first three groups listed earlier whose data was analyzed in this study is provided in Appendix E.

Representing Faculty

The faculty is the academic core "where the essential mission of a college or university is implemented" (Hendrickson et al. 2013, 269). Although a faculty member's role has been morphing with changing social fabric over the ages, it continues to influence how we engage in the process of education. Charting the role's history, Gehrke and Kezar (2015) traced it from a contingent tutor awaiting ministerial position in the 18th century to a specialized faculty member in the 19th century. Post-World War II, the subject matter specialization combined with research made the role scholarly and highly professionalized. Geiger (2011) termed this era as the age of academic revolution of American higher education.

The scholarly role of an academic profession developed in this golden age with three key functions: teaching, research, and service. A profession in a more general sense is "a kind of occupation whose members control recruitment, training and the work they do" based on a "formally organized, theoretical or abstract knowledge for its adequate performance." It requires formal training that is "heavily weighted by book learning. It characteristically takes place today in an institution of higher education where theory is taught formally." In contrast, the skills and knowledge for a "craft," while equally specialized and controlled, are acquired "on the job rather than in school, and [are] based more on practice than on theory or book learning" (Freidson 1989, 425). By this definition, research is a profession that requires formal training in the form of doctoral studies, and teaching has traditionally been practiced more as a craft because, as also summarized by Levine and Sun (2002) in an article published by ACE:

> Universities do not educate graduate students about how to teach; they have always assumed that if a person sits through enough classes, teaches some classes as a graduate assistant, and loves the subject matter, then that person can teach at a college or university.
> Levine and Sun (2002, 3)

It is this perspective that defines academic profession and can be mapped to the 'profession' ideal type in the institutional logic framework.

The profession ideal type is controlled by "a code of ethics and peer surveillance organized by external voluntary associations. This allows workers to have a much greater degree of personal control over their expert knowledge" (Thornton and Ocasio 2008, 42). It is not driven by financial markets or corporate hierarchies and derives its legitimacy from peer reviews. This leads to a conflict between "the compliance with the profit-seeking administrative procedures of the corporation and the adherence to the professional standards in the performance of work" (105–106).

The publications from agencies such as the American Association of University Professors (AAUP) and the American Federation of Teachers (AFT) show that their members subscribe to this ideal type. They define the purpose of a university's existence, as articulated by AAUP in 1915, "to promote inquiry and advance the sum of human knowledge; to provide general instruction to the students; and to develop experts for various branches of the public service" (AAUP 2015a, 7). This mission can be achieved only when academic freedom, tenure, and shared governance are respected by all constituents of the field. Gerber (2010) defines academic freedom, tenure, and shared governance as critical components of the professional identity of an academic. Among the tripartite functions of research, teaching, and service, research has traditionally superseded in importance over the other two. However, the contemporary world of higher education has witnessed some broad-level changes that are disrupting the research preeminence over teaching in several ways. Among these changes, there are two that cast a significant influence on teaching practice.

Changing Academia

In 1970, full-time faculty percentage was about 78% that reduced to 52% in 2015 (IES-NCES 2016b). These full-time positions included tenured/on-track positions as well. The percentage of tenured faculty dropped from 64.8% in 1980 (IES-NCES 1991) to 47.3% in 2016 (IES-NCES 2017c). This change has created a division within the faculty by creating a two-tiered system or bifurcated faculty (AAUP 2016; Selingo 2016). It has also led to a qualitative shift in which there is an increased emphasis on teaching that historically has been considered secondary to research. Kezar and Holcombe (2015) found in a survey that "faculty members (tenure-track and, to a lesser extent, part-time and full-time non-tenure-track) and deans did not find an increased focus on teaching and student development at the expense of research and service to be an attractive idea" (12). One potential reason for such disapproval for the teaching-only role could be that faculty members themselves value research more than teaching. As was argued by Metzger (1987), faculty members are more closely tied to their disciplines than to their pedagogy, even if the emphasis academics place on research varies according to the type and quality of their institution, most of them—even those in teaching-oriented institutions—deem it more severe test of themselves to publish their ideas rather than to utter them, to submit to the judgment of their peers rather than to the judgment of their pupils.

(161)

Irrespective of what the academia feels, the rising concerns about accountability demand pedagogic improvements that shift the focus not only away from research but also from being teaching-centered to learning-centered (Levine and Sun 2002; Kuh et al. 2006).

With research moved out from the teaching faculty's domain, the traditional path to enter academia is also changing. It is teaching and not research that the newcomers are being trained on, changing teaching from being a craft to a profession in itself. Material evidence of such a change is the partnership between ACE and the company ACUE (Association of College and University Educators) formed in 2014. ACUE offers instructor-training programs on effective teaching practices for non-tenure-track faculty members who did not take the traditional academic route whose "primary job responsibility on campus is to teach, and many developed their substantive expertise outside the academy" (ACE 2016).

While the earlier indicators promote teaching over everything else to improve student success, there is a concern that increase in contingent faculty not only de-professionalizes academic profession but also negatively impacts student learning (Gerber 2010; AERA 2013a). As argued by AFT, such changes are the reasons behind why "America is no longer the world leader in college attainment. Student retention rates are far lower than educators want or the nation should accept" (AFT 2011, 6). A study published by the National Bureau of Economic Research (NBER) reported that an increase in part-time and full-time non-tenure-track faculty adversely affects graduation rates in four-year degree programs (Ehrenberg and Zhang 2004). However, another study published by Northwestern University and NBER reported that students performed better after taking a course from a non-tenure-track professor in comparison to those who took the same class with a tenure-track professor (Figlio, Schapiro, and Soter 2015). While it is not relevant to analyze the validity of these studies here, it is important to acknowledge that these attempts reflect a growing tension about whether and how tenure adds value to the academic profession.

In this manner, faculty members subscribing to the academic logic are facing many questions about how they can justify the privileges of scholarly status and academic freedom they have traditionally enjoyed. As expressed by Clark (1987), an eminent sociologist in the field of higher education, the [academic] profession is mainly and increasingly composed of individuals who are caught up in large local and national administrative frameworks, often intensely bureaucratic ones, which systemize their duties and privileges and convert them into employees. In turn, these workers manage to convince outsiders as well as themselves that, unequivocally, they are not mere employees but instead are, and should be seen as, privileged members of a virtually independent professional community. As if it were a birthright, they struggle for self-government, invoking powerful doctrines—academic freedom, community of scholars, freedom of research—which serve both as guild ideologies and as the justification of unusual personal liberties.

(371–372)

Resisting Online Education

The rapid adoption of online education by students and its aggressive promotion by various higher education organizations has further exacerbated academia's concerns. The percentage of higher education organizations offering distance education through the use of technologies such as two-way interactive video and online interactions increased from 33% in 1995 to 63% in 2012 (IES-NCES 1998; NCSES 2014). But agencies such as AAUP and AFT advocate against online learning and perceive the rapid pace of online adoption as the administration's rush to market forces that conflict with higher education's academic mission. In response to the rapid emergence of online education in the late 1990s, there were several statements and reports released by AAUP. In one such report, the authors described the political context of the growth of distance learning as follows.

Distance learning has become increasingly admired by governors, legislators, institutional administrators, and critics and reformers of higher education, all of whom look on it as a more cost-effective way than on-site delivery to make services available to a wider, more varied audience than ever before. Despite mixed evidence as to its effectiveness in answering the needs of higher education, the political pressure to implement distance learning continues to grow rapidly across the country.

(Rubiales et al. 1998, 30–31)

One key concern expressed in these reports is that online education cannot substitute for the face-to-face teacher-student engagement:

The subcommittee recognized that distance learning can be a valuable pedagogical tool to increase access to higher education for students not able to utilize traditional campus offerings, but it is in no way a substitute for the engagement of the teacher with the student.

(30)

In an article published by AACU, the author termed traditional learning as "close learning, a term that evokes the laborious, time-consuming, and costly but irreplaceable proximity between teacher and student" (Newstok 2013, 16). According to this viewpoint, "The old-fashioned Socratic seminar is where we actually find interactive learning and open-ended inquiry. In the close learning of the live seminar, spontaneity rules" (18). Many studies have been conducted to support the argument that the best model for learning is close learning. For example, a study of over 200,000 students in the California Community College system found that the students taking online courses lagged behind those taking the same course in face-to-face settings (Jaschik 2015). Other factors such as lack of opportunities for collaboration and an overall absence of human-touch are among the many concerns that faculty members have expressed about online education (Newstok 2013; Carnevale 2000).

The second significant source of concern that results from online adoption is about who creates, uses, and owns the instructional content. The Statement on Distance Learning contended that "teachers should have the same responsibility for selecting and presenting materials in courses offered through distance education technologies as they have in those offered in traditional classroom settings" (AAUP 2015c, 256). The Statement on Copyright argued that the faculty members should be allowed to retain complete or partial content ownership (AAUP 2015b).

The third concern is that the online adoption has unbundled teaching activities by distributing them to different roles responsible for course design, development, and delivery to achieve economic efficiencies (Paulson 2002; Macfarlane 2011; Gehrke and Kezar 2015). As published by a professor in AAUP journal published on its website:

A professor who does not choose and present educational content in his or her courses is no longer a professor in the traditional sense of the word, becoming instead a glorified teaching assistant.

(Rees 2014)

The unbundling of teaching role is also enabling the use of content developed by third parties such as Pearson or Cengage Learning for custom-developed courses that are hosted on a learning management systems (LMS)—e.g., Blackboard. An article published in AAUP's Journal of Academic Freedom reported how teachers are resisting this trend because they want to "champion instructor involvement and choice" and allow the "essence of inquiry to flourish, which can only be achieved by requiring subject expertise and human intervention in the classroom" (Bossaller and Kammer 2014, 11–12).

Such oppositions have in turn led administrators to rate faculty members as one of the top barriers to online adoption (Allen and Seaman 2015; Green and Wagner 2011). Although faculty's online adoption as reported by Hill (2016b) is at 70%, their acceptance of the value and legitimacy of online education has been hovering around 30% since 2003. Such resistance has led to the perception that much of faculty's resistance to online adoption emanates from a perspective rooted in their identity as an autonomous academician expecting to conduct teaching in a certain way and perceiving online education as a threat to this identity.

Representing Administration

The administration is a structure that supports academic core to deliver education (Hendrickson et al. 2013). Such a structure is hierarchical with roles and responsibilities defined by one's position in this hierarchy. Considering that the individuals representing this group handle everything other than teaching and research required to run an educational organization, their perspective is oriented toward their organization's internal community as well as its external stakeholders. They try to bring together various branches of academia to deliver an integrated view of education in the most efficient and effective manner, and their agenda reflects how they want to engage with their internal as well as external stakeholders.

From a theoretical viewpoint, a corporation emerges "due to the difficulties of efficient exchange where transaction costs are high—those exchanges with uncertain outcomes, few actors, and highly localized knowledge" (Friedland and Alford 1991, 232). It functions through an organization that is influenced by the incentives provided by its stakeholders. Its control mechanism is the hierarchy of authority that operates through administrative procedures focusing on efficiencies. The source of legitimacy, in this case, is the approval from senior administration. It is committed to organizational success rather than to individuals and follows the rules of managerial capitalism (Thornton 2004; Thornton, Ocasio, and Lounsbury 2012).

Therefore, theoretical translation of corporation identity into the field of higher education points to the administrative unit of a higher education organization. The agencies such as ACE, APLU, AASCU, and AACC, whose members are presidents and other senior administrators, represent the constituents of this unit. Their goals and motivations are wide and varied, but their perspective toward teaching practice in general, and online education in particular, reveals some coherent patterns.

Managing Contradictions

> [I]nstitutional contradictions are the bases of the most important political
> conflicts in our society; it is through these politics that the institutional
> structure of society is transformed. A key task of social analysis is to
> understand those contradictions and to specify the condition under which
> they shape organizational and individual action.
>
> (Friedland and Alford 1991, 256)

The contradictions between administrative and academic logics of an
educational organization demonstrate how they have been shaping the
higher education's institutional structure. The manifestation of "corporation" type is articulated less by the administrators about what it is and
more by the subscribers to the academic type about what it should not
be. The academicians express how the administration goes against the
organization's academic mission by adopting a corporate mindset. As
stated in an article titled "How Can We Resist Corporatization" published in an AAUP journal:

> Just about everyone with a stake in the long-term success of U.S.
> higher education worries about the growing influence of free-market
> business practices on the operation of colleges and universities. Most
> faculty, in particular, see the increasing reliance on corporate models
> as destructive to the mission of higher education.
>
> (Andrews 2006, 17)

Various articles and reports published by agencies, whether representing faculty members or the administrators, show an inherent divide
between their academic vs. administrative perspectives. The "administrative culture has tended to become more separated from that of the faculty
and sometimes competitive with it" (Kellogg Commission 2000, 33). The
administration perceives that the academicians lack "identification with
the institution as a whole, with its larger purposes, or even a concern for
how well it is run, so long as their own freedom to stoke the furnace of
knowledge remains undisturbed" (30).

The term "corporation" surfaced in the data along with its related
terms such as "industry" or "commercial enterprise" broadly in two contexts. One, where the discussion was about increasing external influence
of the corporations through means such as corporate-funded research
or corporate executives in the governance boards. This trend is called as
"academic commercialism" (Washburn 2011) or "academic capitaliza-
tion" (Slaughter and Rhoades 2004) that seems to threaten academic
freedom. And two, where the issue was about internal administration
of a higher education organization where "administrators are managers whose decisions make shared governance and due process inefficient

and unnecessary" (Andrews 2006, 17). It is the second context that is relevant to this research, as it was found directly influencing the teaching practice.

Building Community

A 'common boundary' within which members cooperate with each other to increase the status and honor of their group as well as its members characterize the community ideal type. Members share a commitment to a common set of values and ideology and develop an emotional connection to the community as a whole (Thornton, Ocasio, and Lounsbury 2012). A reflection of this community is found where the close-knit community feeling in a small liberal arts college is preferred over "impersonality of the multiversity" (Thelin 2006, 16). Referring to this impersonal character of large universities, a report from the Kellogg Commission to NASCLU (APLU) termed university as a multi-verse because:

> The university has become an institutionally fragmented aggregation of departments. The primary loyalties of scholars are increasingly directed away from their immediate colleagues, students, and institutions toward national and international societies and associations of their disciplinary peers. [. . .] today's university community no longer has a single "culture" but several: an academic culture, made up primarily of faculty and students, fragmented into its own subcultures organized around disciplines, self-governing departments, and professional schools; a distinct and entirely separate student culture, with a bewildering diversity of aims and interests, from fraternities and sororities to student associations and research clubs; an administrative culture that tends to be separated from that of the faculty and sometimes in competition with it; and an athletics culture, perceived to be autonomous and beholden to commercial interests.
>
> (Kellogg Commission 2000, 9–10)

The earlier quote points to the acknowledgment that a conscious effort has to be made to build an educational community that can create a culture conducive to learning. Pertinent to teaching, the pervasive cultural fragmentation in large universities also points to disengagement among teachers and students, which is viewed as one of the reasons for students' lack of persistence in college. A report commissioned by the National Postsecondary Education Cooperative (NPEC) identified "student engagement" as central to student persistence (Kuh et al. 2006). The report cites the theory of student integration laid out by Tinto (1987) according to which studies have found that students' social integration with their peers and faculty is considered a stronger predictor of their persistence in college. It views teacher-student engagement as core to the educational experience and encourages active and collaborative learning within the classroom to create more opportunities for students to interact with their peers and the faculty.

The activities that bind the members of a community together are predominantly conducted in residential settings, and therefore students in a residential setting implicitly associate themselves more strongly with their college or university communities. But such experiences are most often not part of an online learning experience. The higher education organizations that offer online education have very well recognized this gap. In the absence of a physical-campus community, a visible effort is made by students, teachers, and administrators to bridge the gap by establishing virtual communities, societies, clubs, and associations. The underlying motivation is to give a rich social experience to students and contribute to their social development, learning, and success. However, there lingers a perception that "far from an intimate setting among a family-like community, distance learning by nature is mass learning, conceivably involving thousands of students in a single course" (Levine and Sun 2002, 4). This perception is especially strong among the subscribers to academic logic who see online learning less as a community and more as a convenience. As stated in an article published by AAUP:

> Distance learning also plays directly to a recent trend in the way people live their daily lives—a tendency toward not connecting rather than connecting. . . . It seems easier, more "real," to some to "meet" people on the Internet in the privacy of their home than in the "commons" of a classroom. By that standard, one can comfortably bank and invest; shop for a car, clothes, and a house; read newspapers and magazines; play games; and have a romantic relationship on the Internet, all in the privacy of one's home. Why, then, should one not be able to take a college-level class from home?
>
> (Rubiales et al. 1998)

In a similar vein, an article about the MIT's Open Course Ware (OCW) published by AAUP argued, "Posting course materials online would not, of course, be equivalent to offering the experience of an MIT education; that can be had only by enrolling in MIT, interacting with the professors, and living and studying with fellow students" (Lerman and Miyagawa 2002, 25). Similarly, as argued by Newstok (2013) in an article published by AACU, "Even Coursera co-founder Andrew Ng concedes that the real value of a college education 'isn't just the content. . . . The real value is the interactions with professors and other, equally bright students'" (quoted in Oremus 2012, 18). These views exemplify how the academic logic perceives that online education is conflicting with the efforts to build a learning community within a higher education organization.

Promoting Online Education

Agencies representing the administration of higher education organizations promote online education, largely for three reasons. First, they view online education as an enabler for lifelong learning. It democratizes education by extending access to non-traditional students, students with disabilities, or anyone who cannot attend classes in a campus setting (Lewis et al. 2000; Payne 1993). AASCU takes pride in being at "the forefront of the movement to provide online courses and degrees" because "even traditional-age college students are going to class online because it fits their lifestyles" (Aldridge, Clinefelter, and Magda 2013, 14). The emergence of MOOCs symbolizes the idea of democratization as they not only offer freedom from space and time but also from cost barriers that are insurmountable for many (Carver and Harrison 2013). These agencies view online education as a transformational vehicle that would disrupt higher education's traditional ways by

> eschewing the research activities, summer break, athletic teams, and campus infrastructure of the traditional university model, online degree providers enjoy significant advantages in the delivery of instruction. Online courses are developed centrally, allowing for a lower cost of development and more systematic focus on cognitive learning outcomes. Through innovative learning systems, remedial assistance can be provided online at reduced cost relative to face-to-face tutoring. Online learning is both low cost and of increasingly high quality. It is a classic disruptive innovation.
>
> (Christensen and Eyring 2011, 51)

The second reason to promote online education is to resolve quality and accountability issues in higher education. Surveys conducted by AACC and AASCU report that online education is considered to have entered the mainstream of higher education. They report that more than 70% of higher education organization administrators perceive the quality of online courses as equivalent or superior to their traditional courses (Finkel 2015; Aldridge, Clinefelter, and Magda 2013). The trend over a t10-year period, from a survey conducted by Babson Survey Research Group, shows that the perception about student-learning outcomes in online education is increasingly being considered as superior or same as face-to-face education by the administration, although the faculty's acceptance of the legitimacy of online education has been stagnant at around 30% since 2003 (Allen and Seaman 2015).

Agencies such as APLU and ACE promote technology interventions in teaching/learning activities, such as personalized courseware, e-advising, and learning analytics to measure and track the quality of learning. There is a clear impetus to use software for student advising and learning to track student engagement in real time. APLU has reported several success stories of universities that used e-advising and learning analytics to improve student persistence (Lee and Keys 2013; CUSU and APLU 2016). It has also launched an initiative across many universities named Strategic Management of Advising Reform and Technology (SMART) to use data analytics for Integrated Planning and Advising for Student Success (IPASS). The momentum toward tracking and measuring quality using technology is building.

While agencies such as APLU and ACE that represent senior administrators promote the use of such practices, agencies representing faculty members—e.g., AAUP and AFT—view it as becoming "nothing more than a 'widget factory' mass producing educated 'cogs' for the benefit of corporate interests" (Stein, Scribner, and Brown 2013, 5). The *Chronicle of Higher Education* reported in 2000 that AFT passed a resolution to oppose undergraduate degrees that were taken entirely online (Carnevale 2000). The concern expressed by AFT and other agencies subscribing to a similar perspective is that the quality of online education cannot match that of resident education. The subscribers to academic logic argue that the administrators' motivation behind the online promotion is to reduce cost, increase profits, claim copyright for the content developed by the faculty, make decisions about courses and, therefore, force faculty members to give up their content and their academic freedom.

The third reason for the administration to promote online adoption is to ease enrollment capacity constraints and generate revenue, which is among the top-four motivations driving online education as reported by ACE (Oblinger, Barone, and Hawkins 2001). Even small liberal arts colleges that traditionally resisted online because it conflicted with their academic mission have eventually adopted online education to address financial constraints (Thelin 2006). Not only has the number of higher education organizations offering distance learning has increased but also almost the entire enrollment growth in community colleges in the decade from 2005 to 2015 has come from online enrollments (Finkel 2015). The field-level data also shows a similar trend where the overall higher education enrollments are going downward whereas online enrollments are increasing.

As evident from the aforementioned, the administrative viewpoint about online education contradicts that of academic. It is also evident that such contradictions between the two are historical in their origins and have intensified with increasing online adoption across the field. From administrators' point of view, academic culture has walled itself off from the outside world in its "ivory tower" (Kellogg Commission 2000), whereas according to academicians, administration is swayed by market forces, running an institution of higher education like a corporation driven by enrollments and revenue, often compromising on academic priorities (Andrews 2006). The academic perspective views the online world as dominated by administration while, as expressed by an administrator in an article in the *Chronicle*: "Many faculty members wonder whether the rug has been pulled out from under them" (Elias 2016), viewing faculty resistance to online as signs of self-preservation and job insecurity.

Representing Regulators

The field of higher education is regulated in several ways by the state and federal governments. The state governments fund their higher education organizations through an annual budgeting process. Although this budgeting process varies greatly from state to state, there have been two key trends that are of interest here. The first is the trend of retreating state appropriations since the 1980s. According to the reports published by the State Higher Education Executive Officers Association (SHEEO), the percentage educational appropriations per FTE at a national level dropped from about 71% in 1992 to about 53% in 2017 (SHEEO 2018). While the absolute numbers show a steady increase with some fluctuations, the rate of increase has slowed down (Grapevine 2018). A report published by the US Government Accountability Office (GAO) shows that state funding has decreased by about 11 percent from 2003 to 2012 (GAO 2014). More recent reports show that there is a "slow but steady increase in higher education funding as states recover from the recession" (Wexler 2016), but the overall perception that state spending on higher education will cease to exist persists (Selingo 2016; Mortenson 2012). This drop in state support has resulted in a field-wide concern that "public higher education is gradually being privatized," further projecting that "average state fiscal support for higher education will reach zero by 2059" (Mortenson 2012, 27). From an academic point of view, the state government's withdrawal of support is viewed as a threat to student learning, as expressed by AFT:

> Government disinvestment has resulted in higher tuitions which, in turn, have left students assuming unreasonable levels of debt to attend college and, worse, prevented many from enrolling altogether or persisting in their studies.
>
> (AFT 2011, 6)

The second trend relates to how, apart from providing funds to public higher education organizations, the state governments are providing primary oversight and regulating the organizations funded by them. In response to rising concerns about the accountability of state higher education organizations, many state governments have changed their funding from enrollment-driven to performance-driven model in which the state funding is tied to metrics such as student persistence, degree completion, and job placement (Dougherty et al. 2016). Although there have been several misgivings about the unintended consequences of this model (Lambert 2015; Supiano 2016), over 30 states had adopted this model by 2015, and several others were in the process of doing so at that time (NCSL 2015).

While state governments focus on funding the higher education organizations, the federal government directs its funds to students through its Title IV program and lets them choose which higher education organization they go to. As students can apply their student aid funds only toward organizations accredited by the agencies recognized by the federal government, the federal government indirectly uses its "legislative power and purse strings" to influence how colleges and universities function (Hendrickson et al. 2013, 87). In this way, the federal government has expanded its reach within the higher education field through financial aid and accreditation.

Measuring Quality

Accreditation—a tool that the government employs to keep an oversight—tries to address the question of accountability through its attempts to measure quality. Accreditation organizations were started as private, voluntary membership groups in the late 19th century. They matured into six regional accrediting bodies by the middle of the 20th century. As of September 2015, seven accrediting agencies are covering six regions of the country (Hegji 2016). Other than these seven, there are national agencies accrediting faith-based (e.g., Association for Biblical Higher Education) and private career institutions (e.g., Accrediting Bureau of Health Education Schools), and specialized or programmatic accrediting agencies, such as the Association of Collegiate Business Schools and Programs (ACBSP) and the Teacher Education Accreditation Council (TEAC). In 1996, CHEA became the national association for advocacy related to quality assurance and accreditation. The USDE and CHEA set accreditation standards, and CHEA coordinates accreditation activities through these accrediting agencies across the nation. The accreditation process is decentralized and democratic, as it is based on self-study and peer review, followed by a site visit from a team of volunteers sent by the accrediting organization.

Accreditation is viewed as a "signal" to the public about the quality of education and, therefore, a matter of public credibility (Eaton 2015). Its goal is "to provide a yardstick for student achievement, quality assurance, and institutional operations" (Harcleroad and Eaton 2005, 205). But the problem with quality is its elusiveness. The quality criteria started with inputs such as faculty credentials, syllabi, and student-faculty ratio. It has undergone several cycles of revision and readjustments, but its elusiveness persists. This elusiveness became problematic when the public voiced concerns about the rising cost of education, leading the federal government to intervene by including student-learning outcome as one of the elements to be assessed for accreditation in 1989. The accreditors shifted their focus, as documented by CHEA next, to measure what or how much the students have learned.

> One of the most significant changes in accreditation in the last ten years has been the increased attention accrediting organizations have been giving to student learning outcomes. Where once accreditation focused almost exclusively on educational resources and processes such as course syllabi, faculty qualifications, library holdings and physical plant, central to accreditation reviews today is evidence of student achievement.
>
> (CHEA 2002, 13)

CHEA defines student-learning outcome as "the knowledge, skills, and abilities that a student has attained at the end (or as a result) of his or her engagement in a particular set of higher education experiences" (CHEA.org). However, as evident from this definition, putting this definition into a measurable practice is a challenge (Ewell 2001). It has also triggered opposition from the groups representing faculty members, as they perceive the effort to measure learning outcomes as "an attack on academic freedom—both the teacher's and the student's—and a clear attempt to further discipline faculty members who resist the model of the corporate university" (Champagne 2011). Some academics are resisting the measurement-oriented approach to assess teaching effectiveness for two reasons. The first reason is that they view the effort to measure learning as a corporate-oriented "management by objectives" approach. The federal government's efforts to establish "learning outcome" as a critical criterion in accreditation assessment has been seen as "a kind of 'quantaphrenia' that assumes most anything can be reduced to a numeric scale"(Stein, Scribner, and Brown 2013, 9).

And the second reason is that they view teaching as an art and not as a science that can be quantified and measured, as expressed in the excerpt that follows:

> When do mere annoyances become infringements? Perhaps when external assessment becomes the ultimate arbiter of what constitutes quality in the classroom. [. . .] "Management by objectives," once confined to the corporation, is now a common currency in colleges and universities. . . . It is not surprising that educators trained in math, engineering, and other "hard" sciences are often more comfortable with an exercise that reduces phenomena to numeric expression of measured certainty and predictability. [. . .] Whether this approach allows for the conveyance of knowledge in non-science classrooms is another issue. Gilbert Highet suggests

that teaching, whatever the subject matter, is something closer to art than science. To the extent this is true, attempts to reduce the process to a post-hoc, universally agreed upon numeric metric may be intrinsically problematic.

(Stein, Scribner, and Brown 2013, 9)

Online Quality

The criteria for assessing the quality of education were expanded to accredit online education early in the online growth phase with "1.6 million students . . . enrolled in 54,000 college-level, credit-bearing distance learning courses in 1,680 degree-granting colleges and universities" in the 1997–98 academic year (Eaton 2002, 2). The federal government established eligibility for the Title IV program by the 50% rule instituted in 1998, according to which only up to 50% of the courses or students could be fully online. The USDE modified this 50% rule in 2006 by removing this restriction for "courses offered by telecommunications" while continuing it for "correspondence courses and students" (USDE 2006, 2). This move indicates that as far as accreditation goes, the accreditation agencies have fully accepted the online modality of delivering education.

But as articulated in a report by the president of CHEA, "The emergence of distance learning . . . has the potential to undo . . . the delicate balance of accreditation to assure quality in higher education" (Eaton 2002, 1). The challenges introduced by online education range from assessing whether "the Internet can substitute for the campus as a supportive environment for creative learning" to the question of "what we mean by a college degree" because

> the college degree, traditionally the culmination of a distinctive institutionally based experience, is coming to represent a different type of experience: the completion of an idiosyncratic amalgam of educational experiences selected by the student from a number of unrelated institutions and delivered by a mix of technological as well as physical means.
>
> (5–6)

The organizations such as ACE and NCCRS functioning as alternate accreditor organizations that accredit alternate educators in the online world—e.g., MOOCs and other online content providers—are partially bridging the gap between the new and the traditional models. They seek teachers employed with traditional established colleges and universities to create as well as accredit the content which not only gives them the subject matter expertise but also helps them acquire legitimacy and experience of college-level teaching. More recent data also shows increased support from the federal government in terms of funded research to increase the use of technology in teaching and learning, for example USDE's EQUIP program (Educational Quality Through Innovative Partnership Programs) allowed 8 colleges to offer federal grants and loans to 1,500 students pursuing courses from three alternative-education providers and General Electric (Blumenstyk 2016). However, the advocates of academic logic perceive this as a "threat to traditional colleges," as reported in an article in Inside Higher Ed, according to which, Gary Rhoades, the former general secretary of AAUP, said that "not rapid certification but rigorous quality education in which they really engage faculty and peers" will help the country best.

While online education and learning analytics are technology levers being promoted by federal agencies to capture and improve quality, the debate on the definition of quality itself remains unresolved (Bienkowski, Feng, and Means 2014). Not only has the quality elusiveness transferred from the resident to the online paradigm unresolved, but it has also exposed the issue of the basic definition of a credit, which historically is calculated as seat time in class plus the homework time typically in a ratio of 1:2. Inputting a fixed number of hours every week for a semester is considered equivalent to fulfilling the credit requirements and, therefore, meeting the quality criteria. This definition fails to find its equivalence in online education models where there is no seat time per se. With this gap still open, the emergence of new educational models such as Competency-Based Education (CBE) or MOOCs has further strained the credit criteria.

In summary, while the agencies representing quality have tried to define and capture quality, the subjectivity of teaching and learning has made their attempts open to questions. This gap has surfaced vividly in the online paradigm, where critics have not only used quality as the basis to discount online education in comparison to resident education, but they have also resisted the efforts to measure quality to allow comparison. It is this gap that is becoming the focus of emerging alternate entities in the higher education landscape.

The Alternate World

The contradicting views among faculty, administration, and accreditation agencies reveal how the "hidden hand" is failing to make a dent in the "iron triangle." The increasing student diversity, market demand, and competition for students are motivating administration to adopt online to survive in the consumer-driven higher education marketplace. On the other hand, the faculty demand tenure and academic freedom, want research to be a critical component of their role, and disfavor online teaching. The questions of cost and accountability are changing faculty composition to contingent and teaching focused. And among these transformations, the quality of education continues to be elusive and, therefore, a weak link. These gaps are beginning to look bigger as higher education comes increasingly under scrutiny, and it is these gaps that the emerging entities in the higher education field are trying to fill using technology as a bridge.

Alternate Education Providers, Quality, and Accreditation

Alternate accreditors have played an active role in enabling alternative-education providers to make an impact. ACE and NCCRS have been offering college credit recommendation services (ACE since 1945 and NCCRS since 1974) to alternate education providers that traditionally comprised of business organizations such as AT&T and GE. As of January 2017, the ACE website lists more than 130 non-traditional education providers collectively providing more than 35,000 courses acceptable for credit at more than 2,000 higher education organizations. These providers include organizations such as StraighterLine and Saylor Academy which are fully dedicated to education as well as large corporations such as Walmart and Starbucks that provide job training for their employees. MOOCs were approved for credit by ACE in 2013, giving another stamp of approval to online education offered by alternate providers.

When MOOCs emerged in 2011, their massiveness introduced a new dimension that had not existed before—an "unknown" student. The MOOC providers needed to know who their students were, why they enrolled, how they perused the course materials, and what made them complete or drop a course. The motivation to know this unknown student triggered the idea of using data captured by their software platforms to analyze students' learning behaviors (Mackay 2013). It has now led to a field-wide impetus to use technologies, such as adaptive courseware and learner analytics. The urgency is not only because of the excitement around this innovation but also because of its perceived promise to solve the quality problem (Shallard 2016).

But these trends have raised concerns in the teaching community. AAUP published an article expressing wider concerns over such digital tracking used in learning platforms as a mechanism for surveillance and control (Dehaye 2016). In a white paper published by a company that makes adaptive courseware for universities through APLU, the author reported barriers to its adoption, such as concerns about faculty not understanding the inner workings of the analytical algorithms, students not knowing that they are being tracked, and third parties having access to student and faculty data that may create privacy issues. These concerns raise ethical questions related to the adoption of platforms with learning analytics (Shallard 2016). Despite these concerns, the emerging online technologies are attempting to fill many gaps that have been left open so far in the traditional education world. For example, making adaptive courseware based on pedagogical research to compensate for lack of faculty's pedagogical knowledge, employing learning analytics to measure quality in terms of student-learning outcome, and having media professionals produce the content that is edutaining and interactive to engage otherwise disengaged students (ACE-CEAI 2014; Lee and Keys 2013).

Leverage to Disrupt

It is important to note that despite the claims of disrupting higher education, the emerging alternate entities heavily rely on established academia to create and validate their content and make it creditworthy. The alternate education providers recruit faculty members from traditional established universities to build their content. Interestingly, the universities that sponsor these MOOCs do not accept their own MOOCs for credits (Green 2013). But MOOC providers are trying to transform higher education by seeking legitimacy from faculty members, leveraging their established reputation and credibility in traditional settings.

The alternate accreditors are also adopting the same path. For example, the criteria to become an evaluator at NCCRS and ACE as published on www.nationalccrs.org/form/evaluator-request says, "If you are a professor or college instructor interested in serving as an evaluator for NCCRS, please fill out the form below and email a copy of your current resume or CV to NCCRS@nysed.gov." Similarly, the credit evaluator recruitment flyer from ACE-CREDIT (ACE's College Credit Recommendation Service) states, "Eligible faculty must have been teaching for at least five years at an institution recognized by CHEA." These observations indicate how the alternate world is leveraging as well as disrupting the traditional education model.

4 Micro Conflicts

In this chapter, I present findings from six case studies that capture institutional logics and their mediatization at the organizational and individual levels. The next section describes the sample selected for data collection, with a brief description of each of the organizations where the case study was conducted. The subsequent sections elaborate the patterns found in the data.

Organizations

It was important to select organizations that represent widely different missions to capture a wide range of perspective governing higher education field. Taking the social-versus-industry and resident-versus-online debate as the point of departure, two dimensions—mission (social vs. industry) and mechanisms (resident vs. online)—offered the basic categorization to select a combination of private/public, non-/for-profit, and resident/online organizations. This approach resulted in six categories as shown in Table 4.1 that indicates theoretical sampling (Eisenhardt 1989) or "light theorization" as "a tentative but plausible account of similarities or difference that might be revealed by the case comparison" (Kessler and Bach 2014, 173). Within this matrix, using a multiple-case design with a single unit of analysis embedded in each and adopting the case selection technique of "selecting to differences" helped develop a comparative research methodology (Yin 2009; Kessler and Bach 2014).

In each of these organizations, an undergraduate degree program was identified as the unit of analysis which comes under a single administrative department within which the teaching practice was embedded. By limiting the scope of the study to one program in an organization, it helped clearly define the boundary for data collection. After reaching the decision to use an undergraduate degree program as the unit of analysis within a matrix of six types of organizations, I adopted the convenience sampling technique by choosing the degree programs to be in the closely related applied fields of information science, technology, and business. The primary reason to choose degree programs specifically in this set of

Table 4.1 Units of analysis

Dominant Teaching Model	Private for Profit	Private Non-profit	Public Non-profit
Resident	Unit 1: Two-year associate degree program in information technology at Sycamore Institute which is a for-profit college in the US-Midwest with 2,000+ students. The program is in resident-only mode, but online adoption at the college level is 9%	Unit 2: Four-year bachelor's degree program in information systems at Cypress University which is a private non-profit Doctoral University in the US-Midwest with 5,000+ students. The program is offered in resident and online modes. Online adoption at the university level is 9%	Unit 3: Four-year bachelor's degree program in information sciences at Redwood University, which is a public Research 1 university in the US-Midwest with 45,000+ students. The program is offered in resident and online modes. Online adoption at the university level is 13%
Online	Unit 5: Four-year bachelor's degree program in business at Aspen University, which is a for-profit university delivering online adult education with 40,000+ students across the US. The program is offered in resident and online modes. Online adoption at the university level is 71%	Unit 6: A portfolio of courses offered by Cedar Academy that are ACE/NCCRS accredited and acceptable for credit at partner schools in their two- and four-year degree programs. Cedar Academy is a private non-profit organization headquartered in US-East. All courses offered online only. Online adoption 100%	Unit 4: All details same as noted earlier, except that this unit is 100% online

disciplinary fields was my familiarity with them as well as my relative ease of access to the colleges offering these degree programs.

The programs' and their organization's websites were the starting point for data collection for all units, followed by some more data requested from the organization, as needed, on a case-to-case basis. This resulted in over a hundred documents, ranging from reports, news articles, and policy documents to job advertisements, meeting minutes, and teaching guidelines. As many of these documents are available in the public domain, they are not quoted verbatim in the following sections to preserve the organizations' and individuals' anonymity in these case studies. However, wherever required, they are paraphrased to communicate important observations.

One of the challenges I faced in recruiting organizations to conduct case studies was getting access to for-profit organizations. While the four non-profit organizations readily accepted, several for-profit organizations turned down my request for access to conduct a case study. Some of these refusals were clear and immediate, while others came after much deliberation and paperwork. My access to the two for-profit organizations that I eventually got remained relatively constrained and limited to individual interviews only. I bridged the lack of direct access to these two organizations by using relevant documents, such as news articles and annual reports that were available in the public domain.

Unit 1: A Resident Program at Sycamore Institute

Sycamore Institute is a for-profit organization located in one of the Midwestern states in the US. As per the Carnegie Classification, it is an associate's college that also offers vocational and technical degrees and certificates. It has nine schools in a variety of disciplines such as business administration, information systems and technology, criminal justice, culinary arts, and nursing. As per the data provided at IES-NCES, it employs 75 full-time and 55 part-time faculty members across all disciplines. It enrolls about 2,000 full-time students. As per its website, it employs about 300 full-time faculty and staff members. One of its largest programs is the associate degree program in information technology, which is the unit selected for this study.

My access to this organization was enabled by a friend who helped me reach out to Jack, the academic chair of the college. Jack was very forthcoming in accepting my request but exercised some caution in providing access to the participants to be interviewed for the study. I scheduled a certain date and time to visit the college premises, and he set up the interviews with five participants, including himself, on a single day. He selected these participants based on my request to have a mix of students, teachers, and administrators. All interviews were conducted in a closed conference room. After the interviews, Jack showed me around the facility that helped me gain some perspective on the work environment and culture in the organization. The college campus was located in a suburban area. I noticed during the tour of the facility that all staff and faculty members wore lanyards with their ID cards, something which I had not seen in any other academic setting. Jack also showed me the open-seating arrangement for the faculty and staff members and talked with pride about how Sycamore doesn't believe in closed-room offices and how even the dean sits in an open cubicle with the other faculty members.

Unit 2: A Resident Program at Cypress University

Cypress is a private, non-profit university in one of the Midwestern states in the US. It has more than 5,000 students of which about 4,500 are undergraduates, and the rest are graduates. It has one main campus and four small campuses within the state, and an online campus that offers online degrees and certificate programs. About 30% of its undergraduates are enrolled in these online programs. The university has a collective bargaining agreement with its faculty members. As per the Carnegie Classification, it is a doctoral university with moderate research activity. The unit considered in this case is an undergraduate degree program from a college that offers programs in the field of information systems, communications, and technology. It is accredited by ABET-Computing Accreditation Commission. The program is also offered online, and according to the department head, the resident-to-online ratio in the undergraduate program is 5:1. Since the college adopted online education as an alternate model, the resident faculty members are expected to teach in an online model, although it is not mandatory.

My access to Cypress was also through a friend who teaches in one of the colleges in the university. She reached out to seven individuals based on the sampling criteria that I shared with her and then shared their contact with me. I then individually reached out to each of them to set up a date and time to schedule the interview. The college campus, located in a suburban area, looked very similar to any mid-sized university campus. All teachers and administrators had their office-rooms where I interviewed them. I interviewed the two students in the college cafeteria.

Unit 3: A Resident Program at Redwood University

This unit is a four-year undergraduate degree program offering BS and BA degrees in one of the 12 academic colleges in Redwood University, which is a major, state-related Research 1 university in a Midwestern state in the USA. The university offers more than 150 majors at undergraduate and graduate levels. The college employs more than 120 faculty and staff members. Many faculty members also serve in administrative positions. Among the full-time faculty members, about 65% are on research track (tenured or tenure track), and the rest are on teaching track. Some of them also teach in the college's online program.

Redwood University is a large organization and I, fortunately, had direct access to all levels of the college. I could directly reach out to the individuals I knew could provide a rich perspective about the inner workings of the college. I also spent considerable time in the campus and

interacted with many teachers, students, and administrators. All participants were very forthcoming in sharing their views and answering my
interview questions.

Unit 4: An Online Program at Redwood University

This unit is the online version of the program in Unit 3 and therefore
from the same university and the college. Although the program analyzed
in this unit comes under a governing unit different from that of Unit 3,
both units draw from the same resources, such as faculty and administration. The key factors that drive some of the unique characteristics of
this unit are its adult-student demographics and its fully online delivery
model. The online nature of this model then entailed interviewing three
participants (two students and one teacher) over a video conference as
they worked remotely from distant places.

Unit 5: An Online Program at Aspen University

Aspen University is a publicly traded for-profit organization headquar-
tered in one of the Northeastern states in the US. It has more than 80
campuses all over the country. Founded in the 19th century, it started
offering online programs in 1997. The unit analyzed in this case study is
in a campus located in one of the Midwestern states in the country and
is classified as "Master's Colleges & Universities: Medium Programs"
according to Carnegie Classification. It has more than 2,000 students;
about 1,700 of those are undergraduate students. It has 12 full-time faculty members and more than 100 part-time faculty members. The program as a unit in this study is the undergraduate program for business
that has more than 100 students enrolled in it in the branch where this
study was conducted.

My access to this unit was most constrained and only feasible at individual interview level. I interviewed one teacher and one administrator,
although both played a dual role of teaching as well as administration.
I interviewed one of the two participants on the campus of another university where he taught part time, while the other participant in one of
the branch campuses of Unit 5. Both participants were very forthcoming
in answering my interview questions but indicated that they could not
share any organizational documents or data.

Unit 6: An Online Program at Cedar Academy

Cedar Academy is a non-profit organization, funded by a private trus-
tee. It was established in 1999 and has been promoting its free education
initiative since 2009 to make higher education accessible to everyone. At
the time of data collection, it offered 94 free online courses, 22 of which

are accredited by ACE or NCCRS and were accepted for credit by more than 40 higher education organizations that are Cedar's credit-transfer partners. Therefore, although Cedar Academy itself is not accredited to offer degrees, its students can use the credits earned through Cedar courses to earn a degree from partner colleges and universities. Therefore, Cedar can be viewed as one of the emerging alternate education providers enabled by the rise of online adoption. One of the largest set of courses being offered at Cedar helps students earn an associate degree in business administration. Although the nature of this unit made it difficult to draw clear boundaries, I defined the business associate degree program as the unit in this case study.

My access to Cedar was unique in many ways. I had earlier reached out to several similar non-traditional organizations (e.g., MOOC organizations) requesting access to conduct a case study. Only Cedar Academy responded positively. The initial communication was over phone and email with the key-informant in this unit. He shared several organizational documents such as organizational fact sheet and other teaching-related documents, which helped me develop an initial understanding of Cedar Academy as an organization. I followed this up with a two-day site visit during which I met with four participants and conducted interviews with them in a conference room. I interviewed one faculty member over the phone as he worked full time in a resident university in a different state, and worked with Cedar as a part-time academic consultant remotely.

The feel of Cedar's organizational setting was that of a contemporary startup in the digital era. All employees had an open-seating arrangement, and they occupied a few rooms spread across two floors in a building located in the city's downtown area, sharing common spaces such as conference rooms and cafeteria with other organizations. As this unit was completely online, there were no students or faculty members in this office.

Individuals

The day-to-day activities carried out by individuals are "micro-level concretizations" of institutional logics (Friedland and Alford 1991). However, the symbolic interpretation of such concretization varies across individuals, reflecting multiple coexisting institutional logics that they draw from. To capture these interpretations, I conducted semi-structured interviews of 35 individuals playing different roles within the six units of analysis identified earlier (see Table 4.2). As I approached my key informants in the organizations selected for the study, I adopted strategic sampling to capture a range of individual perspectives (Mason 2002). In my request to conduct the case studies, I had stated my requirement of interviewing about five to seven individuals playing the role of a teacher, an

Table 4.2 Research Participants

Unit	Roles	Description
Unit 1	Teacher: 2	Two full-time teaching faculty
	Student: 2	members
	Administrator: 1	The students are sophomores
		Academic chair of the unit
Unit 2	Teacher: 3	Two tenured professors and one on
	Student: 2	tenure track
	Administrator: 2	One sophomore and one junior. One
		program chair, and one head of
		department
Unit 3	Teacher: 4	One tenured, three full-time teaching
	Student: 2	faculty members.
	Administrator: 1	The students are seniors in the
		program
		The administrator is the head of
		academic affairs
Unit 4	Teacher: 3	One tenured, two full-time teaching
	Student: 2	faculty members
	Administrator: 2	The students are juniors in the
	Instructional designer: 2	program
		One director and one associate dean
Unit 5	Teacher: 1	The teacher serves as an 'academic
	Student: 1	consultant'
	Content developer/	The student is a senior
	instruction designer: 2	Two education project managers
	Administrator: 1	One director of education
Unit 6	Teacher: 1	Full-time teaching faculty member
	Administrator: 1	campus dean
Total = 35		
Teacher: 14, student: 9, administrator: 8, instructional designer/content developer: 4		

administrator, or a student. Depending on the level of access, I depended on the list of participants provided to me by my key informants in some organizations while in the other, I could recruit the individuals myself. Within this group, wherever feasible, I contacted individuals directly and elsewhere reached out to them through snowball or chain sampling technique of seeking references from individuals interviewed thus far (Patton 2015). This resulted in the sample comprising of professors, administrators, instructional designers, and students, but their number varied across units. For example, Unit 6 organization (Cedar Academy) has no in-house permanent faculty members and hires them from other universities as part-time academic consultants. It, therefore, has only non-teaching employees in various capacities, which resulted in having more administrators and only one faculty member available to be interviewed. It is important to note that in most of the units, several individuals played more than one role, thereby offering multiple perspectives.

Drawing from the technique proposed by (Mason 2002), the big research questions were broken down into mini-research questions guided by theoretical constructs, which were then used as topics to phrase interview questions (see Appendix C). The interview protocols developed based on these topics were also pilot tested.

The interviewees represented a wide range of profiles in terms of their academic background, types of experiences, and the number of years in their current role, as shown in Table 4.3. This variety of profiles made it necessary for the interview questions to be customized according to the role of the interviewee. The interviews were about one hour in length on average. I conducted all but four interviews in person at the interviewee's work premises. Four interviews were conducted over a video conference with two faculty members and two students. All interviews were audio recorded in two recording devices, with one as a backup, while handwritten notes were also taken to capture in-the-moment thoughts and observations. The open semi-structured nature of the questions allowed for a natural flow to the conversation with contextual probing questions to develop a better understanding of the interviewee's responses.

Micro Foundations

The first step to draw institutional logics at the organizational and individual levels was to analyze their key micro-foundational constructs—goal, identity, attention, and schema, along with three core entities related to teaching practice—teacher, student, and content. The analysis of these constructs uncovered within-case patterns which were then put through cross-case analysis to surface common themes that address the research questions pursued in this research. The highlights of findings are listed next and then elaborated in subsequent sections:

- A multiplicity of institutional identities and organizational goals was evident in all units. This multiplicity, on the one hand enriches the teaching and learning environment as teachers and students exchange educational ideas, but on the other, it also results in internal conflicts that have been exacerbated by the introduction of online education.
- Three dominant teaching schemas—guru, coach, and artist—surfaced to explain how participants viewed their engagement with resident or online teaching and learning experiences. While these three schemas have historically been there, they have been intrinsic to a teacher's teaching and a student's learning styles. With online education separating the content from its creator, these schemas are now manifesting as specialized unbundled roles of subject matter experts as 'gurus,' learning facilitators as 'coaches,' and engaging-content creators as 'artists.'

Table 4.3 Participant Profiles

Unit		Pseudo names	Role/ Designation	Years in current role	Education	Delivery Model (Primary/ Secondary)
1	1	Jack	Academic chair	1	D.Sc.	Resident
	2	Charles	Senior instructor	3	Master's	Resident
	3	Max	Instructor	1	Bachelor's	Resident
	4	Lola	Student	2	Undergrad	Resident
	5	Maxwell	Student	2	Undergrad	Resident
2	1	Coqui	Administrator	15	PhD	Resident/online
	2	Henry	Administrator	44	PhD	Resident/online
	3	Derf	Professor (tenured)	35	PhD	Resident/online
	4	Frank	Associate professor (tenured)	35	PhD	Resident/online
	5	Mary	Assistant professor (tenure track)	4	PhD	Resident/online
	6	Kelly	Student	2	Undergrad	Resident/online
	7	Steve	Student	3	Undergrad	Resident/online
3	1	Marissa	Administrator (director of academic affairs)	10	PhD	Resident
	2	Caleb	Senior lecturer	10	Master's	Resident/online
	3	Emma	Senior lecturer	5	PhD	Resident
	4	Teresa	Lecturer	3	Master's	Resident
	5	Anna	Associate professor	20	PhD	Resident
	6	James	Senior student	4	Undergrad	Resident/online
	7	John Doe	Senior student	4	Undergrad	Resident/online
4	1	Steve	Administrator (associate dean)	10	PhD	Online
	2	Jillian	Administrator (director of education)	13	Master's	Online
	3	Allen	Senior lecturer	15	Master's	Online
	4	Eric	Professor	15	PhD	Online/resident
	5	Chris	Senior lecturer	16	Master's	Online
	6	Christian	Instructional designer	8	Master's	Online
	7	Christine	Instructional designer	5	Master's	Online
	8	Greg	Student	4	Undergrad	Online
	9	Mike	Student	3	Undergrad	Online

(Continued)

Table 4.3 (Continued)

Unit		Pseudo names	Role/ Designation	Years in current role	Education	Delivery Model (Primary/ Secondary)
5	1	Robert	Professor	20	PhD	Online/resident
	2	Harry	Administrator (campus dean)	15	PhD	Online/resident
6	1	Glen	Administrator (director of education)	5	Master's	Online
	2	Robert	Administrator (education project manager)	4	Master's	Online
	3	Sam	Instructional designer (content-development manager)	4	Bachelor's	Online
	4	Dale	Teacher (academic consultant)	5	PhD	Resident*/Online
	5	John	Student	3	Undergrad	Online/Resident*

* In organizations external to the unit

- Separation of content has led to content stratification as a consequence of online education delivery. This has been followed by trends such as content standardization, granularization, and digital tracking, thereby leading to contentious issues of content ownership, and academic freedom. As the repository of such content is expanding, it is becoming a valuable asset for higher education organizations to create, disseminate, track, and control.
- The emergence of instructional content as the face of a higher education organization is creating the notion of a cyber-cultural identity. It has emerged as a descriptor of many new ways to think about and conduct teaching practice with online technologies.

Goal

There are two aspects of this construct in the context of higher education that require careful parsing. First is that entities can have multiple and often conflicting goals because they draw from multiple institutional logics. For example, an organization can have a profit-maximization goal driven by market logic, while at the same time also have a social-welfare goal driven by social logic. Second, there are two kinds of goals in higher education's context: the goal of higher education versus the goal of an entity offering that education. For instance, the goal of education offered by both Unit 5 and 6 is vocational development, but Unit 5's own goal as a for-profit entity is to maximize profits for its shareholders, while that of Unit 6 is social welfare by offering education free from space, time, and cost barriers for students. According to the theory, an entity's goal is tightly linked to its identity (Thornton, Ocasio, and Lounsbury 2012), and therefore the entity's goals are discussed along with its identity in the next section. In this section, I analyze the goal of education offered to students because it helps contextualize participants' experiences in their day-to-day teaching and learning activities.

Analyzing individual responses and organizational documents revealed five goals of higher education: workforce development, citizenship development, academic development, entrepreneurship, and social experience. Not all goals surfaced in all units, and their intensity varied significantly, not only within the same level among individuals but also across levels between individuals and organizations. Workforce development emerged as the most dominant goal across all three levels, perhaps as a reflection of the fact that the units of analysis chosen for this study were career-oriented programs.

The participants' views about workforce development being the dominant goal were mixed. While some considered it to be a strength, others wondered if it is overshadowing the true purpose of education. For example, Eric, a senior professor at Redwood University, expressed pride as he talked about his students who have graduated and are now leading successful careers:

> Through the learning experience, students can get not only new knowledge but also new skill sets. So that will help them, develop them to be ready for the workforce. My past students told me their success stories. They are proud of their work they are doing. In my viewpoint, they are now qualified workforce.

But Robert, a professor at Aspen University, indicated that higher education's goal has changed to something that he had not expected:

> The role of higher education, well I think the role has changed. I think when I started this 20 years ago, the role of higher education was to give young people that transformative experience to make them into better thinkers, which again was partly part of my liberal arts background, that's what I thought college could do. Now college trains people for careers, that's what it does. And if you ask students, most of them do not want that experience. They just want to know when I graduate, what's my job going to be. So that has been an interesting and somewhat sad shift because I think that's what we are now.

The earlier quote also points to the second goal of citizenship development which involves critical thinking, social and cultural development, and increased civic awareness. This goal emerged as the second dominant goal although it was expressed more as what is missing from the contemporary higher education than what it offers. In other words, while participants said that higher education's goal is citizenship development, and the organizational documents mentioned that they pursue this goal, there was no clear evidence at the program or the individual level that this goal was actively being pursued. This gap was also pointed out by James, a senior student at Redwood University, who found the goal of citizenship development to be missing in his experience:

> Almost all of it is just job training. It should be more as somewhere you grow as a person, figure out who you are. You might be able to argue that it happens for some people, but most people are concerned with getting an A in the class than actually learn something in the class. I feel it has become you go there to get a job and not go to learn, sort of thing.

When asked about the goal of higher education, participants often responded with a question, "You mean, the goal that is or the goal that should be?," indicating that they perceive these two to be different. The discussion that followed reflected that while everyone expects the goal to be citizenship development, they realize that it is not. Although the intensity of the perception about this imbalance varied across units, its prevalence was evident. Professors in some units cautioned that this unbalanced focus is making students into short-term thinkers focused on grades and jobs. As Frank, who is a professor in Unit 2, expressed,

> My role, that I view here, is to bring the wealth of experience as I've had in the field, management, and technology. And at the same time demonstrate the strength of the classic liberal arts education. And demonstrate to the students you can be very technical, be successful in business, but it doesn't mean you have to sacrifice thinking and learning about the world. The goal is not just to be the IT person.

The other three goals—academic development, entrepreneurship, and social experience—manifested sparsely and only at the organizational level as none of the participants talked about them. In Unit 2, the organization documents showed how the university promotes engaged learning by encouraging students to take up, among other things, community service and research which is recorded in students' transcripts. However, the rationalization expressed behind these activities in these documents was that these skills attract employers, thus pointing back to workforce development as the underlying motivation.

In Unit 3, the goal of education in university documents was articulated as to help students become entrepreneurs, conduct research, and gain social experience. One of the specializations offered by the college focused on developing entrepreneurial and innovation skills. The program organized events to encourage and award entrepreneurial efforts made by students. There were opportunities for students to participate in clubs and societies to help them engage with their community and create a social learning experience. The college being part of a Research 1 university, its strategic plan mentioned investing more resources in undergraduate research. But no evidence was found in its actual implementation for any of these three goals. All participants mentioned workforce development as the most important goal with a clear focus on getting 'jobs' in corporations. None of the interviewees mentioned research as the focus of their undergraduate teaching or learning. John—a student—expressed disappointment because his interests lay in research but found the program to be "too application-focused." The teachers, as well as the administrators, interviewed in this unit, emphasized "knowledge-application" as their focus with no mention of research in their undergraduate curricula.

The goal of social experience, interestingly, surfaced most clearly in Unit 4 which is an online unit. Steve, an administrator in Unit 4, talked about higher education as a shared social experience that brings people together:

> I would say about higher education in the US today, perhaps in other countries, but certainly in the US is that it is one social experience that a significant percentage of the population share . . . there are not many foundations of social integration in this country that people can talk about as a somewhat shared experience. I understand that the experience at each institution is somewhat different. But I think ultimately higher education is a shared social experience in the US. . . . I would say that socialization side is the one that is may be as little as obvious and not thought about quite as much.

In the same unit, students expressed that they miss knowing their professors and peers, and teachers felt they are not able to communicate with their online students as effectively. Mike, a student, said,

> I think one of the strengths in my experience in a more traditional setting is you are able to see and interact with your teacher very frequently, you are able to develop a rapport and relationship with them as well.

The need for social experience also showed up in the documents in the form of organizational efforts to create virtual student clubs and associations to bridge this gap. The unit has a webpage to "build a sense of community" through efforts such as supporting student-led Information Technology Club that serves as a "networking platform for students," promoting a "student blog," and enforcing teamwork across all courses so that students "form bonds with one another."

Derf, a professor in Unit 2, who occasionally taught online classes talked about how the social setting of his resident classes helps break cultural barriers:

> We have all these different cultures, different people. So I'll bring in food every once in a while, the Saudis will bring their coffee, the Indian students will bring in [food] from their favorite restaurant. So that's the exchange. I watch the students now learning and that interaction that you never get within an online environment. So I think that's the great part, because now people who tend to be prejudicial, and biased, and impressioned, their whole attitudes change.

The overarching goal to prepare students to work in the industry has cast its influence on teaching-learning activities in various ways. For example, all three resident units required group projects within the courses taught in the programs. While some supported it with the rationale of collaborative learning in which students learn from each other, the more common rationale was that an industry job demands teamwork skills. However, not everyone agreed that teamwork is a good pedagogic technique. Unit 2 being an ABET accredited program necessitates group projects to be a critical parameter in the curriculum. Frank, a professor in this unit, considered teamwork not only ineffective but detrimental to learning because "it has no connection to the real world because if someone didn't do their job in the real world, they would get fired, not just pull everybody's grade down!" However, he acknowledged that he assigned in class closely monitored teamwork because of ABET accreditation requirements of his college. In his words,

> We work in teams in the classroom. I do not have them work in teams outside the class. It is such a fake environment. If I was in an environment of a residential campus 30 years ago, I might do it. But the different efforts and expectations of students still would worry me. If we were in an environment where everybody wanted to do their best and get the highest grade, I think group work is fine. But that is not the environment we are in. And I think graded group work outside the classroom, where someone is not standing there, is not going to work when you are sitting in the corner. It is a waste of time. It causes more stress, and stress is the antithesis of the learning environment. [. . .] They don't learn anything because all they are doing is stressed about the group member who is not doing their work or trying to find a meeting time where everybody can meet. It's not conducive to learning. On the other hand, it's very important to

our ABET accreditors that we do graded group projects. Because the educators say that is the way people learn.

The students in these units, when asked about teamwork, did not talk about any particular problem with it, but did mention that they learn less about the subject matter and more about people when working in teams. As Kelly, a student in Unit 2 said,

> I think I would learn a little bit more had I done it myself because I would have to do all the parts of it. Whereas the one I did, I just had to do my part, and then I read over the other parts to proofread, that's about it. So I don't think I learned as much in-depth of the topic or the breadth.

Caleb, a professor in Unit 3, also expressed a similar observation about the effectiveness of having teamwork as a pedagogic technique:

> I don't see how important the team-mate interaction is in terms of individual learning. I might see improved solutions brought about the team interaction, but I don't see student A learning from student B. I am not sure why. If it is common, it has missed me.

The same practice of teamwork showed very different dynamics in online units. There was a common recognition across all teachers that group projects in online courses do not work. Despite this recognition, Unit 4 aggressively promoted group projects in all its courses because its parent college required so for all its programs—whether resident or online. Steve, an administrator in Unit 4 who also teaches some courses in the program, said that he applies "brute force" to get students to work in teams because "students don't like teams." In his words,

> You are not going to have the luxury of sitting down with four people on a consistent basis in a room somewhere and talking through the problem. Not with organizations that are internationally dispersed, and doing international design, development, and manufacturing. I think the need to be able to work in a virtual team environment is increasingly important. And I think we have to do it in our classes, and as I said, I the use brute force method. I am sure there are better methods. But I just say you are going to do it. I know you hate it. And inevitably the [student evaluations] always come back and say, Oh! I hate it.

But Jillian, an administrator in the same unit, said,

> I think we fail to remember that our online students often have been working and have already experienced teamwork. We are trying

to include that in the curriculum so that our 18- to 22-year-olds don't walk out of here and fall down when they get in a corporate environment.

Similarly, Christine in the same unit talked about how the role of her university is different for adult learners from that for traditional 18- to 22-year-olds:

> The role of Redwood for traditional students is different. It is a way for the students to be immersed in something besides just classroom, where they are connecting with something. There is also the social living part of it. Growing up and going to a dorm. And some aspects that will always be there, that kind of transition, from high school to college. But that is a different audience with a different set of priorities than the online student who is here to get a degree and motivated to learn. They are at a different place in their life for what they want out of Redwood. We have had some classes where resident students mix with online students, and if it is done well, they could learn from each other, but you could recognize that they are at very different places, and most of the time it is doing better if they are in separate sections. If you are going to put them on teams together, they are really mostly different in where they are in life and what they are thinking about.

Robert from Unit 5 explained how the challenges have led Aspen University of Unit 5 to stop using group projects as a pedagogic technique across all its programs. In his words,

> We got rid of all team projects by the way; we don't use them at all anymore. . . . Online courses have people all over the world; timewise it's impossible to coordinate them, students hated them, they were a nightmare to do. And you know what it's like with team projects. One person, the smart guy that does all the work, the other people do nothing.

To summarize, workforce readiness as the primary goal of learning is perceived by teachers as making students more short-term focused, ignoring the larger academic value of what they are being taught. This is also influencing the teaching techniques being dictated more by what the industry wants in its work environment and less by what teachers think is a better pedagogy.

Identities

An individual's identity is tied to a group to which he or she belongs— e.g., industry, profession, organization, race, or geography. It may also be tied to the individual's relationship with others, such as a parent, a CEO, or a teacher. An individual has multiple identities, for instance, a parent who is also a teacher and a researcher working in a department within a university. Individuals may have different levels of commitments to these identities, reflecting a hierarchy of identities, which then impacts their relationships with others, and may drive potential identity conflicts. Such multiplicity of identities and inherent conflicts reflected in the data as well. The analysis revealed seven identities across six units.

Academic Identity

Drawn from the professional institutional logic, academic identity's definition is derived from the ideal type of academic profession. The phrases such as "love of learning," "living an intellectual life," "disseminating knowledge," and "conducting research to create knowledge" reveal the manifestations of this identity. This identity has two distinct orientations—teaching and research. When teachers and administrators talked about the goal or identity of their organizations, they invariably talked about both, although with more emphasis on one over the other. For example, Annie in Unit 3 and Eric in Unit 4, both tenured professors, identified themselves more as researchers than as teachers. For example, when I asked Annie, a professor in Unit 3, about her role, she first talked about her role as a researcher. She said that her motivation to join academia was inspired by her love for "intellectual life." When I asked especially about her role as a teacher, she responded,

> Often my undergrad students arrive at my doorstep, arrive at my class with the knowledge that is very narrow, that they believe is wide. That they know a few things about the world and assume that that is the knowledge of the world. Part of my job is to explain to them, show them, expose them to the knowledge of the world that is a better representation of reality so that when they go out into the workforce, they will be wide thinkers

This dual role of teaching and research also surfaced as a conflict between individuals and their organizations creating a dynamic that has been termed as "cross-level effect" (Thornton, Ocasio, and Lounsbury 2012). For example, Jack in Unit 1, which is part of a teaching-focused college, emphasized how he is trying to inculcate more academic rigor by encouraging teachers to conduct research. And he said he was trying this because his organization was undergoing the process of accreditation to get the status of a four-year college. He wanted his faculty members to stretch their academic vision. On the other hand, Robert's organization of Unit 5 wants him only to teach and not conduct research. However, Robert anyways conducts research and publishes in academic journals because he enjoys it. This conflict emerged most clearly in Unit 3 and Unit 4, as they both are part of a major Research 1 university where academic positions are divided into research and teaching tracks. Teachers on the teaching track perceived their university as biased toward research, thereby ignoring teaching at the expense of student learning. Emma on a teaching track in Unit 3 expressed the following:

> I think when a research mission is a pursuit of knowledge in lieu of or as primary, and educating the people that support and pay for their salaries is secondary, I have a problem with that. It wasn't until I came to a Research 1 university that I realized what a big disconnect that was, and the average person doesn't know.

The second conflict within the academic identity was between the perceptions about resident and online teaching and learning. It was visible when teachers, as well as students, expressed inherent difficulties in online education regarding teacher-student interaction, establishing relationships, and the absence of in-the-moment experience. It was most clearly manifest in resident settings (Units 1, 2, 3) where the individuals had experienced some online teaching or learning in the past and had concluded that it was not something they liked to do, or that it was of inferior quality. James, a student in Unit 3, said, "I feel I didn't get as much learning from the online or hybrid courses as I did in the class in person." Coqui—a professor and an administrator in Unit 2—reflected why he doesn't like teaching online:

> I can't read the room in an online class . . . I need to see the faces. . . . I need to figure out what's going on. In online I am blind. I don't know who's there. So I don't feel comfortable.

Steve in Unit 4 expressed frustration because such perceptions make it difficult for him to get good faculty to teach online, leading him to conclude that some teachers don't want to change their age-old ways of lecturing in a classroom setting. As he described,

> I have had the opportunity to interact with both faculty who are very innovative and want to embrace different ways of teaching, but also those who say, no, the only way to do this is to do it in a traditional environment. [They] will say that we are not going to do that distance education stuff, we are not going to do that online learning stuff. That's not as good as having me in front of the classroom. Well, I would argue, that is a very traditional academy perspective, and that's kind of the sage on the stage perspective of education.

To overcome the resistance from some faculty members to teach online, Redwood University has "tweaked the reward structure" for faculty teaching in resident units by making online teaching as part of "on-load teaching." In other words, teaching online has been made mandatory to address the issue of faculty not wanting to teach online.

The third kind of conflict resulted from workforce development being the most dominant goal of education, especially in Unit 1, Unit 2, and Unit 5, which translated into a conflict between teaching job-oriented knowledge vs. teaching theory. Charles, an instructor at Unit 1, although pursuing a doctoral program, took pride in having worked in the industry and therefore was not "just an educator":

> The stories that I have in the field makes it interesting for students because I am not just an educator. I am more of a trainer with experience that has done the work. You can read these information technology books all you want, but that does not make you an IT person. Being in the field [. . .] we were in the server rooms, we were in the data centers till 3 o'clock in the morning, freezing because its 60 degrees in there. We were fixing things. Other instructors haven't really experienced that.

On the other hand, Frank in Unit 2, who also has a PhD with many years of industry experience, expressed frustration, as students seek training in job-relevant skills:

> I had a student in here. He was asking for help on ASP class that I am teaching, . . . And he said, but I don't want to be a programmer. As if . . . the only thing that mattered was getting a job while that's not why you are in school, that's not why you are here [. . .], and so, the students don't value half of what we are forcing them to take. And their employers aren't valuing half of what we are forcing them to take. And that makes trying to do anything outside of what they are rigidly looking for very hard.

And the fourth conflict resulted from teachers' concerns regarding students' inability to learn, attributing several reasons to this problem. Caleb in Unit 3 talked about students' short attention span, while Robert in Unit 5 saw it as students' unpreparedness for college-level learning. These problems, when coupled with the fact that instructional content is now so widely available, especially in the online units, has led to the debate whether a teacher should focus more on subject matter or direct their energies to help students learn how to learn. Steve, an administrator in Unit 4, argued,

> we can go out and find lectures by the most outstanding people, the most recognized people in a field, and listen to what they have

to say about it. So doesn't that mean, if you are not the source of knowledge, if you're not Socrates, doesn't that change the role of the instructor? And what I would argue is it is not so much a role now of instruction, it is a combination of imparting knowledge but also guiding individuals to find the knowledge and to apply the knowledge. So I think the role of the instructor has become much more of a mentorship role than pure 'here are the fact' and this is the way it is.

Robert, a professor in Unit 5, said, "Faculty are good at teaching content, but not enough faculty teach students how to be good students." In the context of teaching online, he said,

> I don't know that you teach a lot online per se. I think the idea is to get them to teach them to engage the material. . . . You are not a teacher per se as much as you are a guide and a coach to teach somebody how to learn stuff in that modality.

Some individuals equated teaching subject matter with 'lecturing' and teaching how to learn with 'problem-based coaching.' As evident from the earlier quote, Steve considers just lecturing to be poor pedagogy, but other individuals who expressed otherwise. For example, Frank in Unit 2 argued that it is not the lecture-based technique, but the art of delivering that determines its effectiveness. As he reminisced,

> I took organic chemistry from the guy that made LSD for the CIA experiments in the '60s. The class held 200 students in it. He kept everybody intensely interested. [. . .] He would ask a question, and if he would get it right occasionally, he would reach into his pockets and say, really good, and throw out whatever change he had. And it would just scatter in front. So something as simple as that, people knew he was excited about what he was teaching. So how could you sit there and fall asleep?

Similarly, James—a senior student in Unit 3—said that he often feels disengaged in most of his classes. But he expressed admiration for a professor who lectures so effectively that he finds himself most engaged and makes sure he does not miss any of this professor's classes. In his words,

> One of the faculty, he does a great job of lecturing, . . . he is also very active in class [. . .] He will wait for people to answer questions if he asked a question [. . .] People don't answer questions usually, but he will wait. He will rephrase the question. It shows he really wants us to engage in the class. Something else I really like is if we ask a question or answer a question, he will raise a counterpoint to that. It is not like he'd say great point and move on even if we know the

answer is wrong [. . .] I like watching how he does it. I don't think I could ever do that.

Community Identity

The community identity refers to how individuals relate to the group of which they are a part, which in this context would be a program, a college, or a university. The criterion of belonging to a community is that its members have a "common boundary." They take pride in being part of their community and feel an "emotional connection" to it (Thornton, Ocasio, and Lounsbury 2012, 73). To trace this identity, I mapped community identity to phrases such as "student and teacher engagement," "learning community," "group activities," "clubs and associations," and "collaboration and cooperation."

The root of this identity emerged as the need to provide social and cultural development to students and to help them engage with their educational environment, thereby fulfilling the educational goal of providing a "social experience" discussed earlier. Individuals and organizations have recognized this need and translated it to activities undertaken within as well as outside the classrooms. The examples of inside-classroom activities, mostly driven by a teacher, were student-team projects, course-related discussion forums, and teacher-student interaction. The outside classroom activities mostly driven by the college or the university were student mentoring and tutoring, voluntary clubs and associations, and community-work as part of the curriculum.

Greg, a senior student in Unit 4, described his experience as an online student:

> Since last few years, it has become much more of a community . . . maybe because I have met more people, the online campus is growing, many things combined. Quite a drastic improvement, 2011, 2012, it was not as strong. Community and family feel have grown. That to me is the most important. For class work, I have noticed an increase in interaction in the college itself. . . . As I have gotten closer to the degree, everybody seems more engaged. The quality of classes has improved, maybe it is the upper-level classes, science classes. My interest has improved, my comfort has improved.

Most of the evidence of community identity for resident units were found in organizational documents. The only way this identity surfaced clearly at an individual level in resident units was when the participants talked about their online experiences, where they felt they missed that community feeling. For example, James in Unit 3 talked about his experience as an online learner in the past: "In person, you also get personal relationships with all the other students and other professors that you just simply cannot get online." In Unit 4, the organizational documents revealed focused efforts to create a student's community in the form of clubs and associations of present students and alumni. One of the documents claimed to offer a "real sense of 'community' for online learners" indicating the realization that online environments otherwise lack a campus community. Interestingly, while individuals interviewed in Unit 3 which is the resident unit of the same college did not express this pride, several individuals in the online Unit 4 talked at great length about how they considered themselves fortunate to be part of the "Redwood community."

Unit 5's efforts to engage students surfaced only in the teachers' interviews where they talked about how they try to have regular one-on-one interaction with their students through videos, e-mails, and online discussion forums. Unit 6 reflected the weakest community identity because of not having any concept of a student cohort. The only evidence of their community was the student-led online discussion forum that the Cedar was trying to promote.

Corporation Identity

The corporation identity was traced by looking at internal policies, procedures, and working culture of the organizations. Phrases such as "status in the organization," "norms and standards," "policies," and "best practices" were coded to infer the presence of corporation identity. For example, Redwood's strategic plan articulated its first foundation strategy as striving for efficiencies to save cost, indicating an economic priority guiding its actions, which in turn points to its corporation identity. Redwood's large and complex bureaucratic structure governed through charters and bylaws also reflected its corporation identity.

Two key factors that accentuated corporate identity concerning teaching practice and its online adoption were the issues related to content ownership and content standardization. The question of content ownership emerged as being addressed differently in different units, influenced by three characteristics specifically: the for-profit status, the online education model, and the university's collective bargaining agreement with faculty.

- Unit 1: Private for profit, resident, content ownership with the organization
- Unit 2: Private non-profit, resident, content ownership with faculty due to the collective bargaining agreement
- Unit 3: Public non-profit, resident, content ownership with faculty
- Unit 4: Public non-profit, online, content ownership with the organization

- Unit 5: Private for profit, online, content ownership with the organization
- Unit 6: Private non-profit, online, creates and uses copyright-free content

In Unit 1 and Unit 3, the organizational policy claimed that the content ownership largely rests with the organization. However, as expressed by the participants, there was a collegial sharing and openness among faculty members and, therefore, they either did not know the policy or did not care. Their organizations also did not strictly enforce the policy. As per Sycamore's policy, the content created by a faculty member is owned by the college. But enforcement is left to the department head, Jack, who said.

> We don't want our material that you have spent time on be shared with other schools. And we can enforce that for that matter too. I can easily contact IT and ask IT downstairs to run a log on all USB ports that have been in our system and furthermore on my forensic side of my own school; I can run a piece of software to check to see how many times they actually have done that. [But] . . . we try to be as free and open as we can.

In Unit 2, the content was owned by faculty members because of the collective bargaining agreement, and, with only a few exceptions, teachers openly share content to help each other. As Henry, an administrator explained,

> In our department all but two people openly share anything they have. . . . And the two faculty who don't want to share, nothing is shared. But the other faculty scratch their heads about that stance. Majority of our faculty will share everything they have. Every on-ground material they have, every online material they have.

Similarly, Derf, a professor in Unit 2 expressed that he doesn't mind sharing his content:

> My own stuff, I don't care people take it. I am a teacher, that's what they are paying for, so they can steal my stuff. I do not care. My philosophy on that is my example of data and information. Anybody wants my shell, I give them my shell because they are going to do a different spin. It's all my stuff but they are going to do it differently because they have a different frame of reference coming out of stuff. I don't care about my stuff, so my things are out there.

All the three resident units revealed high flexibility and freedom for the teachers to create their content. Contrary to this, in online settings, where the core content was much more solidified and created with significant organizational investment, it was explicitly owned by the organization and faculty creativity was severely restricted. The organizational policy, as explained by Steve, was

> the background knowledge that the faculty puts into the course is faculty's intellectual property. However, once you have that, whatever the course may be, PowerPoint with the voice-over, whatever that is, that now becomes the property of the university. The reason it becomes the property of the university is the university paid for you to do it. You used university resources and hence then the university has invested in the intellectual property. And, therefore, I believe the university should own that.

The second factor about the content that reflected corporate identity was its increasing standardization. While most teachers across all units expressed no concerns if their organizational policy made their content owned by the organization, they did express a concern that it took away their freedom to be creative. This concern was especially evident in the online settings. For example, the teachers in Unit 2 were beginning to see restrictions as their online adoption was increasing. In Unit 4, teachers were allowed to modify only up to 20% of the content and Allen—a professor in this unit—said that she "at times finds it stifling." Robert, a Unit 5 teacher, said that their organization was beginning to realize the importance of creativity and flexibility for teachers to enjoy teaching, and had started "experimenting" with letting them modify some content selectively. On the other hand, teachers in fully residential Unit 1 did not express any restrictions regarding their freedom to change content to suit their needs.

Although this content standardization seemed restrictive to the teachers, they acknowledged that the goal is to improve quality and give a better learning experience to students. All participants expressed the need to design content according to the principles of pedagogy to make teaching and learning experience consistent and seamless, which would not be possible if the content design was not standardized.

Another form of corporation identity was observed in Unit 2 where the teachers expressed frustration about the university being managed by "professional managers," instead of scholars. According to them, these managers compromise academic priorities in the interest of short-term results. Derf, a senior professor in Unit 2, talked about an "adversarial relationship" between the faculty and the administration. In his words,

> So there is this adversarial relationship amongst universities and within university, which is far more divisive. And I find that administrators now are not homegrown and not that it is good, or bad, or

ugly, but the bad part about that is they are all about themselves. I have been here 35 years. Everything I have done, I can justify has been done for the institution. Because my view is, what's good for the institution is going to be good for me. Now we have a cadre of professional administrators. What they do is what's good for them to get their next job. [. . .] There is, you'll see the top tier schools like Harvard as an example, the people who become presidents are scholars.

Coqui, a senior administrator in the same unit, who had started his academic career as a teacher several decades ago, said that

they are not about teaching. They are about management. [They have] this incredible focus on short-term goals to the expense of long-term goals. I am really appalled by that kind of behavior. And yet I see it everywhere, not just here. But it clearly shows in our budgeting process and our spending process, our hiring process. Like we are hiring faculty now for next year. Most people would do it in October or September. But we wait to look at March cash-flow before we decide to hire.

In Unit 1, the corporation identity also surfaced in the form of its corporate-like work environment, often not seen in traditional academic work settings. All offices, including those of the instructors and the dean, were set up in open cubicles. The faculty members wore neck lanyards, and the policy required them to be at the campus every day from 9 a.m. to 5 p.m., much like any corporate office.

Market Identity

An entity's orientation toward the external world was interpreted as its identity. Phrases such as "student as a customer," "competition in higher education," "market ranking," "revenue targets," and "shareholder value" were coded as representations of this identity. For example, Christian, an instructional designer in Unit 4, when asked about the role of his university in higher education, responded,

I have never been in an environment that is more about making money and business. I hate to say that, but it is true. ROI is like the most important thing. You know that's the bottom line. But I don't operate that way. In my own individual way, I don't really care about the numbers, but I know that is the truth. And everybody knows that. I hear that all the time from everyone about how much revenue we generate. Revenue, revenue, revenue. That's a contrived model. It is a created model to incentivize more online education because someone feels that we need to increase our enrollment base. There is a lot of that that goes on.

Coqui in Unit 2 also expressed a similar frustration about his disagreement with the university's senior administration that expects him to treat students like his "customers." He found his marketing department's expectation to treat students as customers to be frustrating. In his words, "Student is not my customer. Student is my product. I am not interested in trying to get the student in. I am better interested in what would happen to them afterwards." He also talked about how the university's focus to increase enrollments interferes with good teaching practice. In his words,

> The emphasis on marketing is a problem. Back ten years ago or so we introduced eight-week courses in multiple entry points. . . . And it hurt everything. And luckily the Provost has been benevolent and allowed the department to move back in many courses to expand them back to 15 weeks. We just cannot—there is no way you can cram into people's head that fast. They don't get enough project time, they don't get enough time on tests to build assignments and so many of the courses we moved back. But some are still pushed into eight-week formats [. . .] That was done because they wanted more enrollment. We would have more enrollment if we allowed people to come whenever they felt like. Every eight weeks start a program, take a course in intensive mode, four-hours a week roughly in the classroom.

Coqui also mentioned his observation of the college website in which

> Anything that says Academics and goes down from there is populated from our database is all accurate, is live up to the minute, and is filled in with whatever is happening there. Anything over on Admissions or Graduate or Undergraduate—those stacks—are totally fiction. They are made up by PR people. The right things that they think sound good, and often are not accurate.

Charles, an instructor in Unit 1 at a for-profit organization, spoke about how the mindset that the student is a customer influences students' behavior as they think, "I paid $50,000 a year to go here, you will do what I say . . . and it's a little bit different for this school because we are for-profit."

This identity's material manifestation was most apparent in Unit 5 as it is a for-profit, publicly traded organization. Its annual report to its shareholders shows its focus on revenue and profits, like any profit-focused company in the market. Although Unit 1 is also a for-profit organization, no data was found in the public domain that could surface its market identity. But its implications were observed at an individual level, as a teacher expressed that the for-profit nature of the organization changes student behavior as they acquire a customer's attitude "demanding" to be awarded a degree whether or not they do the required work for it.

The other ways in which this identity was traced was through the use of certain "vocabularies of practice," which according to the theory, is the link between the material and symbolic elements of an institutional logic (Thornton, Ocasio, and Lounsbury 2012, 158). Some examples of vocabulary indicating market identity that were observed in the data are

- the term "target-market" used for the student population, and setting "enrollment targets" in organizational documents (Unit 3, 4, 5),
- emphasis on *US News & World Report* rankings on their websites (all units except Unit 6),
- administrators talking about "competition" in the education market (Unit 1, 2, 4, 5), and
- individuals expressing frustration that the administration is too focused on short-term revenue goals at the expense of academic priorities (Coqui in Unit 2, Christian in Unit 4).

State Identity

The state identity in this study represents governmental influences on the workings of educational organizations which directly or indirectly impact the teaching practice. The only evidence of such an impact found in the data was related to the accreditation mechanism that surfaced selectively only in Unit 1 and Unit 6. Unit 1, gearing up to become an accredited college shortly, reflected the need for a change in faculty orientation regarding teaching and research. Jack, the academic chair, talked about how he is "educating" his faculty members about the accreditation process, measuring student-learning outcomes and class objectives, and running accreditation tests to assess the quality of teaching. In his words,

> When I first came here, the individual I took the place of did not believe in assessments or accreditations. I know that accreditation is so important. Yesterday, at the end of the day, I gave a report from middle states that actually talked about the importance of accreditation and the importance of student learning outcomes. Then I also worked with the department that is kind of like the central source in ensuring our accreditation.

Unit 6 showcased the importance of getting its course credit recommended by ACE and NCCRS to gain legitimacy and thereby making its course offerings more socially impactful. Glenn, an administrator in Unit 6, welcomed the fact that "government is more willing to at least recently be open to the idea of non-traditional types of education and how they can be used effectively to deploy to more people." The impact of regional accreditation in any other units was not evident. Interestingly, when asked about accreditation, most faculty members, as well as administrators, revealed a complete lack of awareness about it.

Social Identity

The social identity represents an entity's altruistic goals which are drawn from the larger goal of the higher education sector to serve its society. While the means to serve this goal vary with the level and type of role played by these entities, the focus is on contributing to the larger community. Some examples of the phrases that were traced to capture this identity are "making a social impact," "helping economic development," "building better citizens," and "solving social problems." There is some overlap between the community identity and social identity, and the manner in which the two were differentiated was by associating community with the members internal to the program, college, or university, and associating social identity with the entity's orientation toward external stakeholders.

All organizations articulated serving the society as one of their topmost goals. One common claim to social contribution was workforce development. But their rationale for how that serves social goal ranged widely from supporting economic growth to helping the students lead better lives, reducing crime in our societies, and ensuring students get well-paying jobs after graduation so that they can pay off their loans, thereby solving the social problem of student debt. Redwood University's website also claimed that it contributes to the state economy as it is one of the largest state universities and employs thousands of employees across the state. The organizational documents also expressed the social goal of making students into better citizens but, as was pointed out earlier, the individuals described the goal of their teaching and learning activities to be mostly job preparation. A few individuals in Unit 3 and Unit 4, being in a research-university, talked about their research as their social contribution.

In the online context, Steve, an administrator in Unit 4, expressed his role in democratizing education by making it available online. In his words,

> I would be motivated by the fact that I am part of the process that is democratizing education if you will. That is providing access to education for people in other environments, in other situations who would not have a chance to pursue higher education.

While Unit 4 and Unit 5 claimed that they make education accessible by removing space and time barriers through online, Unit 6 took it a step further by offering courses free, thereby removing the cost barrier as well. Richard, an administrator in Unit 6, expressed his organization's goal as

> providing access to pockets of population that might otherwise not have access, so within the US and internationally, there are many students who can't afford what traditionally has been seen as higher education, too expensive to enroll in accredited places that offer higher education.

Cyber-Cultural Identity

I found phrases in the data that reflect dynamics of cultural institutions that offer engaging content, such as "capture students' attention," "use humor to keep students engaged," "edutainment," and "tell stories to communicate ideas." These were found in resident as well as online units. Frank and Coqui, both teaching for more than 30 years in Unit 2, argued that teaching is an art and not a science. Similar expressions, such as telling stories in the class, and entertaining students to keep them interested in learning, were used by individuals in other units to emphasize the cultural aspect of teaching. Many of them talked about their unique "styles" when talking about how they create their presence in the class. Teachers in online units gave high importance to creating their virtual presence through videos to be able to relate to the students. Frank, a professor in Unit 3, expressed frustration that he cannot "tell stories" on videos the way he can do it in his resident class because "people are expecting no 'uhs,' 'ifs,' no backtracking. In a video presentation, they are expecting Hollywood." He said that he teaches by telling stories in the classroom hates online because

> to teach the same way I teach in person would require a vast amount of time, effort, and expense. The expectation of me in the class telling a story is fine. A video of me telling that story is not fine. [. . .] I cannot do that online. That's why I hate online.

Aspen University has recognized this need and has set up a studio with professional media experts to create instructional videos to be used in their courses. Glen in Unit 6 said that it is important to have "production value" in their videos. So instead of individual faculty members making their own videos, they tried having them fly down to their office to make high-quality videos. However, due to financial reasons, they eventually hired an internal media team to create videos with surrogates who present the 'script' written by faculty members. These manifestations point to the artist schema where it is not just about the content, but also about how it is packaged and presented to its audiences.

In online units, the cultural elements showed a heavy dependence on the underlying technology used for their manifestation. For example, digital technologies help create high-quality videos, host them on digital platforms, and then disseminate them globally, thereby enabling the practice of creating engaging video-based instructional content. Unit 5 and Unit 6 took it a step further by attaching data analytics tools to these platforms for tracking learning behavior and measuring the quality of teaching.

As two of the three online units—Unit 4 and Unit 5—also offered resident programs, their resident counterparts also showed the presence of cyber elements such as digital content, interactive simulation software, and electronic tracking of teacher-student interaction. In all these manifestations, the primary motivation to use technology was to keep students engaged and their attention captured. This cognitive aspect of teaching was also talked about by instructional designers, perhaps indicating that the increasing emphasis on pedagogy, especially in the online education world, is a reflection of their cyber-cultural identity. In this identity, teachers use their creativity to navigate the cognitive pathways of student learning. It combines the elements of both teaching as an art as well as teaching as a science, thereby transcending this debate.

Schema

The schema is one of the four micro-foundational units of institutional logics, the other three being identity, goal, and attention. Schema represents the top-down knowledge structures that individuals have to process information and guide decisions (Thornton 2004). These structures "shape attention, construal, inference, and problem-solving," and "guide expectations of behavior by helping individuals resolve ambiguities" (Thornton, Ocasio, and Lounsbury 2012, 88).

However, unlike the other three constructs, schema is an individual-level construct that could be interpreted only from interview data. It was traced by analyzing the analogies used by individuals to express how they perceive teachers or teaching, and what they focus on when teaching or learning. This analysis yielded the sub-constructs through which various schema manifested in my study. These sub-constructs are essentially schema's attributes (Walsh 1995). The attributes that I found in my analysis are first, their orientation toward teaching and learning; second, how they assess the quality of teaching and learning activities; third, the challenges they faced in teaching and learning activities; and fourth: what they perceive as positive contributors to the students' learning process. Each of these attributes further showed variants which when analyzed together distilled into three schemas that I have termed as guru, coach, and artist. As shown in Figure 4.1, these schemas are not mutually exclusive, and many individuals showed more than one of them. In the following sections, I first describe these three schemas and their attributes and then analyze how these schemas interact with different contextual settings and modalities of teachings.

Teaching Schemas

GURU

Individuals subscribing to this schema viewed teaching as a scholarly activity and teachers as scholars. They assigned a high priority to the knowledge a teacher demonstrates, or a student acquires during teaching and learning activities. They used analogies such as—a subject matter expert, a consultant, or a priest—to convey how they think about a

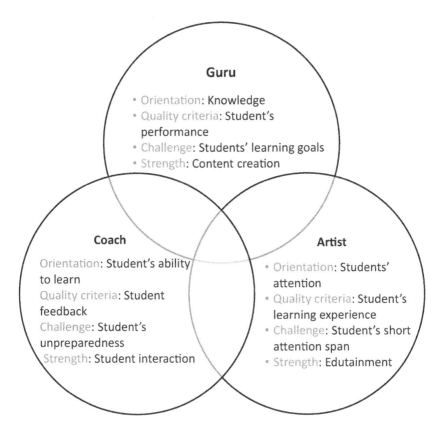

Guru
- Orientation: Knowledge
- Quality criteria: Student's performance
- Challenge: Students' learning goals
- Strength: Content creation

Coach
Orientation: Student's ability to learn
Quality criteria: Student feedback
Challenge: Student's unpreparedness
Strength: Student interaction

Artist
- Orientation: Students' attention
- Quality criteria: Student's learning experience
- Challenge: Student's short attention span
- Strength: Edutainment

Figure 4.1 Teaching schemas

teacher. For example, Annie—a research track professor in Unit 3—used the analogy of a priest or a clergy to express her views about teaching:

> Both have the sacred knowledge, and they are the mediator between this sacred knowledge and the congregation that they serve. The professor is also the mediator for a body of knowledge. I take this knowledge from this academic world; I contribute to it with my research. And then I translate it or mediate it for my students, so I am the robed clergy of this knowledge and sometimes that can be, I imagine, a wonderful experience of sharing something with someone else, and sometimes it can also be very protectionist. This is a sacred place you cannot enter until you've gotten a PhD.

Teachers themselves expressed pride in creating new knowledge, or developing content to be used in their teaching. For example, Eric in Unit 4 and Dale in Unit 6—both senior professors—expressed pride in having written eBooks for the courses they teach. Eric claimed his course to be the "best on the planet." Dale said he used his eBook to teach in his resident classes and said, "That was great for me because I think for the students to see my name on a book probably raised my profile a little bit in their mind."

From a student's perspective, several of them pointed out how they expect teachers to be experts in their fields and expressed disappointment if they saw them lacking in that respect. As Steve, a resident student in Unit 2 expressed,

> They are sort of our leader in a way. They are a source of knowledge that we need. [I assess the quality of my classes by assessing] how much I learned, how knowledgeable the professors are, sometimes they are just reading from the book, not really bringing in their own knowledge and experience. Mainly that, mainly how much they are really bringing in their own rather than just bringing up a PowerPoint and reading off of it. [. . .] I had one class in psychology where the professor honestly didn't know very much know at all [. . .] So it didn't make sense.

A similarity found among teachers with knowledge-orientation was that they use their intuitive judgment to assess the quality of their teaching, mostly relying on the quality of work produced by students in their coursework. They either completely discounted or did not give much weight to student-evaluation surveys administered by their organization because they think that students lack competence or are biased in their responses. Annie from Unit 3 said that the student surveys are a "waste of time," and expressed her approach as follows:

> I have in mind things that I want the students to be able to do and to know. I assess whether they have got there or not. In courses where

I say ok there are ten topics, ten theories, ten issues, and they have to be able to employ them at the end of the semester, in some way, I can usually tell whether they have been able to do that or not. Beginning of the semester—no idea, end of the semester—used them. That's it. I don't have a better system than that.

Similarly, Eric in Unit 4 expressed that he uses his assessment based on students' ability to solve the problems that he assigns to them. He also uses his judgment by comparing his content with that produced by other experts in his field. While he tries to explore the reasons when his student-evaluation ratings go too low or too high, he mostly doesn't pay much attention to them. Coqui in Unit 2 attributed his lack of faith in these surveys due to their poor design.

They can tell you did they learn. They don't tell you did they do the work. . . . It turns out to be a survey of the population where you don't know the causal variables. So the overall average gives you a sense of how satisfied the student was. But none of the other metric, none of the sub-classifications are worth anything.

Teachers with knowledge-orientation expressed frustration about students being too focused either on grades or jobs. Derf, as well as Coqui in Unit 2, saw it as a short-term materialistic goal that keeps students from engaging in deep study and failing to see the big picture as "they are all under the task-mode of operation."

This evidence shows that the guru schema showcases knowledge-orientation and assesses teaching quality based on students' performance. Its greatest challenge is students' misaligned goals. Teachers subscribing to guru schema view themselves as scholars and pursue activities such as conducting research or writing books that contribute to their discipline in some way. These activities are closely related to the subjects they teach, and they take great pride in their contributions to the field. Individuals with guru schema get frustrated when they see students too focused on grades, or jobs, or any short-term benefit that demonstrates that they are not interested in knowledge but only in its material benefits. The subscribers of this schema did not endorse any specific teaching technique, nor did the teachers express any particular problem with the online modality of teaching.

COACH

This orientation surfaced as individuals emphasized the importance of teachers being approachable, mentoring students to help them learn. They used analogies such as a mentor, a coach, a parent, a nurse, or a doctor. They gave high importance to understanding students' learning needs and customizing teaching style accordingly. For example, Marissa—an administrator in Unit 3—compared teacher to a nurse as follows:

> They see things differently. A nurse has to find out what is going on so far . . . they are the first person who takes down what are your symptoms. . . . So that parallel to teaching is that a good teacher is trying to understand where the students are coming from, and understanding some of those contextual issues also.

Individuals with this orientation talked about how learning is achieved through a constant dialog between students and teachers where teachers do not 'lecture' but 'discuss' the subject matter with their students. Teresa—a professor in Unit 3—explained how she tries to help students explore their true potential and encourages them by setting herself up as an example. In her words,

> My role is to introduce them to their own ability to succeed in those classes. So I really have to peel away at them to get them to say OK I can do this. My role also, being a woman in a field like this, I represent women, and its ok to like programming. That doesn't make me a geek, a nerd, a bad person. It's ok to be good at math. I need to make sure that they see that in themselves.

Teachers emphasized knowing their students personally and being approachable to them so that they do not hesitate in seeking their help. Teresa said, "I have found that by using their name, by sharing an interest with my students, all those little things have made a huge impact on my students' attendance, interest . . . I try and make myself approachable." Similarly, Caleb—another professor in Unit 3—took great pride in having students come to meet with him at his office, as he said,

> It is this week, which is 3rd week of classes. Today I have had eight students come through the door and talked to me, two of whom were from the previous semester. That's pretty cool that they have that level of comfort, or I have that approachability or something.

Mary—a teacher, and Kelly—a student in Unit 2 compared teaching with parenting. Kelly said that professors take students under their wings and help them out, while Mary talked about how teachers mold students' minds and students look up to them as their mentors. Teachers with this schema placed relatively much higher emphasis on student surveys to assess the quality of their teaching. Mary in Unit 2 and Caleb in Unit 3 not only considered end-of-semester surveys as useful but also took feedback every week to assess what difficulties students were experiencing in learning. Similarly, Robert in Unit 5 valued student surveys highly and took immense pride in being one of the highest

rated professors not only in his university but also in the social platforms such as ratemyprofessors.com. Allen in Unit 4 calls her surveys
as 'pulse-checks' and thinks that she not only gets feedback, but it also
helps keep students engaged.

> What I ask them before they get the opportunity to fill out their eval-
> uation, what they like so that I don't throw that out, and what they
> don't like, and why they thought it wasn't important. I think the effort
> that you make throughout the semester asking for feedback allows
> you to make corrections and clarify why you are doing what you are
> doing, which keeps their attitude positive, engaged, motivated.

One of the reasons behind viewing teachers as a coach that many interviewees gave was that they feel students are not prepared for college-level
learning. Robert in Unit 5, whose students are mostly non-traditional
(over 25 years of age) in a university that has an open-admission policy,
said that he has to spend first two weeks of his courses in teaching students how to learn. When asked about his key challenges, he said,

> For me, it is the unpreparedness of the students. [. . .] I usually teach
> a lot of very freshman level courses [. . .] So you get a lot of people
> that quite frankly aren't ready for college. They just don't know it
> yet. And it's challenging.

Marissa, an administrator, expressed similar views and reflected that
there is an untapped potential where along with telling teachers how to
teach, the higher education field should focus on coaching students how
to learn.

However, in the online world, teachers with this schema expressed
difficulties as they found coaching using online technologies either very
laborious or ineffective. Allen in Unit 4 said she had to learn how to
communicate with her students using email in the absence of non-verbal
language. Robert found e-mails to be ineffective as they cannot express
emotion. So he creates short videos for each student on a one-on-one
basis to provide feedback and establish a rapport so that they are encouraged to participate in their learning activities actively. But he acknowledged that it is "labor intensive." As described by him,

> And so I started using a ton of video in my teaching. [. . .] either
> at my office, or my home, I have a little webcam, so I have high-
> definition webcams in both and, in a normal discussion where type
> that, type, type, type, you'd see my face. "Hi, great job on the dis-
> cussion today." You know you can't type empathy; you can't type
> enthusiasm; you can't type—humor is hard for me to type. But when
> I am talking to you, and you can see me laugh. I have heard so many
> reviews from students that just see me smile at them, talking to them,

and here is what they know. Every video they make, because I talk to them by name, its individual, they know that. It's not like I type something and then copy and paste, copy and paste, copy and paste. It's not. It's very individualized. It is usually labor intensive.

Caleb, a professor in Unit 3, who has taught some courses online, expressed this difficulty:

> It is uncommon in the online realm for someone to raise a coachable question in the midst of doing an exercise. In the classroom you see a different approach, that is, students coming in, seeking all kinds of guidance throughout the entire process.

In summary, student-orientation guides the coach schema. Its quality criterion is student feedback, and its greatest challenge is students' unpreparedness. Individuals drawing from this schema laid emphasis on guiding students on their learning path, and some also expressed their disapproval of guru schema saying teaching is not about teacher's knowledge but student learning. They prefer problem-based learning over lecture-based teaching because it gives them a chance to interact closely with students and coach them in their learning activities. They value student evaluations, and often administer additional frequent surveys to assess how well the students are learning. They try to personally know their students and take pride when they are approached by the students for some guidance. They find students' lack of preparedness for college-level learning very challenging and try to address this problem by coaching them as best as they can, whether in resident or online settings.

ARTIST

Individuals with this orientation expressed the importance of teaching techniques. They focused on how teachers capture students' attention to communicate complex ideas engagingly, comprehensible to diverse audiences. The analogies ranged from a performing artist or a standup comedian to a psychologist who can 'look' inside a student's mind and figure out a way to get the message across. Maxwell—a senior student in Unit 1—expressed this orientation as follows:

> Maybe like a psychologist. [. . .] because I have had some [teachers] who actually try to get into the head of people either positively or negatively. And I have had some [. . .] they kind of scare information into your head and they know how to get it into your brains, so it's stuck in there. [. . .] Other people, [. . .] kind of like know how to get it in a positive way through humor and different teaching methods

[. . .] how to inject stuff into your head without you having to try to keep it in there.

Teachers with this orientation valued getting instant feedback from their students in a classroom and seeing the 'light-bulb go on' in their eyes. Emma called herself an entertainer who enjoys having a captive audience, challenging their thinking, and having that "in-the-moment discussion that happens on the fly." In her words,

> I spend a lot of time on making it entertaining. And it's interesting because I have had this conversation with people. They say you are not here to entertain. You know what, you don't understand the first thing about basic attention span if you don't understand that you have to engage and entertain in a way that is not hand puppets. So I spend a lot of time to figure out how can I create a class that is provocative in some ways and that couches the content in a way that forces the students to engage. And while I may yak at them a lot, there is really little time when it is not pointing out what you think, [. . .] I think making it interesting and relevant for students.

She compared teaching with 'marketing' as:

> The thing [that teaching and marketing] share in common is that they are disseminating information to a targeted group of people and you want them to walk away with a particular message. They are exactly the same. Being able to understand the motivations and the incentives of the person you are delivering it to is very similar. I think, the way you have to understand how to break down content, and what is important, and the order in which you say things, is very important and similar. I think, understanding the channels that people best take in information is important.

Mike, an online student in Unit 4, remembered his experiences with resident teaching earlier and found parallels between teachers and standup comedians who are

> upfront commanding whole room. The whole room is kind of following with them. [. . .] Their goal is to, in their own way, through humor, kind of educate people, and kind of give them something to think about. [. . .] the underlying theme would give the people who are listening to it something to think about. [. . .] They may not necessarily utilize humor, but they'll, I think they'll at least try to make the material as engaging as possible. [. . .] They'll introduce their own experiences or try to teach the material with the same kind of passion

that may try to accomplish the same goal of getting the students to think.

When describing how they assess the quality of teaching and learning, individuals portraying attention-orientation talked about their "in-the-moment learning experience." Some participants mentioned student surveys and peer reviews, but their answers to other questions revealed a little more nuanced focus on how to work with students' minds. For example, Frank in Unit 2 used the analogy of an engineer to explain his approach:

> You think about an engineer; you are trying to get some piece of hardware to work with its environment [. . .] It's the same thing. When we teach, we are trying to get what we need to teach into the students. It is not like stuffing information in it. We have to change them to work with the information and the environment. So we have to engineer that change. [. . .] Because we are not just credentialing. It is one thing to stuff the content, and it is another thing to change the student and have them fit it into their new schemas of the world, and that's the tricky part.

Sam in Unit 6 used the analogy of an actor or a musician for a teacher that revealed a similar focus on in-the-moment teaching and learning experience:

> I think that classroom teaching has a lot of similarities to acting and to musicianship. Where the ability to improvise is important but most actors have a script that they can go back on, or in musicianship, where there is a score in certain genres of music, you might improvise. And I think that kind of more beautiful interaction between teachers and students can happen in those unscripted moments.

Almost all teachers with attention-orientation stated that the students' attention span is getting shorter and so they find ways to capture their attention by using whatever means available at hand. They talked about techniques such as using humor, telling stories, or creating interesting content so that they remain engaged.

They play videos in class at frequent intervals to keep them engaged while also ensuring that videos are not too long. Marissa, Christian, and Robert in Units 3, 4, and 5, respectively, talked about 'chunkable' content not only in videos but also other materials such as text, discussions, and lectures. In the online context, the focus on creating a good learning experience was especially evident in the responses from instructional designers who considered long walls of text or long videos that were not designed keeping in mind short attention spans as poor quality.

However, it is important to note that all these experiences and analogies related to the participants' educational experiences within a resident classroom where a teacher takes the stage to engage. In an online setting, this schema translated to the content that captures students' attention. It manifests as best practices of instruction design such as creating granular content, making engaging videos, or designing navigable content, which now is becoming increasingly video based. Unit 4 revealed it in having instructional designers ensuring that the content is engaging and modular to capture short attention spans. Unit 5 and Unit 6 took this a step further by having professional video production teams and media specialists work with faculty members to create content that is movie-like or "viral-worthy." This schema shows relation to the cyber-cultural identity discussed earlier, as it perceives teaching as an art, focuses on the cultural aspect of focusing on students' attention, and uses cyber technologies to create, disseminate, and track digital content. It reinforces that, while technology allows the digitization and dissemination of the content virtually, the schema of a teacher as a performer continues to surface in the online world as well.

In summary, the artist schema focuses on student attention during teaching and learning activities, considering their learning experience as the key quality criteria. It finds students' short attention span as their greatest challenge. It views a teacher as someone who captures attention, persuades, and challenges students' minds while also entertaining in a manner akin to a stage-performer. While seeming as entertainment, this schema focuses on understanding the learners' minds to figure out what it will take to get the message across, persuade them, and then provoke thinking.

Contexts of Schema

These three schemas emerged in a variety of units and roles in the study, indicating that perhaps an individual's schema is more deep-seated than the influences of his or her contextual settings. It is also noticeable that several individuals expressed more than one schema, indicating that schemas are not mutually exclusive. For example, Eric in Unit 4 who has taught extensively in resident as well as online units, portrayed all three schemas with strong emphasis on his knowledge and research, his passion toward mentoring his students, and amount of time he invested in designing his 'content' (overhead slides, videos, lab-assignments, eBook) so that his students can understand complex material easily. He talked about how he had perfected the use of blackboard in classroom settings, which he now tries to emulate in his video recordings. In his words:

> For residential, if you can do perfect blackboard, your presence is the
> blackboard because the logic is so rigorous, the students just enjoy

the blackboard. . . . They get how you do analysis, what's your logic, step by step. [. . .] If the blackboard can be made perfect, that is the highest level of classroom teaching. [. . .] Online is different. I rely on my voice, to reconstruct the logic from the bullets on the slide. The bullets on the slide have some gap in terms of what I want my students to learn. So I use my voice just to fill in the gap [. . .] I focus on the voice, clear voice, in a quiet room. It is a different challenge. I usually write a sketch. If I am not happy with the recording, delete it, record again. Try several times, until you think the rigorous logic is in your voice. Then I will stop.

While schema emerged as independent of a resident or online setting, when individuals talked about their experiences, there did emerge a pattern in their adoption and use of online modality. With the increasing availability of digital content in residential as well as online settings, the need to disseminate knowledge through classroom lectures is diminishing. This trend is especially apparent in the online units, as was argued by Steve in Unit 4. Robert, a full-time online professor in Unit5 for last ten years, said that he doesn't really 'teach.' He just helps students get through the content prepared by someone else. To enjoy 'teaching experience,' in its traditional sense, he works as a part-time faculty member in a resident university.

You know this is therapy, that's why I teach it. I miss teaching in a classroom because that's real teaching. And I don't mean real in a pejorative way, but you don't teach a lot. They learn online. Material is presented; they have to go learn it somehow. They'll ask questions. But I am not presenting as much. [In my resident class] I love the students, and I get to feel like a college professor while I am here. And so I do this primarily for therapy [. . .] so I can validate my existence as an educator by teaching.

Although Steve's views express guru schema as unfit for 'teaching' online, there are those who have been using their content in their online courses and have expressed pride in doing so. They consider content creation to be their strong suit and a critical factor in student learning. None of them expressed any particular dislike for teaching online except that they lose flexibility in changing the course content, as was discussed earlier.

The teachers reflecting coach schema find coaching difficult in an online setting because of having to wait for a student to seek help proactively. This lag between the moment when coaching is needed and the time when it can be provided is the biggest challenge for this role, especially since online teaching is more about coaching and less about teaching as was expressed by Robert. These challenges are overcome by some teachers by creating short videos for their students for several reasons such as to portray themselves as more approachable, to give them individualized feedback, and in general to connect with them so that students feel comfortable to reach out to them when they need help.

As the artist schema focuses on how the content is presented and tries to capture attention, its manifestation in an online setting is difficult. Emma in Unit 3 who calls herself an entertainer in the classroom hates online because

> I think the in-the-moment discussions that happen on the fly which are difficult to do in discussion based online type of things is where a lot of rich stuff comes out. I think connecting with students in a more personal face-to-face way is a sweet spot for me. [. . .] It's that dynamic because I need that. I crave that, so I want to look that student in the eye; I need feedback in some ways. I don't get that feedback in online. It is just better for the way I teach.

The artist schema when taken to the online world often fails unless it is given the tools to produce high-quality videos. As was pointed out earlier, Frank in Unit 3 made videos but had to change his teaching style by focusing on just the subject matter and not 'tell stories' to engage his students because the students expect high-quality production in videos. He talked about how he uses videos to connect his stories posted by him on the discussion board with what he says in the video.

> I try to do short videos. And I try to not do them in the same spot. So I'll do some from my kitchen, from here, from my dining room, from my office. Trying to get that same level of connection. Sometimes [the camera is] on me, sometimes I have the camera down at the desk, and I am doing something, but I'm talking. Just talking. And the goal is to try and make a connection so that when I write those stories on the discussion board, they will actually read them and make a connection.

Making videos also represents some elements of coach schema through which teachers try to establish their presence and make a connection with their students. As Caleb in Unit 3 put it, who occasionally teaches online,

> I made a two-minute video every week. And that two-minute video talked about essentially, where I was in grading different things, and what to expect in the next week, and what the assignments were like, and other sorts of announcements. And this was me making a dumb video. So they got to see what the guy's office looks like. What is his attitude? Is he a grumpy old guy? Which one of the seven dwarfs is he? That was my way of having a stage presence in the online

classroom. It seems to have worked because it is not uncommon to receive comments from students about the things that happened on the video. It was pretty funny.

These patterns indicate how different schemas leverage technology to improve their teaching but at the same time struggle with the limitations that technology imposes. Guru leverages technology to create academically rigorous content but feels constrained by such a content's inflexibility. Coach schema uses it to have more interaction between students and teachers but feels constrained by the time lag. And artist schema uses technology to create engaging content but misses to experience 'in-the-moment' expressions of ideas and responses.

Arguably, the guru schema has its roots in the traditional image that has been downplayed significantly in recent times as an outdated concept of 'sage on the stage' (King 1993). As this schema focuses on knowledge, it appreciates scholarship as integral to teaching and expects pedagogy to be tailored to the discipline, as argued by Rowland et al. (1998). This perspective is also evident in (Pratt 1998), where one of the five perspectives of teaching is the 'transmission' where the "primary responsibility of the instructor is to structure or organize the content and create educational materials that can be efficiently delivered within the allotted course time" (Boldt 1998, 59–60). But the author notes that although widely prevailing, this is the most negatively perceived perspective. This negative perception prevails perhaps because most of us have experienced its poor examples through disorganized teachers who "jumped without connection from topic to topic, overwhelmed students with facts, offered convoluted explanations and responses to student questioning, or mismatched what they taught (usually by lectures) and what they based their evaluations on (usually in tests)" (Boldt 1998, 60).

The coach schema often referred to as a 'guide on the side' (King 1993), has gained much popularity as teaching practice is shifting its focus from teacher-centric to learner-centric methods. This study also shows a similar emphasis whose expanse is illustrated by its parallels across two of the five perspectives identified by (Pratt 1998). These are apprenticeship (Johnson and Pratt 1998) and nurturing (T'Kenye 1998). While pedagogical advancements are proposing a teacher to be less of a guru and more of a coach, the interpretation of what exactly a coach should do varies widely across individuals and contexts. As the analogies offered by participants in Table 4.5 show, this schema ranges from coaching (similar to an apprenticeship) to parenting (similar to nurturing). It is also important to note that one of the reasons distance education struggled to achieve widespread adoption was the inability to establish rich interaction between teachers and students, which is a key element in coaching. As online technologies have made such interactions feasible, there is an effort not only to strengthen but also to measure interaction by using learner analytics as an effective tool (Ferguson 2012; Siemens 2012).

The artist schema has been sparingly mentioned in the education literature and can be related to the age-old debate about whether teaching is an art or a science (Highet 1954; James 1899; Villegas-Reimers 2003). As my findings indicate, it is a combination of both. Some of its manifestations can also be seen in the form of adoption of computer games for formal as well as informal 'edutainment' to improve learner engagement (Egenfeldt-Nielsen 2011), engaging trained actors in recording video-lectures (Šlaus et al. 2013), and producing Hollywood-style course videos to attract students (Gross 2015). As evident, this schema cuts across content development as well as content delivery, as both need to be interesting and engaging. The five perspectives identified by Pratt (1998) do not cover this schema as it is more about a teacher's style than any method of teaching.

With increasingly digitized content, the transformation in a teachers' role can be explained using these schemas. A guru provides subject matter expertise in content development, whereas a coach helps students by guiding and encouraging them to get through the content. This doesn't imply that the guru doesn't have to think about student interaction or that coach doesn't require subject matter expertise. The critical balance was emphasized by Glenn in Unit 6 who said that their criteria of selecting academic consultants for content-development is not only that they have a terminal degree in their fields, but also to have strong teaching experience in the resident as well as online settings. These prerequisites assure that the content developer is familiar with students' profile and their learning behaviors. Artist cuts across both knowledge-orientation and student-orientation to focus on how to make the content and its delivery attractive. The instructional designers fulfill part of this role as they focus on the structure, navigability, and length of the content that makes student's learning experience as seamless as possible. This unifying perspective helps establish the importance and contribution of each role—content creation, content delivery, and student mentoring—to the overall process of education, thereby also addressing the concerns about unbundling of teachers' role due to the emergence of online education and how it can impact academia (Gehrke and Kezar 2015).

Attention

Attention is the fourth micro-foundation of institutional logics, and it represents "what problems and issues get attended to and what solutions are likely to be considered in decision making" (Thornton, Ocasio, and Lounsbury 2012, 90). The data for this construct was obtained by analyzing the challenges regarding teaching practice that the individuals and organizations are focusing on, and the decisions they are taking to address them.

Student Engagement

While each unit reflected its unique challenges, student engagement emerged as a common concern consistently across all units. At the organizational level, this pertains to students' engagement outside the classroom while teachers expressed concerns about student engagement within the classroom.

University- and college-level documents showed a concerted effort to engage students in activities such as internships, extracurricular activities, and experiential learning initiatives to address the student-engagement needs outside the classroom. While there are different levels of technology adoption across organizations, programs, and individuals, one consistent pattern that emerged was how the focus of technology usage has shifted from enabling education access to offering a learning experience. The term "learning experience" surfaced across all units, and especially in online units where they try to compare themselves with resident education and try to create an "experience" through means such as social networks, discussion forums, online office hours, virtual student clubs and communities.

Redwood University of Unit 3 and Unit 4 articulated one of the six foundations in its strategic plan as student engagement. It implements this strategy by supporting professional clubs and societies for students to come together as a community. These initiatives echo the field-level concerns where there was a call made by agencies such as APLU to create communities within universities and colleges to improve student engagement, which in turn will improve their retention and graduation rates.

Student engagement also emerged as a key concern expressed by all faculty members. Annie, a professor in Unit 3, expressed, "I think there are always problems with teaching in terms of engagement. . . . It plagues every teacher, not just me." Harry, an administrator in Unit 5, emphasized how student engagement and retention is a university-wide concern, "Today we spend a lot of time helping our students trying to make sure that they stay in class. Make sure they are doing their work. If they are failing, why are they failing."

These concerns about within-classroom disengagement manifested in two variants: students' unpreparedness and students' lack of interest or attention span. Both impact teaching practice, as teachers need to coach students on how to learn to address the former and try to make their teaching interesting and engaging to address the latter. The move toward creating an 'experience' is also observed as teachers try to create the teacher's presence in online settings by creating their videos. Teachers come up with their own style to reflect their personality and help students "know" them.

Student Unpreparedness

The problem of about 20% of students requiring remedial education at a field level was also reflected in individual interviews as faculty members talked about students' lack of readiness for college-level learning. Lack of student preparedness makes teachers focus not so much on the subject matter but on how to help students learn the content, as was reflected by Charles in Unit 1, Caleb in Unit 3, and Eric in Unit 4. They focus on problem-based learning as it allows coaching opportunities when students try to work through the problem. Eric said that he finds lecture-based techniques to work well for his more prepared graduate students whereas his undergraduate students, being less prepared, need hands-on, problem-based learning to be effective.

> I did some experiments in the classroom . . . so I tried lecture-centric style which is more like liberal arts theory. I also tried a teaching style that is more hands-on, more problem-based learning. . . . I have some evidence through my class-teaching experiments, and I have some tentative conclusions that are for undergraduate students, especially in our college. I found hands-on labs are very important because our students in our college are less prepared in their hands-on skills, so I think a hands-on lab can enhance their learning most effectively. That is my tentative conclusion. For graduate level, depends on the students. If the student is already a professional, has a lot of hands-on experience, then you can teach the student other things. Like more critical thinking, more analytical things and less hands-on. [For] grad students, typically I will first check the background of students. If they are good at hands-on, then I will adjust. Then my teaching will be more lecture, critical thinking, analysis-oriented. For some of my graduate classes, if they are not much hands-on experienced, then I increase hands-on. I do it adaptively.

This problem was most acute in Unit 5, which has an open-admissions policy coupled with the trend of students moving toward online. The resident enrollments in Unit 5 remained flat in absolute numbers and dropped by 7% in relation to the total enrollment in the period from 2005 to 2015. These factors have aggravated the problem because as online makes learning more difficult, the risk of dropouts is increasing. As student retention and completion rates are critical metrics closely monitored to prevent high dropout rates especially in for-profit organizations, Aspen University has started digital tracking of students' as well as teachers' online behavior. It acquired a software tool which, when plugged into its learning management system, provides data on time spent by students on learning activities, use of resources, and discussion board posts. It is using predictive analytics of students' online behavior to trigger warnings so that teachers and administrators can proactively engage with the student to prevent dropouts. This data is then displayed in a faculty dashboard app visible to the faculty and administration, and used later as an input for faculty performance evaluations. According to Robert,

> People quit online not because they are stupid, but because they are disconnected. I don't know anyone; I don't care; I am on an island. It's easy to quit when you won't be missed. Right? When you think no one is there, you don't know anybody; I think it's so easy to walk away.

More than 80% of the student population in this unit are over the age of 25, working full time, have families and have come back to school for career advancements. According to university documents as well as individual interviews, this student demographic has lower retention rates and, therefore, needs novel approaches to engage. While, on the one hand, the university is trying to engage them by creating cohorts, Robert tries to engage them by creating personalized videos, having them post their videos, and asking them to respond to daily bonus questions that brings them to the online discussion board. Similarly, Unit 4 is working toward measuring student interaction on their newly instituted online learning platform. Unit 6 is trying to track how students are using the online content to assess students' learning behavior.

Student Attention Span

The reasons given by the interviewees about the lack of student attention varied across all units. Some attributed it to students' disinterest in anything that doesn't directly translate to some form of immediate material benefit, such as a job. Others pointed to digital devices such as laptops and cell phones at their disposal that keeps them perpetually distracted. But one common implication was that teachers need to make extra effort to capture students' attention by making their content much shorter and interesting to alleviate any boredom and keep them actively engaged. Caleb, as mentioned earlier, observed students' shortening attention spans and addressed it by designing his classes that have multiple switches at short intervals:

> It appears that students' attention spans are not what they once were. Certainly, much briefer today than I remember it being when I was a student. . . . It has to be seven to eight minutes and change something, something to do. Have a discussion, raise a question, show a related video. Those are my kind of two go-to kinds of things to do. Because you can introduce a discussion question at most any time. But for me

coming off with observing the phenomenon of short attention span was one thing and figure out how to deal with it was another one.

In online settings, this translated into creating granular content so that it doesn't require long periods of focus. Unit 6 not only creates granular content but also has an in-house production team to create framing videos in which individuals as surrogate faculty members provide a human face to the content. Unit 5 has set up a full-scale movie production studio to create Hollywood-style movies.

Another common pattern related to this concern was that teachers and administrators who have been in education for several decades reported it to be more of a recent phenomenon. For example, Caleb in Unit 3 expressed the following:

> The preparation of materials has morphed over the recent years. Many moons ago when I was teaching, I could rely on students to focus and concentrate for almost an entire hour and a half session. That's not the case today, at least in my experience. So I have had to evolve the materials in sufficiently modular lumps, interruptible lumps, and changed something, put a video up there that is related, ask a question for discussion, have to do something approximately every seven to ten minutes. Otherwise, I lose them to some other semi-innocent distraction, typically smartphone.

Marissa, an administrator in the same unit, said,

> I was told when I was in school that we should never have lecture more than 20 minutes. Now it is eight minutes. So the digital mind has a different attention span, a different kind of thing that they are tuned to, a different way that they read things, a different way they want to see things presented. I do think that it influences how they desire to receive information, and the patience they have for it.

One could argue that this is just a manifestation of the older generation's perception about the next generation. But the implication nonetheless remains that it requires an effort to address this concern by altering teaching techniques.

5 Mediatization

My data analysis ran in three parallel tracks to trace the mediatization of teaching practice. In the first track, I chronicled the critical events that reflected any of the four phases of mediatization over a period of 120 years of history of distance education. Some of the significant events relevant to this study are listed in Table 5.1. The second track comprised a more granular manifestation of mediatization at all three levels of analysis—i.e., field, organization, and individual—specifically focusing on core entities of teaching practice—content, teacher, and student.

The third track related to the premise that the field of higher education has some characteristics of a cultural institution as it engages in the creation and exchange of symbolic content. This then entailed looking at other fields that have cultural characteristics and finding parallels, if any, in the way they were transformed when their communication processes were digitized. Finding such parallels, in turn, allowed a better comprehension of the contemporary dynamics as well as the possible projection of what could unfold in future. Scholars have done a similar exercise by comparing higher education with manufacturing, retail, healthcare, and other service industries (Scott 2010; Anson 2007; Christensen and Eyring 2011; Ljoså 1993; Martin 2011). I extended this line of thinking by bringing out parallels with cultural institutions, focusing on three entities of teaching practice—content, teacher, and student. I discuss these three tracks in the following sections, highlighting the findings from each as relevant.

Distance Education

Education has always been aided by the prevalent technology of the times, starting with written text in medieval ages and then printed books in the modern era to aid the core of teaching and learning in a face-to-face setting (Wedemeyer 1981). These technologies changed from being a supplementary aid to a mediator when distance education emerged in the late 19th century. Some accounts trace the beginnings of distance education to 1878 when the Chautauqua Literary and Scientific Circle

Table 5.1 Critical mediatization events

#	Year	Event	*Phase*
1.	1881	Chautauqua Correspondence College offered first college-level course by mail	Mediation
2.	1892	Major universities: Penn State University, University of Chicago created first college-level distance courses (Moore and Anderson 2003)	Adoption
3.	1921	The federal government issued the first educational radio license to the Latter-Day Saints' University of Salt Lake City (Saba 2011)	Mediation
4.	1926	Distance Education Accrediting Commission (DEAC) founded	Adoption
5.	1934	The University of Iowa used television broadcasting (Syed 2009)	Mediation
6.	1963	Instructional Television Fixed Service (ITFS) started as low-cost licensing systems to offer distance education (Syed 2009)	Mediation
7.	1971	Commission on Non-traditional Study created, funded by Carnegie Corporation (Gould 1973)	Adoption
8.	1973	National College Credit Recommendation (NCCRS) founded (www.nationalccrs.org)	Adoption
9.	1974	ACE established credit recommendation service CREDIT to connect workplace and non-traditional learning with academic credit	Adoption
10.	1985	National Technological University became the first school to offer online degree courses via satellite transmission	Mediation
11.	1991	Interactive television (one-way video over satellite with multipoint audio conferencing) for distance learning began at Air Force Institute of Technology (Moore and Anderson 2003)	Mediation
12.	1998	Federal government included new rule to make distance program eligible for Title IV funding	Adoption
13.	1999	AAUP released Statement on Copyright and Statement on Distance Education (www.aaup.org)	Reciprocation
14.	1999	Jones International University founded as the first fully online accredited university	Adoption
15.	2001	Massachusetts Institute of Technology (MIT) launched OpenCourseWare (OCW) funded by Mellon and Lumina foundations	Mediation
16.	2001	Carnegie Mellon University launched the Open Learning Initiative (OLI) funded by Lumina Foundation	Mediation
17.	2006	Federal government removes 50% rule restriction for Title IV eligibility	Adoption

(Continued)

Table 5.1 (Continued)

#	Year	Event	Phase
18.	2009	ACE recommended nine courses from Straighterline (www.straighterline.com)	Adoption
19.	2011	First MOOC launched by Stanford University (Crotty 2012)	Mediation
20.	2012	Gates foundation fund research on new learning models (www.gatesfoundation.org)	Reciprocation
21.	2013	ACE accredits MOOC courses delivered by Coursera	Adoption
22.	2016	ACE partners with the Association of College and University Educators (ACUE) to offer training programs for college instructors	Reciprocation
23.	2016	USDE launches an experiment with non-accredited providers to provide education eligible for Title IV funding	Reciprocation

offered a four-year correspondence course for summer schools at Lake Chautauqua in upstate New York. This was followed by teaching higher education through the mail by Chautauqua Correspondence College in 1881 (Moore and Kearsley 2012; Wedemeyer 1981). Other major universities followed suit with Penn State University and University of Chicago offering their first college-level distance courses in 1892 (Moore and Anderson 2003). Since then there have been several generations of distance education through broadcast radio and television, open universities, teleconferencing, and now the Internet.

With communication technologies at our disposal since the late 19th century, distance education has helped to address the social need to expand access (Garrison 1993) and the economic need to leverage existing resources to increase profitability of higher education institutions (Peters 1967, 1994). However, this alternate model of education has introduced multiple challenges at the pedagogical or transactional level (e.g., see Lloyd, Byrne, and McCoy 2012; Picciano 2002; Anderson 2008; Garrison, Anderson, and Archer 2003), as well as at the structural or institutional level (e.g., Moore and Kearsley 2011; Salmon 2005; Peters 1967, 1994). These challenges vary with the meaning of "distance," which changes with the technologies employed to impart education. Its origins are rooted in the non-traditional means of learning, such as independent learning, open learning, part-time learning, and correspondence study, that were collectively referred to as "learning at the back door" by Wedemeyer (1981). The key characteristics that have been emphasized in literature to define distance education reflect the ways in which distance education deviates from traditional forms of education, thereby changing the definition of "distance" in education.

The transactional theory of distance (Moore 1993) explicates "distance" as a continuum where the degree of dialog between the teacher and the learner varies with the degree of structure in the content. The higher the structure, the lesser the need for dialog, and thus the larger the transactional distance. Therefore, according to this theory, it can be argued that online education has reduced the transactional distance by increasing the level of mediated interaction between teacher and student, as well as student and student, which perhaps has led to its accelerated adoption.

This reduction in transactional distance can explain the unpredicted growth rate in online adoption that has also been viewed as the second wave of massification of higher education (CHEA 2002). Looking at the history of higher education, the first massification wave involved physical expansion in the number of higher education organizations. It began in the 1920s and led to qualitative changes in higher education, the primary ones noted by education historians as transition from elite to masses, increased vocationalism, bureaucratization of academic institutions, and the rise of student subcultures (collegiate, vocational, academic, and non-conformist) (Clark and Trow 1966; Geiger 2011; Altbach 2011; Rudolph 1962).

The second wave of massification led by mediation technologies started at the turn of the 21st century and is currently unfolding. The debate this time is about the effectiveness and quality of education and related accreditation that were developed over many decades and based on traditional institutional forms (Meyer 2002; CHEA 2002). There are several sides to this debate, the foremost being a concern about the lack of means to ascertain quality in a distance environment (Novak 2002), while the other is arguing that distance education has shaken the status quo and introduced pedagogical rigor in higher education (Guri-Rozenblit 1990; Swail and Kampits 2001). Some argue that distance education is casting itself in the conventional model of an educational provision, thereby failing to tap its full potential (Powell and Keen 2006), while others recognize that the pace of growth has made the field fairly uneven, especially in terms of quality (Willinsky, Fischman, and Metcalfe 2011).

This "virtual massification" has been studied from the research point of view at multiple levels. The macro-level research focuses on social issues, such as access and quality of education, globalization and industrialization of academic institutions, and cross-cultural implications of this phenomenon (Zawacki-Richter, Bäcker, and Vogt 2009). The meso-level research has focused on organization models, structures, hierarchies, and institutional priorities (e.g., Moore and Kearsley 2011; Peters 1967, 1994). And the micro-level research looks at pedagogy and instructional design (e.g., Holmberg 2003; Moore 1993; Anderson 2008), trying to make online education a student-centric or learner-centric experience.

Mediatization Phases

Mediation

Mediation occurs when technology mediates a social or an institutional communication process. Tracing the history of distance education in general, the phenomenon of mediation of teaching practice started with the emergence of distance education in the 1890s and with online education in 1990s. The Institute of Education Sciences—National Center for Education Statistics (IES-NCES) defines the term distance education as follows:

> Distance education uses one or more technologies to deliver instruction to students who are separated from the instructor as well as to support regular and substantive interaction between the student and the instructor synchronously or asynchronously. Technologies used for instruction may include the following: the Internet; one-way and two-way transmissions through open broadcasts, closed circuit, cable, microwave, broadband lines, fiber optics, satellite, or wireless communication devices; audio conferencing; and videocassettes, DVDs, and CD-ROMs, only if the videocassettes, DVDs, and CD-ROMs are used in a course in conjunction with the technologies listed above.
> (McFarland et al. 2017, 121)

While the contemporary definition, as shown earlier, implies the use of electronic communication technologies in distance education, the earliest distance education was paper-based. Since then the mediation technologies have continued to change with the Internet being the most recent form and MOOCs as one of its recent formats. Although higher education has tried to use all communication technologies to mediate teaching practice as evident in Table 5.1, the most recent form of Internet technologies has gained the widest adoption of all.

Adoption

Adoption occurs when the use of mediation technology widens. This, in the context of higher education, translates to accepting online education to be legitimate. Therefore, the accreditation of online education by established agencies reflects adoption. This phase started in 1926 when the Distance Education Accreditation Commission was founded. The need to find an alternative and a more flexible way to deliver higher education was felt way before the current online revolution. The Commission on Non-traditional Study in 1971 is a material manifestation of this need, which reported that:

> Most of us agreed that non-traditional study is more an attitude than a system and this can never be defined except tangentially. This

attitude puts the student first and the institution second, concentrates more on the former's need than the latter's convenience, encourages diversity of individual opportunity rather than uniform prescription, and deemphasizes time, space, and even course requirements in favor of competence and, where applicable, performance. It has concern for the learner of any age and circumstance, for the degree aspirant as well as the person who finds sufficient reward in enriching life through constant, periodic, or occasional study. This attitude is not new; it is simply more prevalent than it used to be.

(Gould 1973, xv)

The earlier quote points to what some members of higher education field have been trying to address through technologies ranging from paper to radio to television, and have finally found some resolution with the advent of the Internet. The real adoption took off when the federal government extended its Title IV program in 1998 to online education. It was first introduced as a 50% rule that only half of the courses or student in a higher education organization could be in a full distance-delivery mode. This 50% restriction was lifted in 2006. Soon after, MOOCs and the other alternate education providers began getting credit recommendations from alternate credit recommendation services such as ACE and NCCRS.

Reciprocation

In the reciprocation phase, the new and the old reciprocally influence each other, for example, change in an old policy or practice to accommodate the new. One such critical event that is significant in this context is when AAUP released two statements in 1998, one on distance learning and the other on copyright (AAUP 2015b, 2015a), signifying their adoption but at the same time bringing policy changes directing how mediated teaching would fit into the traditional academic organizations. More recently, ACE, which accredits online courses provided by non-traditional providers, partnered with a newly formed third-party ACUE to offer training programs for college instructors, thereby reflecting the new trying to change the old. There are also some signs of emerging entities trying to modify the old ways of doing things. For example, the Gates Foundation has funded research to create new learning models (GatesFoundation.org 2012). Among the initiatives planned through the $9 million grant funding, $1 million is for

Massachusetts Institute of Technology (MIT) to develop and offer a new, free prototype computer science online course through edX, a joint venture between MIT and Harvard, and partner with a postsecondary institution that targets low-income young adults to experiment with use of the course in a "flipped classroom" where lectures take place outside the classroom and homework is done in class.

Lessons learned will be captured and shared to advance understanding of how faculty and students use and benefit from online learning tools, as well as how these courses may be adapted to support on-campus learning and a broader range of learners.

The aforementioned indicates online technologies trying to change how things get done in resident settings. Similarly, the USDE launched an experiment where it is taking content created by non-accredited providers, using it in existing courses at universities, and approving it for Title IV funding (Blumenstyk 2016).

There were several pieces of evidence of reciprocation at the organizational and individual levels as well. The first most prominent evidence was the extensive use of learning management systems across all units analyzed in the case studies. All organizations showed efforts to standardize the use of a single system such as Blackboard, Canvas, Moodle, or any other such platform so that their resident, as well as online courses, offered similar 'learning experience' to their students. Redwood's rationale was to "advance teaching and learning by keeping current with the most modern technologies," and extend the benefits of online education to their resident student population by offering "blended education." Having such a platform at the disposal of teachers for resident teaching allows them to use a variety of digital content for students to peruse inside as well as outside classrooms. For example, Caleb who taught resident classes in Unit 3 talked about how he used the course management platform provided by the university:

> The technology of course management is an amazing find for me. Now I have a central repository for all the materials. The students can look at the material. If I organize it right, they will be able to find things. Oh, by the way, they have related the assignments to maintaining of the grade book. There are just so many capabilities. All these were manual when I started. Now I can reuse it for future semesters. . . . There is the ability for people to schedule tests elsewhere at other times. So students with special needs, it has been really good to keep them up with the classroom in ways they are comfortable with. There is also the analytical part of assessments—like best or worst questions in the quiz. Gives you an idea of what should be reinforced or what falsehoods need to be dispelled.

Caleb and Emma in Unit 3 played videos extensively in their classroom. Teresa had her students watch videos before coming to the class. All three of them used video content extensively in their resident teaching. However Anna, who also taught in Unit 3, tried using technologies in her resident classes, but her experiences were not as positive. She tried incorporating technologies in two ways in her resident classes several times, but according to her, they failed every time. The first thing she tried was to have her students write about a certain topic in their personal blogs. She found that students don't like that "level of exposure about their own writing" and prefer to write "privately" only for their teachers and not for everyone to see. Anna's second attempt to use technology was when she tried to play videos in her classroom but found that it proved to be more of a hindrance than a help. In her words,

> I have tried to use some videos in the classroom, YouTube videos or academically produced videos. And I find that it often fails too. Students are too accustomed to turning off their brains when the video comes on. And so they have a reading mode, a writing mode, and they have a viewing mode. And in the viewing mode, they stop being critical. And I would love to have the ability to watch a minute of a video, pause it, have a discussion about what we just saw, start it, have another minute or two of video, pause it, have a discussion, and that is really jarring to the students, because that's not how they watch anything. And so that is another difficulty in teaching.

While not all teachers employed digital platforms in their resident classes in the same manner, a consistent pattern was that they all attempted to do so, and many found them to be very useful in improving student engagement. For example, Derf, a senior professor in Unit 2, showed his resident class content hosted in a Blackboard shell (a course site) during his interview and said,

> I don't like online, but that being said, all my on-ground courses—I have a very detailed shell that supports that. Some of the students tell me they are probably more developed than some of the online courses. So . . . because I know their attention span is very limited, I have PowerPoints, I have just little snippet articles, I have multiple videos, I have a variety of things, and a series of discussion questions. I support them all to do that.

And the second evidence, although not as prominent, was the potential of an emerging debate about copyright issues for content created by faculty for resident classes. Such a debate was already noted in Unit 2 because of the university's collective bargaining agreement according to which the faculty owned all the content created by them. Steve, an administrator in Unit 4, which is closely affiliated with Unit 3's administrative unit, cautioned that although the content copyright issues in resident teaching were never a "bone of contention," they may soon become so because at the time of this interview, Redwood University was undergoing a major initiative revamping its learning management system platform to Canvas. According to Steve,

> I mean it's a huge investment for the university. And as faculty begin to use it, and begin to put their content into the canvas system, whether it is teaching online or in residence, there has to be a question of who owns that, right? So I think this is probably an issue. And we've established a boundary around online education, but I think this is an issue that has not been resolved completely. I think it will begin to become an issue in the resident world as well.

Finally, domination begins when the new media logic begins to govern or control the prevailing institutional logic. No evidence of this phase was found as the alternate accreditors and education providers still rely on the traditional establishment for legitimacy.

Core Entities of Teaching Practice

While mediatization has impacted all three core entities of teaching practice—content, teacher, and student, the instructional content has undergone the most significant transformation. The following sections first discuss the key transformations related to content and then, subsequently, analyze their influence on teachers and students.

Content

Content Stratification

Among the six case studies, the three online units showed a pattern where the instructional content is split into two layers: a rigid core layer and a flexible outer or supplemental layer. The core is developed much before the course is launched, often with the help of a course committee comprising faculty members as subject matter experts, instructional designers as pedagogy experts, and IT-team as technology experts. In Unit 4, Eric designed his course with some assistance from instructional designers, authored an eBook used in the course, and created videos that explain the concepts using PowerPoint slides with his voice-over. Having used this material for several years, it became the core of the courses that Eric taught. Similarly, Chris and Allen also designed and developed their own courses and then used it as a core for all future deliveries of their courses. Christian, an instructional designer in Unit 4, who has worked with several faculty members to develop online courses, explained the process:

> Usually, the standard process in developing a course is two semesters. . . . So we'll start to talk to people in advance just to get an idea

of what the scope of the project is going to be like. [. . .] And usually the first semester we really try to concentrate on getting out all the materials. And then starting to get it all together. In second semester, we work out a lot of the technological pieces that might be involved [. . .] A lot of people like to write content or make videos, so that's where we spend a lot of time. [. . .] So it's like, ok what are the big ideas, is there a larger unit that all these lessons are going into. That's how I like to think of things. I like to think of things from a larger context. What is it you are trying students to accomplish and then work backward. [. . .] So here is this unit, this unit, this unit, ok let's go ahead and do that. [. . .] I try to really impress upon the faculty that think about the course as a course instead of thinking about it as a time unit, like 15 weeks. Yeah, eventually we have to break it down into that, but let us just think about the course as a whole, and then we can break it down from there.

In Unit 5, Robert used the core content created by a centralized team. In Unit 6, a course-development project team started with course blue-printing phase that involves listing the topics and the related learning outcomes. This team had internal instructional designers and external academic consultants who were faculty members from other higher education organizations engaged on a project basis The project then moved on to content development that had several steps such as sourcing openly licensed content, pairing content with learning outcomes, adding framing videos or notes, and adding assessments. The course was then sent for peer review to other academic consultants. Once cleared by the peer reviewers, the course was finally launched for students to peruse. Across these three online units, the freedom to change the core content ranged from very limited (Unit 4) to none (Unit 5 and Unit 6).

The supplemental layer in these units was very different from the core in many ways. First, it was created not before but during course delivery. Second, it was created by the persons directly participating in the course—e.g., teacher, teaching assistants, or students. Third, it focused more on the interaction between the teacher and the students rather than on the subject matter. This dynamic made this layer highly volatile and customized to each unique course setting. While most of the teachers in online units talked about following a certain process, they exercised complete freedom on how they did it. Christian, an instructional designer in Unit 4, argued that while it is good to standardize some aspects of online courses such as syllabus and course-navigation, the teaching approach should not be standardized. Chris, an instructor in the same unit, said,

> just like in the classroom, students don't want all of us to be the same. I don't want to be the same as you. . . . Cookie cutter for an instructor for online is not a good thing.

So he created his unique presence in his courses by conducting live-web conferences that also get recorded for students to watch later. Robert in Unit 5 added his supplemental content to help interact with the students in the form of grading feedback, discussion-forum posts, and videos to interact with students. The case in Unit 6, where there is no cohort or teacher, the idea of supplemental layer manifested only as a discussion forum where students post questions and browse for answers posted by students who took the same course earlier at some other time.

These two layers show the model of content stratification in which the core is about the subject matter and the supplemental layer is about interaction. This model has significant implications regarding how courses are designed and delivered, and the role played by various constituents in teaching practice. The core is getting standardized to ensure high-quality presentation. A combination of pedagogic and entertainment techniques is being used to achieve this goal which requires significant investment and therefore the core content is solidified to minimize variation across individual teachers. This content investment is then passed on to teaching in resident settings, wherever applicable, to maintain uniformity across course offerings, and because online content is perceived to be of better quality.

Content Variety

Observing the way the content has been morphing, one can see a blending of a variety of content forms as synchronous/asynchronous, text/audio-visual, one-way/interactive, and static/adaptive. The variety of content used for teaching ranges from plain old textbooks to professionally created videos and sophisticated instructional software. This content that forms the core of content-stratification model discussed earlier is often prepared by third-party publishers—e.g., Pearson Education that operates at both ends of the variety-spectrum. In between this spectrum is the content developed either by the faculty or by an in-house team with expertise ranging from instructional design to professional video production. Several other dynamics reinforce the manifestation of content variety at a field level:

- Internal content: The faculty members and the instructional designers within the organization create the content and host it on the LMS platform. The platform itself though is gradually moving to third-party cloud platforms—e.g., Canvas with Instructure hosted on Amazon Web Services (Hill 2016a).
- MOOC content: The third-party platforms, such as Coursera and EdX host content externally, often aligned with college-level courses and produced by established higher education organizations.

- Partner's content: The third-party content producers that are partnering with universities to create course-specific content to be used by the faculty members. One such example is Acrobatiq that has partnered with APLU to develop adaptive courseware (APLU 2016). Cedar Academy analyzed as one of the case studies is one such third-party content provider that partners with universities to provide credit-recommended courses.
- Commercial content: Companies such as LinkedIn that provide content to the world at large. These companies are not aligned with any college or university courses. As published in an article titled "A 'Netflix for Education'? Why LinkedIn's New Product Should Give Us Pause," the author reports that LinkedIn views higher education as its secondary market where its content can be used in flipped class formats (Hill 2016b).

Content Commoditization

As the core content is becoming an organizational investment, it is getting commoditized and raising the issues of content ownership. The scholars in cultural and media studies have extensively analyzed the issues of content commoditization. They find content commoditization as one of the first outcomes of the rapid adoption of mediation technologies across cultural institutions ranging from mass media (Durham and Kellner 2009; Curtin 2009; Lull 2000; Thompson 1995) to performing arts (Katz 2010; Auslander 2008; Chanan 1995).

Commoditization results in "massive profusion" of the content that, on the one hand, expands access to masses (Hesmondhalgh 2007, 57), while on the other raises the issue of ownership as the content changes from being an artifact of individual creativity to that of an organized production (Lipinski 2003). As mediated content development engages myriad specialists and technical experts, each contributing to the overall quality of the content, the ownership gets handed over to the institution (Hesmondhalgh 2007). The issue of copyright is raised not so much to protect the author's rights but those of the institutions, printers, or sellers, from where they are produced and distributed (Thompson 1995).

A similar phenomenon has been unfolding in the educational field since the issue of commoditization was raised when distance education started gathering steam (Peters 1993; Jarvis 1993). Institutional ownership is replacing the traditional norm of individual ownership (Moore and Kearsley 2012; Zemsky, Wegner, and Massy 2005; Lipinski 2003). Scholars have voiced concerns about academic capitalism and have identified distance education as one of the contributing factors (Slaughter and Rhoades 2004, 2011). The issue of copyright is one of the key focus areas in policies of online education (Oblinger, Barone, and Hawkins

2001), directly impacting the practice of teaching that requires creation, dissemination, and the use of content.

As recording technologies commoditized music, telecommunication technologies enabled free broadcast platforms such as radio and TV (Chanan 1995). A similar phenomenon has occurred in higher education where, after some attempts to broadcast education through radio and TV, MOOCs seem to have emerged as education's new "radio." They offer increased access and are also being used as a promotional platform (O'Connor 2014), much like the way radio fed off record labels, which in turn used radio as an "acoustic showcase" (Chanan 1995, 61). Interestingly, it was radio that improved the quality of recorded sound by introducing better amplification and microphone technologies that also benefited the record industry. A similar parallel can be seen where MOOCs opened up a new frontier in pedagogical research, motivating the traditional higher education organizations to revisit their traditional methods and content (Šlaus et al. 2013; O'Connor 2014). Online education, in general, has increased the focus on pedagogy thereby contributing to content quality (Qvortrup 2008).

Content Quality

There are two ways in which content quality is being (re)defined as it is getting mediated. The first is in the form of its adherence to principles of pedagogy. The most common principle that came across all online units in the case studies was the need to make content as granular as possible. The reasons attributed to this granularity were students' inability to concentrate on long walls of texts or videos longer than seven minutes; and the need to digitally track how students peruse the content. The content quality is measured based on the standards set by agencies such as Quality Matters, whereas the teacher-quality is being assessed by looking at the data generated by online interaction and engagement between teacher and students.

The second aspect of quality is its legitimacy through accreditation, which is creating new kinds of challenges. For example, the concept of credit units is becoming increasingly difficult to transfer to the online world. The higher education system in the US codifies learning in terms of credit units (in degree-granting institutions), clock hours (in non-degree-granting institutions), or continuing education units (non-credit courses, such as adult education) (Wellman 2003b). The federal government uses this code as a measure for provisioning financial aid and a regulatory tool to enforce quality standards (Ehrlich 2003). This codification system represents traditional institutional logic based on the seat time spent by students in a classroom setting and fails to apply in the context of distance education. This logic is being challenged and revisited to accommodate the new logic of distance education by coming up with alternate forms of measuring education and learning progress (Ehrlich 2003; Wellman 2003b, 2003a).

Content Spectrum

Scholars in media and culture studies have proposed several typologies of content, based on aspects such as content characteristics (Fuchs 2011; Wurtzler 1992; Pavlik 2013), amount of attention paid to consume it (Tunstall 1983), and its effects on consumers (Lasswell 1948; Narula 2006). These typologies bring out inherent properties or tendencies of the content, which, in turn, influence their distribution and consumption. Examples of such typologies are as follows:

* Media as print, audio, or visual; production by hands, mouth, or body; reception by eyes and ears (Fuchs 2011)
* The degree of originality: original, repurposed, or hybrid (Pavlik 2013)
* Consumption activity: primary, secondary, or tertiary (Tunstall 1983)
* Time, temporality: synchronous/asynchronous, simultaneity/anteriority (Fuchs 2011; Wurtzler 1992)

The shift to online education with a widening range of communication technologies has generated the need to build similar typologies of content to define effective creation and delivery mechanisms (Tsai 2000; Rungtusanatham et al. 2004; Twigg 2003). Although this need has not been adequately addressed, there have been some efforts in this direction, examples of which are as follows:

* effect of content format on learning (Nugent 1982; Wisher and Curnow 2003; Moore and Kearsley 2012),
* typologies based on audience, location, time, information display, information extension, information updating, content structure, content flexibility, interactivity with instructional content, interactivity with other learners, production cost, cost of use, teachers' training and students' training (Tsai 2000).

The similarities in the typologies of content present the first parallel between cultural and educational domains. Within this parallel are two noteworthy observations. The first is that media and cultural studies have historically been biased toward the study of its consumption rather than the creation side of the value chain (Williams 1991; Hesmondhalgh 2007). The political economics studies have focused on the production process (Hesmondhalgh 2007) but mostly at the institutional or industrial and not at an individual level. This "consumption-bias" is also prevalent in educational research studies where the focus is on how students learn while overlooking how teachers teach (Jarvis 1993). The second observation is that these typologies focus mostly on technology-mediated content, such as those available over radio and television, thereby missing the characteristics of content in its most organic and unmediated form.

To overcome the limitations of these typologies, a categorization at the more fundamental level is proposed here that allows comprehending the creation as well as consumption ends of the content value chain and helps articulate the emergence of content spectrum. Some content, such as music, theater performances, and lectures have existed in their most organic forms for many centuries before mediation technologies altered them. Such content forms need co-presence of the provider and the peruser. Their organic representation has non-material properties such as aura, ephemerality, evanescence, or presence (Benjamin 2006; Chanan 1995; Garrison and Anderson 2003). On the other hand, content such as text or paintings are born separate from the provider and reach the peruser spatially and temporally removed. The very act of writing separates speakers from listeners, as through writing "one speaks to the multitude" (Gleick 2011, 31). Writing itself is an act of mediation between the speaker and the listeners (Peters 1998), and such mediated content has material properties such as tangibility, portability, durability, and reproducibility (Thompson 1995; Katz 2010). Therefore, one criterion to classify content is as mediated or unmediated. Unmediated content forms, such as music or speech in their organic forms, are attached to their providers and, therefore, have non-material properties, whereas mediated content forms, such as written texts or paintings, are unattached from their providers and have material properties.

This categorization offers three advantages. First, it allows the spanning the entire content lifecycle from creation to perusal. Second, it views the content in its organic form as mediated or unmediated. Third, it reveals the most fundamental transformation brought by technology mediation in the content's characteristics. Organically attached content, when mediated by technology, loses non-material properties but acquires new material properties. For example, music loses aura or evanescence when recorded, but it acquires properties such as tangibility, portability, repeatability, and manipulability (Katz 2010). Therefore, content viewed at its development stage can be defined in terms of its characteristics as attached (unmediated) or unattached (mediated) to the provider.

When the focus is shifted from the provider to the peruser, the attached content affords direct interaction between the provider and the peruser, whereas unattached content affords independent perusal. The former offers provider's "presence," whereas the latter allows in-depth independent exploration by the peruser. The characteristics of content can thus be defined along a spectrum by the degree of independence and interaction afforded by the media of its delivery. This view then translates to the concept of "transactional distance" discussed earlier and defined as a continuous variable based on the extent of dialog between the teacher and the learner, the learner's autonomy, and the structure of the content shared between them (Moore 1993). Attached content has the least transactional distance while unattached has the most. In between the two extremes are various communication technologies that allow a continuum to emerge, which can be configured to suit the contextual needs of the transaction. The content can thus be positioned along a spectrum that defines characteristics between the two extremes of attached and unattached, as shown in Figure 5.1.

Distance education started on one extreme of the content spectrum with the predominant mode of learning being independent study. With increasing technology options available to content providers, especially computers, and the Internet, other possible technology configurations emerged that led to the research on mediated interaction among students and teachers (e.g., see Beldarrain 2006; Picciano 2002). On one side of the spectrum lies the research on Computer-Mediated Communication (CMC), which analyzes various modalities in terms of the degree of interaction and presence. On the other side is the research on Human-Computer Interaction (HCI), which strives to enrich the content itself, allowing independent examination and peruser-driven exploration (Garrison, Anderson, and Archer 2003; Garrison 1993). Finally, the research on social networks extends independence to "interdependence" where perusers can engage in interaction with or without the provider's presence, an emerging pedagogical practice that promotes constructivism as its learning paradigm (Ally 2004). Therefore, this perspective also lays out the three existing paradigms of education, viz. traditional face-to-face

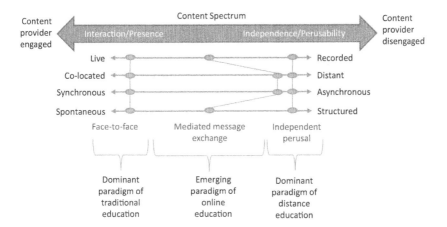

Figure 5.1 Content spectrum

teaching, dominant independent study form of distance education, and emerging collaborative learning of the networked era.

Teacher

Stratified Schemas

Teaching is getting unbundled as online is gaining a foothold in higher education (Macfarlane 2011; Paulson 2002). The content-stratification model captures how the new unbundled roles map to the stratified layers of content. As the guru schema focuses on creating high-quality core content with high subject matter expertise, it maps to the development of the core. The coach schema manifests as supplemental material shared by the instructor to help students get through the core content. It focuses on providing non-standardized and highly customized content that is unique to each course delivery. And the artist schema cuts across both to capture students' attention by employing best practices from pedagogy as well as entertainment. These mappings are presented in a pictorial form in Figure 5.2.

Learning How to Teach

Teaching is increasingly being seen as an activity that requires formal training in pedagogy or andragogy, a trend that was started with the emergence of online education. APLU, in the context of distance learning

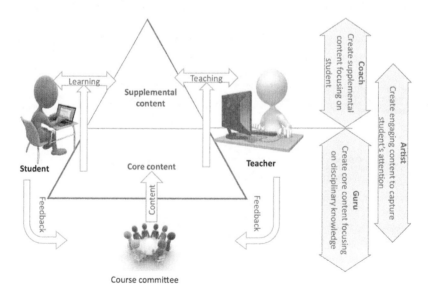

Figure 5.2 Content stratification

in 1999 called for an increased focus on pedagogy and "to invest in professional development and incentives for acquiring the skills needed to create active-learning environments and experiences in classrooms, laboratories, and service learning." More recently, the MOOC phenomenon has been considered instrumental in shifting the focus to "teaching, pedagogical practices, and how to better understand student learning" (Selingo 2016, 6). Focusing on faculty contribution to student success, the NPEC published an article that states:

> Because most faculty members are not trained in pedagogy as part of their doctoral studies, the choice to engage in the scholarship of teaching, ask higher order questions in class and on examinations, use active learning, and use cooperative and collaborative learning requires some learning by faculty members to implement them successfully.
>
> (Braxton 2006, 19)

As a teacher's training in pedagogy is being viewed as critical to student learning, teaching is gradually moving from being a craft to a profession. The ACE-ACUE partnership and the mandatory pedagogic training requirement for teachers to teach online in the three organizational case studies are clear evidence of this trend.

Digital Quality

Combining the science of learning and cognition with the power of data analytics to study student's learning behavior is trying to address the challenge of not having measurable indicators to assess the quality of teaching. The e-Advising tools are tracking student behavior to keep teachers and administrators alerted about students at risk, thereby addressing the issues of student retention and graduation. Both for-profit units in the case studies—Unit 1 and Unit 5—used this mechanism. Jack in Unit 1 explained how Sycamore requires every interaction a student has with any faculty member or administrative staff to be recorded in a centralized system. This information is accessible to all faculty members and administrators so that "you can see the mindset of our student and understand." The Aspen University of Unit 5 has a tool called Civitas attached to their learning management system which tracks students' online engagement levels by tracking their usage of course materials and shows them as colored icons. As Robert explained about the software interface,

> Every icon is a student, and they are color coded. Very high engaged, those are blue dots. Engaged are green. If I click on the dot, it will tell me who the student is. And now I can drill down, how many

discussion posts did they make this week. How many they made total. How many different discussion views have they had? When was the last time they checked their grade book? I can drill down tremendously, and Civitas will give me feedback. Two students have recently dropped from high engagement to low engagement. Oh, I click on them, it will tell me who they are.

An article published by APLU cited Georgia State University implementing a similar system in which the instructors across the organization enter data about their students' class performance, and this data is analyzed against historical data to predict and send alerts to advisors to take action (Lee and Keys 2013). Another example is SMART, which is a toolkit developed by APLU to use technology and data analytics for proactive advising.

Coupled with the use of technology to track learning is the use of instructional software that provides a personalized learning experience. An article published by APLU describes how the Florida International University used predictive analytics to identify college algebra as one of the greatest risks to on-time graduation, and used computer-based Mastery Math Lab supported by learning assistants in the classroom. The success of this initiative is now being replicated across other high-risk courses to improve student retention and graduation rates (CUSU and APLU 2016). A similar instance was found in Unit 5 case study in which Harry explained how he teaches math in a classroom which is set up like a lab:

> And for our math courses, we have specific labs setup that students are required to spend at least 5 hours a week in that lab practicing what they are learning. And a lot of it is being taken away from the instructor. I mean it's really in the lab itself, way the labs are being put together today, it's adaptive teaching. They'll introduce some subject material to the student, see how the student reacts, depending on how the student reacts, then the program will automatically adapt to introduce whatever material should be introduced to bring that student along. So more adaptive kind of learning.

Another evidence is the Personalized Learning Consortium (PLC) launched by APLU that followed from the success of the Gates's Courseware Challenge funded by the Bill & Melinda Gates Foundation grant. Nineteen APLU member universities in partnership with two learning platform vendors are participating in this initiative. While the outcomes of this initiative are not yet known, the objective is clearly defined to improve the student-learning outcome (APLU 2016).

But the digital tracking of learning is raising questions related to privacy. Christian in Unit 4 expressed frustration when his college would not let him use the data generated by the interactive textbook. In his words,

> Because one of the things that happens in this interactive textbook is it collects data. OK, based on FERPA concerns, people throw all this stuff out. I am like, I don't understand, this is helping my students learn. This is helping me do a better job. I use the data, I pull that data down, and it talks about their participation in the interactive textbook. I use that to grade students, or give them a grade for participation in the course.

One of the vendors of personalized courseware a company named as Acrobatiq, which calls itself to be a learning optimization company, and is backed by Carnegie Mellon University. While promising in its potential, the company, as well as APLU, recognize that the idea of capturing content in software and using it to track student performance raises several issues, some of which are

- students' privacy and security from an ethical perspective and FERPA (Family Educational Rights and Privacy Act) laws,
- the black box nature of algorithms that students and teachers may not have insight into,
- the enormity of data generated by such application, and
- the copyright issues related to the content and the software (Shallard 2016).

In summary, it is evident that the technologies described earlier are transforming teaching from an activity grounded in intuition-based human interactions to a system of data-driven digital interventions. These changes reflect the penetration of online pedagogy into resident settings as well which requires the resident teachers not only to understand how to use these technologies but also to know the underlying algorithms used in it to draw inferences.

As the content quality is being measured by its adherence to the principles of pedagogy and its perusal is being tracked digitally, the teaching quality is getting centered on the "interaction" between students and their teachers. In Unit 4, the administrator challenged those who question the quality of online education, as according to him the quality of resident teaching is far more elusive than online. In online, the teacher-student interaction is digitalized and can be tracked almost in real time. Similarly, Unit 6 has installed an application named faculty dashboard to display students' performance in real time. Therefore, digital tracking enabled by the online content is also being used to assess the quality of teaching, which in turn is used to assess teachers' performance.

Interaction is central to the quality of the distance education paradigm (Garrison 1993; Holmberg 2005). While the objective of interaction is to generate discourse that enables higher-level cognitive learning, the "danger is to remain within the dominant paradigm of prescribed and prepackaged course materials and simply using two-way communications as optional 'add-ons'" (Garrison 1993, 12). The lack of intellectual motivation to engage in mediated interaction accentuates this concern, as (Archibald and Feldman 2011) expressed succinctly in these words:

> Perhaps we are biased but we think that the job of the distance-education instructor would be quite unappealing. Making up new test questions or designing new course materials can be creative and stimulating. But once the course is developed, the job boils down to answering e-mail all day or perhaps moderating a chat room. [. . .] We wonder just how easy it will be to keep high-quality instructors interested in being at the other end of a stream of student e-mails.
>
> (122)

Such expressions reflect the lack of motivation by experienced faculty to engage actively in distance education. Perhaps this explains why the organizations that are scaling up online education to recover the cost of capital-intensive technologies are strategically choosing to engage less-qualified teaching assistants for teacher-student interaction needs (Hanna 2003).

Dual-Mode Qualification

A teacher in the contemporary higher education organization needs to have all the qualifications of a resident teacher, including resident teaching experience, plus an online teaching certification to qualify to teach online. This combination of skills and experience was a requirement even in Unit 6 even though the teacher's role was that of a subject matter expert who only prepares content and is not involved in any way when the students peruse the content. When asked about why the subject matter experts are required to have some years of classroom teaching experience to be able to work for Unit 6 as academic consultants, Richard explained,

> Because I think we want people who understand the challenges that students face when they approach the materials. If we got somebody who had a degree in the subject, but never had to engage with students on the subject, kind of, we want people who have already anticipated the kinds of questions the students will have around the material and had to field them before, so they kind of know what students struggle with, what was easy for them, and that allows us

to tailor our courses based on the faculty's experience working with students. I think we have a tendency toward people with PhDs, but I think the classroom aspect is probably most relevant. If someone has been teaching a subject for a long time that would probably need us to take a harder look at that person vs. someone who hasn't taught.

Virtual Teacher

The emergence of a virtual teacher is much more than the teacher just moving from the physical to a virtual space. It is altering the definition of who the teacher is and what teaching involves. In cultural fields, the separation of content, such as music into a recording medium, was considered the destruction of "aura" (Benjamin 2006, 21) or "disembodiment" of content (Chanan 1995, 7). Media and cultural industries found alternate means to recreate the aura by supplementing their content with images and stories about the artists who developed the content as the "listening experience must be supplemented by additional artifacts" to fill this gap (Auslander 2008, 86).

Similarly, the problem of missing "presence" has been noted as a critical concern for teaching and learning according to the body-phenomenological paradigm (Qvortrup 2008). But the educational institutions have relied on faculty members themselves to fill the "presence" gap by helping students create their "social" and "cognitive" presence, and create their own "teaching" presence through techniques, such as learning communities and online discussion forums (Garrison, Anderson, and Archer 2003). Although a team designs the content, any mention of content creators and designers is conspicuously hidden from the students' view, akin to folk music where composers or lyricists are anonymous and unlike popular or art music where they are duly recognized (Tagg 1982). This aura gap points to two potential reasons. First, this exclusive reliance on teachers to create their presence reflects that distance education is still modeling itself after the traditional teacher-centric model. And second, the recognition of content developers is perhaps not considered an important factor that could influence students' perception or engagement with the course.

Mediation of cultural content resulted in the need for performers to acquire special skills that suit the new medium. For example, the skills for a musician to conduct live concerts are different from those to create studio recordings (Chanan 1995). Similarly, stage actors employ different techniques than those acting in a movie (Kracauer 2005; Knopf 2005). A similar shift in terms of skills and qualities are emerging for faculty members to be successful in online initiatives in higher education. Technology has become a critical skill to be acquired to succeed as an effective teacher in an online environment as content provisioning is now split into "presentation" and "interaction" in online education (Moore and Kearsley 2012). The new medium is demanding a new set of skills from teachers to fulfill their role in online teaching—e.g., technology skills, flexibility in teaching methods and schedules, planning, and a fair appreciation of pedagogical principles (Meyer 2002; Tabata and Johnsrud 2008; Kanuka et al. 2008).

The emergence of pedagogy as a critical skill required in the online environment also originates from the argument that it is not technology but the instructional strategy that influences the quality of learning (Ally 2004; Clark 1983). This has resulted in the skills required by online faculty to extend far beyond just subject matter expertise, resulting in fragmentation of the teaching role.

According to the history of cultural institutions, content commoditization de-emphasizes the role of content creators as the institutions in industrialized mode develop market strategies "based on repertoire rather than the artists" (Chanan 1995, 169). It standardizes the content-development processes, and the developers largely follow the "logic of repetition," thereby "rationalizing the creative stage of production" (Ryan 1992, 155). In other words, the more the content gets pushed toward the recorded, remote, and asynchronous end of the content spectrum, the lesser is the creative input provided by the content developers. It also engages various specialists, technologists, and administrators in the content-development process. For example, recording technology led to the emergence of recording and mixing engineers in the music industry and cinematographers and editors in the movies (Chanan 1995; Knopf 2005).

Similarly, as knowledge is being captured in online content, professors are becoming content providers, while the content structure, design, and layout are being decided by instructional designers and technology experts. The resulting differentiation and specialization in the content-development function in higher education have been termed as unbundling of the teaching role and is creating newer forms of hierarchies (Paulson 2002; Moore 2012).

Student

Motivation and Influence

When describing student demographics, the 18–25 years of age group is referred to as 'traditional' whereas above 25 is considered the 'non-traditional' group. Out of nine students interviewed in this study, four were in the traditional age group enrolled in resident programs and five were in the non-traditional age group with three of them attending online programs. All resident students had had some online learning experiences in the past in at least a couple of courses. While all students expressed that they prefer resident over online education, their approach to education, in general, showed some patterns relevant to online education.

All students expressed motivation toward their higher education efforts, but when asked about why they chose to go to college, the traditional students reflected that their families made the decision for them and they just followed their direction. Kelly in Unit 2 said, "I don't know how I decided to come to college. I guess my parents kind of like expected me to. They didn't go themselves, but they wanted me to, and so I did." Similarly, John in Unit 3 said that going to college was never a question as it was considered "mandatory" in his family. On the other hand, the non-traditional students clearly articulated their motivations as career growth and self-development and expressed how it was a difficult decision for them to set aside other priorities and come back to school. Mike, a non-traditional student in Unit 4, recounted his educational journey as,

> I guess I was a little bit of a late bloomer as far as my interest in education. After high school, I entered the workforce for a number of years. In all honesty, as I was younger, I didn't have the maturity at that point to kind of grasp, you know, college, or even decide what major I wanted. So went up in the workforce for years and I was a lazy student in high school too. Once I reached 25-ish, I decided that now is better than to keep putting it off, so I gave the boots to myself to look around, and I looked at the traditional options as well. . . . And it has been awesome so far. It has been a really good experience for personally, stepped up my career professionally in earning technical certifications now as a reward for studies I have been doing. I feel very rewarded.

Two key learning influences emerged from student interviews. All students—irrespective of their age group and their mode of education as resident or online—indicated the importance of a teacher in their learning experience. When asked how they decide the quality of a class, the students talked first about the teacher and then anything else; and when asked about their online learning experiences, all of them said that they don't like it because they don't get to interact with their teacher face-to-face. John, a student at Unit 3, said, "There has to be some interaction with the professor. And they should be accessible and willing to answer questions."

The second influence emerged in collaborative learning in which students are assigned to group projects in resident and online settings. While all students expressed their like or dislike to this approach differently, there was a common theme about what it helped them learn. They all expressed that they learn less about the subject matter from each other and more about social interactions and how to work with people. They valued knowing their peers through such collaborative exercises, but when it came to studying the subject, they preferred to study alone. Studying with their peers, whenever done, was mostly for socialization purposes.

This pattern indicates that group-learning is appropriate where students' social development is one of the learning objectives. Jillian, Christine, and Allen in Unit 4 also expressed a similar observation that non-traditional students often do not expect to learn social development and want to focus only on the subject matter. The lack of motivation to know their peers coupled with their other conflicting priorities of family and work further makes them disinterested in collaborative learning as it requires significant effort to coordinate across space and time.

This aspect, when combined with the student demographic in online units that has a significant segment of non-traditional students, makes collaborative learning as a pedagogic technique largely unsuitable. For example, 80% of the student population in Unit 6 is non-traditional for whom this socialization aspect may seem unnecessary. Therefore, while online adoption is improving the content as well as teachers' pedagogic and andragogic awareness, there is a clear need to understand what works or doesn't work across the resident and online settings.

Virtual Student

The student has been the most heavily researched entity in the content-teacher-student triad. In a review of distance education literature from 2000 to 2008, research on learner characteristics was found to be the third most frequent topic of research after interaction and instructional design, respectively (Zawacki-Richter, Bäcker, and Vogt 2009). Analyzing changes in the student's profile due to increasing adoption of online technologies reveals two parallels with those that the peruser's profile underwent in cultural industries.

Listening to music in its most original form was a communal activity, but recording technology changed this centuries-old tradition into "solitary listening" (Katz 2010, 21). This change redefined the audience by making it "atomized" and "dispersed" (Chanan 1995, 9). The Internet has continued this atomization by shifting the source of media consumption from TV or radio to personal computers, thereby making it even more private, and giving it a "sense of exploration and discovery [that] has elements that are similar to the privatized experience of reading" (Marshall 2009, 85). Some virtual communities have helped overcome the cultural isolation for fans as they allow "a feeling of community between themselves and between them and the performer, facilitating a belief in a commonality, although they are dispersed geographically and disparate in needs and experiences" (Kibby 2000, 91).

Similarly, distance education has made students into solitary learners who rely on their own ability to be independent or autonomous, one of the foundational elements in the definition of distance education (Peters 2003; Wedemeyer 1981). This solitariness originated in the earliest model of correspondence-based learning that continued as the dominant paradigm in distance education (Garrison 1993). But the notion of peer influence has traditionally been considered the second-most important factor in shaping students' educational experiences; the first being the characteristics that they bring to the institution (Newcomb 1966). While distance education has made learning a solitary pursuit, peer influence is becoming an increasingly important area of research where colleges, as well as teachers, are providing various means for students to connect with their peers (Zawacki-Richter, Bäcker, and Vogt 2009). The pedagogical emphasis on collaboration and learning communities as critical enablers for effective learning has reinforced this focus. Anderson and Garrison (1995) found in a study that learning communities support the development of critical thinking skills and are therefore should be created in a distance learning environment.

Schulte (2003) argued that interactivity among students is an important strategy that facilitates learning and reduces isolation in online courses. Similarly, Song et al. (2004) surveyed graduate students about their online experiences and found the perceived lack of sense of community to be one of the challenges that the online students need to deal with. However, with the emerging technologies such as social networks, students are moving into the center of the content-exchange ecosystem, not only having access to more content for perusal but also having the ability to create and share it through technologies that enable user-generated content, a phenomenon also observed in the cultural industries (Lash and Lury 2007; Hartley 2009; Marshall 2009). But in the educational context, such a free-flowing, content-exchange ecosystem reinforces the need for critical thinking skills for students to sort through the rising glut of fake content.

The second similarity is that increased pedagogical focus on learners offers a bottom-up perspective of education, a shift similar to the one observed in cultural and media studies in the past. Starting with the emergence of the concept of "masses" as media technologies proliferated in the early 20th century, content perusers became an active area of research. Coming from the field of political economics and applying a critical cultural approach, the Frankfurt school viewed them as passive consumers of commoditized culture created by commercial media and the large-scale media industries molding the minds of masses to suit their capitalist agenda (Holt and Perren 2011; Adorno and Rabinbach 1975; Fuchs 2011). British cultural studies viewed consumers as actively creating meaning and making use of what media has to offer (Durham and Kellner 2009; Rayner, Wall, and Kruger 2004). An alternate view offered by studies in mass communication took a bottom-up view and focused on the consumer as the unit of analysis. Its theories on media effects' uses and gratifications analyze user attitudes and behaviors in terms of their media adoption and consumption (Brandtzæg 2010; Holt and Perren 2011; Lull 2000).

The field of education has also observed a similar shift where educational psychology has recognized the active role of learners in the learning process, leading to theories of constructivism and connectivism (Ally 2004; Moore and Kearsley 2012; Qvortrup 2008). Various classifications of learners have been created based on cognitive psychology—e.g., types of experiential learners (Kolb 1984) and field dependent/independent learners (Witkin et al. 1977). This variety of learning styles has been recognized as a need to customize the process of teaching and learning to individual differences among learners (Lengnick-Hall and Sanders 1997), a trend similar to the emergence of new genres in music to suit a variety of tastes. The ability to manipulate content after its creation afforded refinements that were not possible in live performances (Katz 2010). Genres such as rock and pop emerged largely as a result of electroacoustics that was not the domain of traditional artists but of the recording engineers (Braun 2000). The way pedagogy is using technology to provide learner-centric content that can suit a broad spectrum of learning styles, recording technologies allowed mass access to music and theater, generating a hugely expanded corpus of music to suit a wide range of musical tastes (Chanan 1995).

6   An Integrated View

In this chapter, I combine the findings from the field and case studies to capture multi-level themes. Starting with the integration of ideal types into an inter-institutional system of logics, I apply the theory of mediatization to analyze its influence on these logics. In the final stage, I develop findings of the impact of these logics on teaching practice. The key findings of the integrated analysis show the following:

- The higher education sector is a complex inter-institutional system of logics that conflict with or support each other in varying degrees.
- This institutional pluralism is reflected across individual, organizational, and field levels differently, creating a dynamic of cross-level effects, such as individuals accepting or rejecting the organizational policies or field-level norms.
- The inter-institutional dynamics are influencing the way the use of online technologies in teaching is taking shape, or in other words, the way the teaching practice is being mediatized.
- This mediatization is leading to the emergence of a new cyber-cultural logic that is altering its prevailing logics in significant ways.

I elaborate each of the identified institutional logics and its category elements in the following sections.

The Inter-Institutional System of Logics

Academic Logic

The agencies representing academia view an academic as a complete scholar engaged in teaching, research, and service. The faculty members subscribing to this logic derive their identity from their disciplines. They associate themselves with conferences and publications in their disciplines from where they get their peer recognition which they value more than what they get from their organizations where they work. They consider academic freedom, tenure, and shared governance to be the norm for any educational organization to be able to fulfill its mission. They consider that without these three tenets, not only an academic's ability to fulfill his or her role is diminished but student learning is also negatively impacted.

Addressing the problem of student engagement consumes most of a teacher's attention. The students' unpreparedness for college-level learning coupled with their lack of attention is making teachers extend their teaching styles from being a guru to a coach or an artist. They are revising their teaching techniques with the increasing focus on pedagogy and trying to learn new technologies with increasing mediation. They value student-teacher face-to-face engagement because not only do they consider it to be the most effective form of teaching, but they also derive from them a more direct and intuitive sense of how students are learning. They believe that learning occurs in an academic setting where teachers and students engage in face-to-face dialog to exchange knowledge and teachers have the freedom to dynamically tailor their content and teaching techniques to adapt to students' learning styles. They view the use of learning outcomes metrics to assess the quality of education as ineffective because they consider learning to be too broad a concept to capture in numbers.

Online education seems to threaten most of their beliefs, but the demand to teach online is increasing. For a contemporary academic, teaching online is at least expected, as it was at Cypress University, and sometimes even mandatory as it was at Redwood University. Individuals who subscribe to the academic logic discount the quality of online education because they value face-to-face engagement more than having students peruse digitized educational content on their own. Teachers not only view these technologies as negatively impacting student learning, but they also oppose content stratification, loss of content ownership, and the resulting content rigidity. Despite AAUP's strong opposition documented in its Statement on Copyright since 1999 (AAUP 2015b), organizations such as Redwood University and Aspen University are making instructional content an organizational property. Content stratification is taking away the teacher's freedom to alter course content. As content is becoming an organizational property, teachers either are not able to make any changes—e.g., in Aspen University, or make them as less as 20%, as in Redwood University. Whether the content is developed internally within the organizations or procured from a third party, its core is expanding. Teachers are being asked to use this rigid core, limiting, or eliminating the potential for any creative contribution from their side.

These changes are also changing the parameters of assessing the quality of teaching and learning. As the student-teacher interactions in an online setting take place over digital platforms, they become amenable to measurement and tracking by the administrators, which then is being used to assess faculty effectiveness. Such platforms are allowing organizations such as Aspen University and Cedar Academy to use third-party analytical tools to track student-learning behaviors. While APLU is promoting the use of such technologies, AAUP views it as "a Trojan horse, bringing hidden and multilayered problems such as monopolies and surveillance to the culture of the university" (Bossaller and Kammer 2014, 12).

The academic logic strongly opposes market practices such as treating the student as a customer, privatization of educational organizations, or exploiting market opportunities at the expense of the academic mission. This aversion toward market-oriented behaviors makes academics more aligned with the state-funded education system rather than leaving education to the market forces. But all these foundational values are changing in ways that are threatening academic identity and creating significant concerns for the subscribers to this logic. In this way, the academic ideal-type conflicts with several other perspectives prevailing or emerging in the higher education field, especially in reference to online adoption and technology interventions used in the teaching practice. Based on the all the above findings, the academic logic is explicated by summarizing its characteristics under the category elements with a brief description in Table 6.1.

Community Logic

There were two forms of community logic manifesting in the data. The first one pertains to the larger community within a higher education organization. It connects various departments and disciplines creating a common identity and a set of values that tie diverse cultures into one cohesive whole. And the second is the smaller learning community inside a classroom, engaged in collaborative learning guided by a teacher. Both types of communities focus on creating higher student engagement in their learning process. While the first one draws its legitimacy from the organizational identity, the second draws it from peer-learning and faculty interactions.

APLU views the larger communities as learning communities that are "supporting and inspiring faculty, staff, and leaners," being "learner-centered," and providing a "healthy learning environment" (Kellogg Commission 1998, 33). They try to bring the fragmented parts of multiversities together to create opportunities for social associations, clubs, and sports, which makes the students, staff, and teachers feel as if they are part of a larger community. These efforts bring tangible benefits because they increase student engagement thereby improving their academic performance as well. The case study at Sycamore Institute demonstrated this logic through organization-wide services for mentoring, tutoring, and student activities to make students "feel personally connected [. . .] resulting in higher rates of persistence." Redwood University had college-level societies and professional associations that provide venues for students to be part of a community.

Table 6.1 Academic logic

Category element	Value	Description
Root metaphor	Scholar	Academicians as scholars
Source of identity	Scholarship, research, teaching, service, disciplinary knowledge	Academicians identify themselves with research and teaching in their academic disciplines
Source of legitimacy	Credentials, reputation, research eminence	Academicians derive legitimacy from their academic credentials, reputation, and research eminence
Basis of norms	Shared governance, academic freedom, employment tenure	Academicians expect their universities to provide shared governance, academic freedom, and employment tenure to be able to fulfill their duties
Basis of attention	Changing faculty role, content ownership, student engagement	Academicians are concerned with the way the field of higher education is changing, especially in terms of changing faculty role and increase in contingent faculty. These changes are adversely impacting student engagement. With respect to online education, they view it as a threat to content ownership, academic freedom, and shared governance
Basis of strategy	Scholarship, face-to-face teacher-student interaction	Academicians engage in their day-to-day work through scholarship. The teaching function is founded on face-to-face interaction with their students
Economic system	State support	Academicians believe that higher education should be funded by the state and should not be left to market forces, as otherwise its integrity will be compromised

The second manifestation of this logic emerged at a unit level as an effort to create a learning community within a classroom by designing team activities for students to promote collaborative learning. The reasons behind this approach varied from making students learn *from* each other to make students learn how to work *with* each other, or making students learn *about* each other. Their common justification was to learn how do work with people in the "real world." But this argument revealed a varying degree of acceptance of this approach across individuals as well as organizations. And this practice, when taken online, revealed even more issues as Eric from Redwood University found online teamwork to be a challenge. Robert from Aspen University called it a "nightmare to do" because of which the university has completely removed all teamwork from its curricula. The challenges or failure of teamwork, especially in online settings, ranged from coordination issues to a different student demographic that doesn't need teamwork for its social or cultural development. From the students' perspective, almost all students across all units expressed that group work had coordination challenges. However, several of them said that they enjoy its social aspect and the chance to make friends. Greg, a non-traditional student in the online unit of Redwood University, said that he enjoyed connecting with his peers in various courses, especially when working on group projects. He recounted meeting another student in one such project and said that "we have made lifelong friends."

The third manifestation of trying to build a learning community by encouraging collaborative learning in online settings was the use of discussion boards where students engage in group discussions by posting their responses to some questions posed by the teacher, often in pursuit of grade points. Most individuals, including teachers, students, and the administrators called it out to be an ineffective pedagogical tool. Annie in Unit 3 tried to use it for her resident class but found that "students don't want that level of exposure about their own writing. They might write for me, but they write for me privately." Kelly, a student at Cypress, said that it "didn't feel genuine" in comparison to classroom discussions. In Unit 6 where there is no teacher or a student cohort, Richard reported,

> we struggled for a long time in kind of building a community around our courses. . . . It has started to pick up, but in the absence of a professor that you could go to ask, it encourages students to go to one another. It has a varying degree of success. It is kind of contingent on who is taking the course and where they are in the course, and that is harder to not have any cohort or anything like that.

These findings show how community logic manifests in educational settings and faces challenges in the online education models. Table 6.2. provides a summary of this logic with the values for its category elements.

Corporation Logic

As this study focused on teaching practice, I interpreted the manifestations of corporation logic from the perspective of the academia, which houses the teaching function. This perspective viewed the administrative function representing the corporation logic, essentially handling all activities other than teaching and research. And since academic and

Table 6.2 Community logic

Category element	Value	Description
Root metaphor	Community	University is a community of students, faculty members, administrators, and governing board that is bound by a common mission and values
Source of identity	Learning community, multi-cultural/diverse	Students experience shared learning as part of a community by interacting with other members coming from diverse cultures and perspectives
Source of legitimacy	Community engagement	The university community legitimizes itself by getting all its members actively engaged in establishing and promoting its values and goals
Basis of norms	Shared learning experience, peer-learning, interactions	It is expected that all community members work toward shared learning goals
Basis of attention	University culture	The community focuses on building a coherent culture across all groups in the university
Basis of strategy	Student social integration	Promote group activities within and outside classrooms to integrate students into the community and deepen their learning engagement
Economic system	Organizational	The organization supports the fiscal needs to support communities

administrative units have often found themselves at odds with each other when faced with the question of how to achieve their organizational missions, the corporation logic manifested mostly in issues where it conflicts with the academic logic. These conflicts range from high-level policy-related issues, such as research-versus-teaching priorities and the adoption of online teaching to more operational issues such as instructional content creation and ownership. Coqui, the associate dean in Unit 2, spoke about his frustration with the university's senior administrators as "they are not about teaching. They are about management [with an] incredible focus on short-term goals to the expense of long-term goals. I am really appalled by that kind of behavior." Such sentiments were also found at the field level where increasing managerialism is perceived as "corporatization" of higher education organizations.

When seen from an administrator's point of view, the corporation logic focuses on bringing various communities together within the organization to create a cohesive learning environment, finding innovative means to overcome the iron-triangle challenges, and adopting technology wherever possible to increase efficiency and standardization. It equates standardization of content with improved quality because investing in standardized content allows pedagogic benefits and therefore improved learning outcomes. Steve, an administrator in Unit 4, argued that online quality is better because its "design process of using a team approach improves quality of the course. You probably have a much more structured process than you do in the resident environment." But those who subscribe to the academic logic expressed their opposition to this view. For example, Frank, a professor at Cypress University said that he hates teaching online and thinks the quality of online education is based on "bogus educational theories." Others feel that standardization has reduced faculty members' flexibility to alter and adapt the content to their teaching needs, which in turn negatively impacts student learning. Despite such oppositions, corporation logic promotes the use of technology in teaching and learning, invests in developing instructional content that is owned by the organization, and measuring and tracking the quality of education using digital tools.

These findings reveal the manifestations of corporation logic through its contradictions and conflicts with the academic logic. A summary of this logic with the values for its category elements and a brief description is given in Table 6.3.

Market Logic

Market logic attempts "to convert all actions into the buying and selling of commodities that have a monetary price. [It, therefore] cannot exchange unpriced human activities that may be rational for an organization or useful to individuals" (Friedland and Alford 1991, 249). Its mission is to build its competitive position in the market and increase profit margins for which it employs various marketing techniques. In an educational context, it identifies with higher education organizations as "quasi-corporate entities producing a wide range of good and services in a competitive marketplace." They are "managed based upon the values of economic rationality." The laws of supply and demand govern teaching and research. "Students, parents, state legislatures, employers, and research funders are seen as customers." The faculty is presumed to participate out of "calculative involvement." Guiding principles for the organization are to "know its liabilities and assets, to anticipate costs and benefits, to enhance efficiency and flexibility" (Gumport 2000, 71–72).

As evident from the interpretations of market logic noted earlier, the vocabulary used in the field often conflates the idea of being corporation-like with that of being market-oriented. For example, in an article published with the title "Market Forces and the College Classroom: Losing Sovereignty" by AAUP (Stein, Scribner, and Brown 2013), authors refer to market forces as "competition, standardization, bureaucracy, mass production, and technology." However, according to the theory, while

Table 6.3 Corporation logic

Category element	Value	Description
Root metaphor	Company	A higher education organization is a legal entity that represents a group of stakeholders
Source of identity	Administration, management	A higher education organization is run and managed by administrators trained in management practices
Source of legitimacy	Governing board, policies, and procedures	A higher education organization seeks legitimacy through its governing board members, its hierarchical structure of reporting, organizational bylaws, policies, and procedures
Basis of norms	Management practice and principles	Administrators run the higher education organizations according to managerial best practices and principles
Basis of attention	Faculty resistance to online, teaching quality, content quality	Administrators are concerned about lack of support from faculty members in online teaching. They focus on improving the quality of teaching and learning to address accountability issues
Basis of strategy	Data-driven decision making	The administration wants to use the power of data analytics to improve organizational efficiencies as well as student engagement
Economic system	Governing boards, investors, state, and federal governments	The administration is answerable to the board members and investors for financial sustenance and to state and federal agencies for accountability and funding

competition is an external market dynamic, bureaucracy is a corporation's way of managing its internal operations. Similarly, standardization could either mean product standardization to expand markets or standardization of internal processes to gain efficiencies.

To overcome this conflation, I coded the data as an element of corporation logic when it referred to the internal aspects of higher education organizations, as was done in the previous section, and as market logic when it referred to its external dynamics in the field. While corporation logic maps to the internal administrative function of a higher education organization, market logic maps to the entire organization's approach toward its external world. The former focuses on internal efficiencies, hierarchy, standardization, and control, whereas the latter focuses on external customers and competitiveness.

Material Manifestations

The purest manifestation of market logic is the privatization of the higher education field. Although much smaller in terms of the total revenue as compared to the rest, the number of for-profit organizations offering four-year degree programs went up from 207 in 2000–01 to 700 in 2015–16. In terms of its overall percentage, the for-profit component of the sector increased from 18% to 28% in the same period (IES-NCES 2016c).

The second material manifestation of this logic is the emergence of market-ranking platforms. According to the theory, market logic focuses on improving 'market-status,' whereas corporation logic seeks legitimacy through 'market ranking.' As the data did not show any difference between the two, the word 'market' was used to code this aspect under market logic. The *US News & World Report* has been the most widely cited platform since the 1980s although its rankings have often been questioned (de Vise 2011; Freeland 2017). More recently, newer ranking systems, such as the College Scorecard from the US government, and a few other from venues, such as the *Economist* and LinkedIn are increasingly based on factors such as return on investment and job opportunities for graduating students (Economist 2015; Selingo 2016). Such rankings fuel the market-like behavior and lead to "positional arms race" based on the difference in rank rather than a difference in performance (Frank 2004, 49). The emphasis on college ranking was evident at the organizational level as well where across all the units in the case studies, the websites of all five units except Cedar Academy boasted about their market rankings.

Markets exploit opportunities, and online education has unleashed a variety of such opportunities to create new forms of business models and partnerships. Online technologies allow leaders to engage in outsourcing teaching activities, such as course creation by content providers, partnering with third parties for financial gains, or partnering to deliver courses and share revenues jointly. ACE supports such trends, as expressed next:

> Although the gold rush attitude and the corporate cowboys of a few years ago have subsided, there is still enough good news to make online higher education attractive to entrepreneurs. Success stories such as the University of Phoenix and DeVry Institutes fuel continued interest. Jones International, a wholly online university, has now received regional accreditation. In addition, Kaplan has created an online college and UNext, a for-profit online company, plans to offer an MBA in conjunction with Columbia University, Stanford University, Carnegie Mellon University, the University of Chicago, and the London School of Economics.
>
> (Levine and Sun 2002, 7)

But some mismanaged initiatives are also the reasons for the academic type to rally against such market-exploitation efforts, an example of which was published as a news release by AFT:

> Rutgers University faculty were dismayed when they learned last year that the university had entered into a secret seven-year agreement with Pearson Inc. to provide online degree programs to Rutgers students and split the revenues. Consultation with faculty, who are represented by the Rutgers chapter of (AAUP-AFT), was not part of the process.
>
> (www.aft.org/news/rutgers-faculty-say-no-pearson-ecollege dated 10/31/2013)

Similarly, faculty at Amherst College voted down the contract with edX and faculty at Duke University voted not to join a consortium for offering online courses (McKenna 2013). These new forms of market-arrangements are a sign of increasing competitiveness in the higher education field, aggressively looking for new business opportunities. MOOCs that started with a philanthropic motivation to share knowledge freely are now perceived as advertisements for elite institutions to "market" their product in the form of prepackaged courses delivered by their star professors (Lane and Kinser 2012). In this way, as market ideal type tries to increase revenue and improve its market share by using online education as its strategy, it conflicts with the academic ideal type in its mission.

Symbolic Interpretations

There is a widespread perception that higher education organizations are focusing on "short-term profits over long-term investment in education, and they regard students not only as products but also as customers. Professors are commodities to be bought and traded" (Andrews 2006, 17). These behaviors make higher education field perceived as an "industry" (Gumport 2000) and compared with industries such as healthcare or manufacturing (Ljosa 1993; Anson 2007). The theory of academic capitalism (Slaughter and Rhoades 2004) explains how knowledge as a capital good has turned higher education into a marketplace. Higher education organizations are increasingly engaging in strategies that explore emerging market opportunities.

Much like the manifestation of corporate logic, this logic also surfaced through conflicts over its very academic core. The first conflict that directly impacts its revenue-generating activities is the question of whether students should be seen as customers or products. The proponents of academic logic oppose when the "school's being referred to as a 'business' and students as 'customers' or 'consumers'" (Stein, Scribner, and Brown 2013). They worry in the context of online education as online will make higher education "viewed as dissemination of knowledge . . . accomplished by the 'virtual university,' linked to the idea of information as commodity and student as customer" (Boyte and Kari 2000, 51).

The third conflict relates to the kind of education offered by higher education organizations. The USDE has analyzed the changes in enrollments across various majors over the years. These majors are grouped under two categories—academic field and career field. The academic field of study represents most of the liberal arts covering subjects such as language, literature, humanities, psychology, social sciences, and history. The career field covers majors such as business, communications, engineering, biomedical sciences, homeland security, military, and public administration. In a 45-year period from 1970 to 2015, the percentage of bachelor's degrees conferred across majors in academic fields has dropped from 42% to 27% whereas degrees in career fields has jumped from 57% to 70% (IES-NCES 2017e). Chasing market demand and offering what sells is perceived as the emergence of "two cultures of higher education" where in one culture the purpose of higher education is to make "the whole person," whereas in the second it is "job training pure and simple. . . [that gives] return on investment" (Buller 2014, 2). This aspect was also evident at the unit level as the dominant goal of higher education emerged as workforce development, which led professors and students to express that higher education has become job training. These manifestations of market logic are mapped to the logic's category elements with a brief description in Table 6.4.

State Logic

The state type represents

> rationalization and the regulation of human activity by legal and bureaucratic hierarchies. . . . Bureaucratic state organizations attempt to convert diverse individual situations into the basis for routine official decision and cannot easily handle conflicting claims over the substantive ends toward which bureaucratic rationality is directed or demands for popular participation in them.
>
> (Friedland and Alford 1991, 248–249)

A bureaucratic governance is built upon democratic participation and welfare capitalism that tries to increase community goods through redistribution mechanisms. It derives legitimacy from legislation and uses the power of regulations to achieve its goals (Thornton, Ocasio, and Lounsbury 2012).

There are two ways in which the state logic manifested in this study. The first was about increasing higher education's accountability through regulation exercised by the state and federal government agencies. This is done primarily by attaching government funding to the quality of

Table 6.4 Market logic

Category element	Value	Description
Root metaphor	A buyer or a seller	A higher education organization selling education
Source of identity	Business model	A higher education organization sells education to students and its business model is designed to exploit market forces
Source of legitimacy	Market ranking, brand, revenue	A higher education organization uses its market ranking, brand, and size to claim legitimacy
Basis of norms	Revenue-focus, customer-orientation	A higher education organization competes to increase revenue and customer satisfaction
Basis of attention	Competition, return on investment, cost	A higher education organization focuses on increasing student enrollments, ensure return on investment for them while keeping its cost down
Basis of strategy	Expand, diversify, innovate	A higher education organization increases revenue through student enrollments by expanding into new markets that attract more students and explores new business models to diversify
Economic system	Market	It is governed by the principles of market capitalism

education being offered by the higher education organizations. While the focus on measuring and tracking quality is steadily increasing, the state-funding appropriations are seeing a downward trend. The academicians are concerned that this will privatize higher education, drive up the cost, and negatively impact student learning.

The regulating agencies assess quality in terms of the metrics that reflect some aspect of accountability and performance of these organizations. These metrics can be grouped into three categories. The first category represents organizational characteristics such as the faculty-count, student-faculty ratio, and faculty qualifications. These have historically been used for accreditation purposes by USDE and CHEA. The second category represents an overall efficiency of the higher education system in terms of graduation and retention rates tracked by USDE, and similar but more granular performance metrics such as student persistence, degree completion, and job placement. The third category is the most recent and still evolving which focuses on learning outcomes. All these metrics have influenced teaching practice one way or the other, but the most impactful has been the learning out-come metric whose use has been accelerated by its adoption into the digital learning environments. It is evident that all these efforts are geared toward increasing student success and higher education sector's accountability. Online technologies are also enabling a much closer monitoring of how students are interacting with their teachers and the instructional content. The regulating agencies are finding these tech-nologies very effective in increasing accountability, but the subscribers to academic logic are resisting their adoption. Capturing and meas-uring student-teacher interaction to evaluate a teacher's performance is being seen as digital surveillance, and the use of learning analytics to assess student learning is being viewed as forcing 'management by objectives' approach by administrators, and a threat to the student's and teacher's privacy.

The second way in which the state logic manifested in this study was the promotion of online education to increase access. Both state and federal governments are promoting the use of online education mod-els to broaden their access. Online technologies in some cases are also reducing or completely removing cost barriers, as was seen in the Cedar Academy case study. In this way, state logic manifests as the means to fund, increase access to, and accredit higher education, thereby trying to improve its quality and legitimacy. From a teaching practice perspective, the academic logic favors state funding as it reduces the sway of market forces, but it questions some of the measures employed by regulators to assess quality especially using digital technologies. A summary of this logic with the values for its category elements and a brief description is given in Table 6.5.

Social Logic

Unlike the ideal types identified thus far, the social ideal type does not map to any societal-level logic from the institutional logic framework. It instead surfaces in the extant research as well as in its manifestations in the field data that views the higher education field as a responsible citizen serving our society. It identifies with an "organized activity that main-tains, reproduces, or adapts itself to implement values that have been widely held and firmly structured by the society." Higher education as a social entity is

> devoted to a wide array of social functions that have been expanded over time: the development of individual learning and human capital, the socialization and cultivation of citizens and political loyalties, the preservation of knowledge, and the fostering of other legitimate pursuits for the nation-state.
>
> (Gumport 2000, 73–74)

Table 6.5 State logic

Category element	Value	Description
Root metaphor	Regulator	The federal and state governments regulate higher education
Source of identity	Accreditation, funding agency, setting quality standards	Metrics and accreditation determine quality
Source of legitimacy	Democratic participation	The accreditation is based on trust and peer reviews
Basis of norms	Compliance with government policies	The accreditation standards set by state and federal level agencies
Basis of attention	Focus on student-learning outcomes	Accreditors have to increase accountability to ensure that student learning is being measured
Basis of strategy	Measuring quality in education	Accreditors have to ensure that higher education organizations demonstrate accountability
Economic system	Welfare capitalism	Government funds appropriated to fund higher education

APLU articulated this ideal type in its publications where it urges higher education faculty, administrators, and students to actively engage with their external communities to make a social as well as an economic impact. As expressed in one such report published by APLU, "The engaged university is one that achieves impact by maintaining high standards for scholarship and by expanding collaboration and partnerships with entities and organizations outside the academy" (Fitzgerald et al. 2012). This social engagement is achieved by contributing to the communities that they are a part of, making higher education accessible to a diverse population of students, and helping students become better citizens. While these three manifestations were found across the field as well as the case studies, a common theme was that higher education is not fulfilling its social role to the extent it should. As pointed out by APLU,

"it is time to go beyond outreach and service to what the Kellogg Commission defines as 'engagement.' By engagement, we refer to institutions that have redesigned their teaching, research, and extension and service functions to become even more sympathetically and productively involved with their communities, however community may be defined.

(Kellogg Commission 1999, 9)

The document analysis of the organizations analyzed in the case studies showed that each of them claimed to be serving a social purpose in its own way, ranging from conducting research that makes a social impact to simply making education more accessible.

This ideal type has some similarities with the community ideal type as it pertains to helping students engage with their immediate environment. However, the key difference is that community ideal type looks inward within the boundaries of students' higher education organization, whereas the social ideal type looks outwards to the larger society which the organization is a part of. This ideal-type manifests itself in two ways in the context of teaching and learning: increasing access to education by encouraging diversity and educating students to be responsible social citizens.

Increasing Access

Making higher education accessible revealed two forms. First was in terms of social equality for all races, ethnicities, social status, and backgrounds. This change in demographic ratios, as was discussed in Chapter 3, clearly indicates that higher education is becoming more accessible with increasing diversity across races. The second form of access emerged in the form of freeing up education from space and time barriers by promoting online education models, and thereby "democratizing education." The Cedar Academy case study revealed the removal of cost barriers by offering free online accredited courses, replicated at the field level by MOOCs that are now becoming accredited.

Making education more accessible has been one of the key strengths of online education regarding space and time, but the cost barriers are only partially addressed as higher education organizations either are not realizing cost benefits or not passing them on to their students. The emerging education providers such as MOOCs are trying to address this challenge but lack the support of credit approvals. Some philanthropic organizations, such as Saylor Academy and University of People, are also using online technologies to offer online education and trying to offer credit-approved free education (Pappano 2013; Vedder 2016).

Developing Citizens

The second aspect is about building social citizenship among students, and it has been the center of debate around liberal arts vs. career-oriented education. There is a perception that career-focused education such as engineering is "associated with increases in materialism and conservatism and declines in concern for the larger society" (Sax 2000, 14). In the case studies, when interviewees were asked about the role of higher education in our society, they often responded with a question, "You mean what the role is, or what it should be?," indicating that they perceive a gap between the two. The discussion that ensued surfaced the gap between education for "citizenship development" and making a "whole person" vs. job training. The former was found to be associated with "helping students develop the values and skills of citizenship through participation in public and community service," as reported in an AAUP article (Hollander and Hartley 2000, 29), and argued by the scholars in the field of higher education (Gumport 2000; Clark and Trow 1966).

In terms of online adoption across different fields of study, there is a significant increase across all majors, although the increase is higher in career-education programs than in academic programs, for example, 18% in computer and information sciences degrees versus 7% in humanities (Levesque et al. 2008). Analyzing the issue of citizenship vs. workforce development in the context of online education, it is not evident from the data whether this difference is because of higher demand for career-education programs or because of some factors that make the administration of these programs easier in an online setting. There were three instances where the factors that could influence online adoption surfaced in the case studies:

- Virtual mode of learning: In Unit 1, the reason given by Jack for not offering online programs was the inherent inability of online modality to have students do real hands-on lab work where they can open up a computer box and carry out various activities such as fixing hardware issues, disassembling and reassembling the circuits, etc.
- Market demand: In Unit 3, Annie expressed how she wanted to create a MOOC for her course, but her proposal was turned down by her administration because her course is not as popular or in demand to justify the investments required to develop a MOOC course.
- Content flexibility: In Unit 4, Steve talked about a course related to tax-accounting that was launched in an online setting. But the course was later dropped because the tax codes change every year, requiring the content to be changed frequently, making it very resource intensive.

These instances indicate that higher online adoption in certain programs is a result of many complex factors and not necessarily a factor of its orientation toward workforce development.

The goal of offering general education in the course curricula for undergraduate studies is to develop social citizenship through teaching. Service learning as a pedagogical tool is promoted through which students learn as well as serve their communities, as suggested next.

Chemistry students engaged in service learning might, for example, study instrumentation by taking lead paint samples in older urban neighborhoods. At the same time that they learn how to take these measures, they develop information useful to those interested in reducing lead-paint risk in homes. They also learn about the connection between science and societal improvement. In other examples of service learning, composition students hone their writing skills by producing newsletters for nonprofit neighborhood organizations, or psychology students help residents in a home for the mentally ill as part of a course on mental disability.

(Hollander and Saltmarsh 2000, 30)

However, service learning is perceived as something that cannot be replicated in an online environment and, therefore, "Some believe that the availability of distance education will force campuses to articulate the unique educational advantages of campus-based education, including the practices of service-learning and other opportunities to learn and exercise civic skills" (Hollander and Hartley 2000, 359).

In this way, the social logic manifests in the field of higher education through its attempts to serve the larger society that it is a part of. The findings noted earlier are summarized to develop the category elements of the social logic with a brief description in Table 6.6.

Cyber-Cultural Logic

The ideal types identified thus far have been around in higher education field for some time with varying degrees of influence. The use of symbolic content was always the central part of teaching and learning. It underwent its first mediation with printing press and adoption of textbooks. The emergence of digital content represents the second major upheaval, bringing the content once again to the center stage. It is bringing two forms of changes into the field: first, change in teaching practice and second, new contradictions amidst prevailing logics. Both indicate the potential emergence of a new ideal type as "creation of new practices and variations in existing ones are central to the emergence of and change in institutional logics" (Thornton, Ocasio, and Lounsbury 2012, 149). Contradictions among institutional logics "are likely to trigger the activation of alternative logics" that may be "available but less accessible" (92).

This new ideal type has two key features: It mediates instruction, and it uses technologies, such as online platforms, learning analytics, and adaptive courseware in learning. The former represents the feature unique to cultural institutions such as performing arts that engage in creation and distribution of symbolic content (Thompson 1995), and the latter represents the new resource environment provided by online technologies that have triggered this phenomenon. I bring these two symbiotic elements together into one cyber-cultural ideal type to represent the new emerging

Table 6.6 Social logic

Category element	Value	Description
Root metaphor	Social citizen	A higher education organization as a responsible social citizen
Source of identity	Social equality	A higher education organization provides equal access to all members of the society
Source of legitimacy	Social citizenship, engagement	Higher education providers and seekers actively engage in social causes and bring social change and improvement
Basis of norms	Well-rounded education	A higher education organization provides a well-rounded education through a combination of liberal arts and workforce development
Basis of attention	access, diversity, social engagement	A higher education organization engages with its community to improve its social and economic environment, increase access, and welcome diversity
Basis of strategy	Service learning, use of technology to enable access	A higher education organization offers education programs that develop strong citizens and use technologies to broaden access, especially to underserved populations
Economic system	State support	A higher education organization should be state funded to allow access to students from all walks of life

institutional logic in the field of higher education. The manifestations of this ideal-type manifests are discussed next.

Teaching's Cultural Component

There were three distinct forms in which the cultural component of teaching manifests in higher education. The oldest manifestation is the debate about whether teaching is an art or a science. James (1899) James (1899) argued, "Psychology is a science, and teaching is an art; and sciences never generate arts directly out of themselves" (7–8). In a persuasive series of essays, Horne (1917) argued that teaching is not only an art but a fine art because the former is just an activity involving intelligence and skill while the latter also has aesthetic value. The author delineated the difference between art and science as follows:

> In contrast with science, which is knowledge, an art is action. In science, the intellect is primarily involved; in the art, the will. In science,

truth is our goal; in art, performance of some kind is the goal. It is true that this contrast is not absolute, for there is no science without the will to know and there is no art without the intellect, as the definition itself indicates.

(5)

But the debate nevertheless continues, indicating perhaps that it is both. As stated in an APLU report, "Good teaching is a form of creativity that links discovery with integration and application" (Kellogg Commission 2000, 14). A similar sentiment was echoed by Frank in Unit 3 who argued that "regimentation and the expectation that [teaching] is some sort of scientific activity is all bogus."

The second manifestation is the qualifying criteria for organizations to be termed "cultural." Cultural organizations engage in creative pursuits to produce content that has a varying combination of entertainment, education, and information. Creation of such content, termed as symbolic content, differentiates them from other entities such as economic entities offering products and services or political entities offering ideologies (Thompson 1995). Considering teaching as an art that requires creating symbolic content as its core function makes academia belong to the category of creative industry with education as its cultural reproduction (Gibson and Klocker 2004; Williams 1981). Higher education thus gets positioned in the cultural/creative domain, which is "concerned with the transmission of acquired symbolic content" (Thompson 1995, 17). The current economic challenges in the higher education sector represent the tension between commerce and creativity that is a "fundamental feature of cultural industries" (Hesmondhalgh 2007, 69).

Further extending this perspective, the professors can be seen as artists who pursue their intellectual passion for creating and disseminating knowledge (Bramwell et al. 2011; Sawyer 2004). Thus positioned, the transformations shaping higher education can potentially be compared to similar changes that cultural institutions of performing arts went through in the first half of 20th century when recording and mediation technologies first mediated the creation and dissemination of art

The third manifestation was the appearance of performer schema in the case studies that brought forth the cultural aspect of teaching in this study. The debates about the teacher as a "sage on the stage" vs. a "guide on the side" (King 1993) have been discussed extensively in the literature, but the art of a teacher who "takes the stage to engage" emerged as a new aspect that points to the cultural element of higher education. As was expressed by Emma in Unit 3, who argued that while others say that she is "not here to entertain," she uses entertainment to provoke students to think by couching her "message" in some kind of humor. This theme recurred in case studies, reflecting once again the cultural aspect of higher education.

6.1.7.2 Teaching's Cyber Component

While the earlier three indicators provide an insight into the cultural aspect of teaching, its cyber aspect emerged through the use of technology to make it flexible, scalable, and analyzable. Emergence of online content that can be disseminated globally to any student any time (e.g., in MOOCs), and the use of learning management systems that can not only host the content but also provide analytical tools to track and adapt teaching and learning processes (e.g., in Aspen University), are manifestations of the "cyber" aspect of this logic.

There is a recognition in the field that online education has surfaced the need to improve pedagogic awareness among teachers. There is also an acknowledgment of the educators' responsibility to integrate and engage students within their organizational settings to help them succeed in their academic endeavors. In this way, student engagement has become the central focus, making teaching learner-centric. One of the ways that this issue is being addressed is by trying to capture students' attention by making content interesting, making it granular, and using technology to exploit its multiple modalities. Such attempts include integration of computer-simulations, gamification, videos, interactive and adaptive courseware, and social networking into the traditional classroom that not only scales but also engages (Mangan 2016; Egenfeldt-Nielsen 2011).

The resident, as well as online case studies, also showcased this pattern. Teachers used short videos in the classrooms, for example, Caleb at Redwood University used videos, discussions, and music to keep students engaged. Robert at Aspen University created his videos to connect with online students and give personalized feedback to each student. Interdisciplinary teams with media professionals, pedagogy researchers, instructional designers, software developers, and subject matter experts are trying to reunite art and science into a "virtual teacher" using technology advancements now available to higher education (Hibbert 2014). Increasing use of online content that not only engages students but also tracks and adapts to their learning behavior reflects the emergence of a virtual teacher. The most noteworthy trend was the creation of a media studio in Aspen University and a special media team in Cedar Academy to create professional videos. Tracing the focus on student engagement to making "viral-worthy" videos surfaced how teaching is moving from educating to edutaining.

The MOOCs exemplify this face of teaching in which media technologies render professionally recorded videos of professor's lectures on-demand across the world while cyber technologies track each student's mouse click. MOOCs are predominantly pre-recorded lectures but packaged and presented using professional recording techniques and advanced software (Diwanji et al. 2014). It is this combination that led to an article in Forbes, titled "The coming age of the teaching megastar." It compares the new face of education with the world of movies and views professors as emerging megastars (Crotty 2012). Perhaps it would be more appropriate to say that the cultural identity was always an integral part of teaching, but has now become visible due to cyber intervention. Such transformations observed here are a combination of cultural logic that is surfacing with the new cyber resource environment. While in a resident-setting, the art and science of teaching resided in one person, it is getting 'unbundled' into different entities in an online environment. It is the difficulty of capturing this "art" that has perhaps made online education focus more on the "science" of pedagogy than ever before.

The second type of technology intervention in teaching practice is to measure the quality of teaching and learning in which learning analytics, educational data mining, and e-advising are some of the attempts directed toward this goal. While the elusiveness of quality persists, the resident teacher's intuitive assessment or a student's post-semester survey are getting augmented with tools that track "quality" in terms of student participation and teacher-student interaction in real time. Many of these initiatives, such as APLU's project to develop adaptive courseware, or Purdue University's "FitBit for academics" are in their nascent stages, but they point toward how the cyber-cultural logic is gaining a foothold.

Increasing the number of non-traditional education providers that are creating and offering such content (e.g., MOOCs, StraighterLine Academy, Cedar Academy) accredited by alternate accrediting agencies (e.g., ACE and NCCRS) shows the emergence of an alternate virtual world of education. This alternate world uses resources, especially faculty members, to create and validate the content to gain legitimacy. All the alternate education providers and accreditors listed earlier use faculty members from traditional higher education organizations to establish their presence in the field. Drawing from the typology of change in field-level institutional logics, cyber-cultural logic is rising out of the traditional academic logic, exemplifying segregation as a type of change in which "different field-level logics emerge from a previously shared common origin" (Thornton, Ocasio, and Lounsbury 2012, 164).

The Contradictions With and Independence From Other Prevailing Logics

It is important to analyze whether cyber-cultural logic is just a variant of one of the prevailing logics or an independent logic in itself. Analyzing how cyber-cultural logic aligns with the other prevailing logics can help address this question. The first logic that comes closest is the academic type, but as was seen in the findings, almost all cyber-cultural interventions introduced in teaching contradict academic theories and practices. Issues of loss of content ownership, restricted academic freedom, de-skilling of a scholarly role, loss of spontaneity of face-to-face student interaction, and potential digital surveillance are some of the intensely contested issues presented against online education by academic agencies.

The community logic also contradicts with cyber-cultural primarily because online education makes a student more solitary and severely restricts the possibility of face-to-face engagement between a student and a teacher or among students themselves. Although terms such as collaborative learning and learning communities are often used in the context of online education, the space-time distances make community building a challenge (Anderson 2008). The social ideal type supports cyber-cultural logic as it makes education more accessible, and in some cases a lot cheaper, but the larger goal of making students into better citizens through service learning and social engagement fails to materialize in a distributed space-time continuum.

The cyber-cultural ideal type supports the corporation, the market, and the state logics in many ways. To the corporation logic, it gives measurement tools and insight into teaching-learning processes in the form of data analytics, which then enables monitoring, standardizing, and controlling various organizational policies and procedures. It offers new business opportunities to the market in terms of new partnership arrangements, ability to expand markets beyond local boundaries, and provide a platform for promotions and outreach. The cyber-cultural logic also promises potential solutions to the issue of quality and accountability to the state in the near future. However, the state logic's regulated control on quality accreditation by USDE and CHEA, expressed as the "evil duo" by (Vedder 2016), continues to pose a roadblock for the cyber-cultural agency. Despite the alignment with the corporation and the market logic, the cyber-cultural cannot survive without the legitimacy of academic or the support from community and social logics.

Theories, Frames, and Narratives

Online education's new resource environment and the iron triangle's tightening grip have triggered the emergence of cyber-cultural logic. As questions about higher education's cost and accountability became more and more urgent and severe, the teaching practice gained importance, moving out from the shadows of traditional academic logic's scholarly research. A parallel impetus came from online education offering an alternate resource environment making a teacher into a 'virtual teacher.'

Cyber technologies have provided a platform to design content that adheres more to pedagogical theories evolved within the last few decades, than to teachers' teaching style or their scholarly status. Theories ranging from the theory of transactional distance (Moore 1993) to more recent theories of online learning (Anderson 2008; Picciano 2017) have given cyber-cultural logic its own space in the larger context of the academic profession. While these theories provide coherence to what cyber-cultural represents, various agencies articulate frames used to mobilize resources and bring change. As discussed earlier, the ideal types supporting cyber-cultural theories, such as the corporation, market, and state are using the iron triangle as their primary lever to support cyber-cultural adoption. Increasing adoption of online education models, promoting the use of technology in teaching, and defining teaching as a profession independent of the traditional academic identity is how cyber-cultural logic is changing the teaching practice. Learning analytics are replacing teachers' intuition as students are receding away from collocated classes to the space behind a computer screen. Teachers' presence is transforming into a virtual persona that is constructed by a team of instructional designers, media professionals, and subject matter experts.

Table 6.7 summarizes the categorical elements of this newly emerging logic.

Table 6.7 Cyber-cultural logic

Category element	Value	Description
Root metaphor	Virtual teacher	Teacher on a separate space-time continuum
Source of identity	Digitalized symbolic content designed through a combination of art and science	The content is developed by a team of experts in fields ranging from subject matter expert to professional film-making and pedagogic researchers
Source of legitimacy	Association with established higher education organizations	A cyber-cultural entity is associated with a well-established university to attain legitimacy in the form of credit approvals
Basis of norms	Computerized, massively scalable, data-driven	A cyber-cultural entity uses the computer as its platform and scales globally. Its emerging technologies are making it increasingly data-driven
Basis of attention	Quality, interactive learning experience, privacy	A cyber-cultural entity needs to not only match but exceed the quality expectations. It needs to create an interactive learning experience without invading privacy
Basis of strategy	Innovate, engage, track, measure, and adapt	A cyber-cultural entity uses the latest technologies to innovate new ways of teaching and learning so as to engage its students, as well as measure their learning while adapting to their individual needs
Economic system	Part of or in partnership with universities	A cyber-cultural entity is emerging from within a university, funded through a research grant or its online division, or in partnership with third-party content provider

Inter-institutional Dynamics

Having identified the spectrum of institutional logics, the inter-institutional system can now be analyzed as a whole, as shown in Table 6.8. There are several ways in which these logics can be grouped. The first grouping is based on where their constituents reside in the higher education's ecosystem. The academic, the community, and the corporation logics pertain to the members within a higher education organization such as students, teachers, and administrators and are therefore inward facing. The other three logics—market, state, and social—reflect higher education's face toward the outer world. The seventh cyber-cultural logic cuts across all six as it serves different purposes to each of the other six logics. This intersection gives the cyber-cultural logic the greatest potential to bring change. For example, the academic logic wants to draw from the cyber-cultural logic to bridge student-engagement gaps in online education without compromising the educator's status and legitimacy in the professional world. The social logic uses cyber-cultural logic to resolve iron-triangle problems while at the same time ensuring the economic sustenance of the higher education field. This multiplicity of purposes threatens the integrity of cyber-cultural logic's identity and diffusion of its potential as it tries to be many things to many people.

Another way to look at the dynamics is to consider these logics' primary orientation and inherent priorities. As was pointed out in the discussion on findings, there is considerable overlap between social and community logics as both of them focus on how various actors in the higher education world relate to their immediate surroundings. While community logic draws its boundaries within the organizational settings with individuals being at the center, the social logic positions the organization at the center surrounded by the society within which it exists. But both are oriented toward contributing to the growth and welfare of the world around them. Similarly, the corporate and market logics represent the inner and external faces of the industrial orientation of higher education, respectively. The corporate logic focuses on the inner workings of higher education organizations and the market logic prioritizes the external market dynamics in the field. Both draw their theories and frames from the world of business and industry. The academic logic orients itself to its subject matter or disciplinary priorities. It tries to stand independent of the community-social or the corporate-market duos. This is where the state logic intervenes. If state logic is dominant in the higher education system, the academic logic tends to favor community-social duo so that both state and academic logics can focus on serving the society. As the state logic loosens its grip, which is what is currently taking place in the US with the ongoing retreat of state appropriations, the corporate-market forces gain a stronger foothold. This is also where the differences in disciplinary orientation come to play in the form of the goal of higher

Table 6.8 An integrated system of institutional logics the higher education field

Category element	Academic	Community	Corporation	Market	State	Social	Cyber-Cultural
Root metaphor	Scholar	Community	Company	Buyer or seller	Regulator	Social citizen	Virtual teacher
Source of identity	Scholarship, research, teaching, service, disciplinary knowledge	Learning community, multi-cultural/diverse	Administration, management	Business model	Accreditation, funding agency, setting quality standards	Social equality	Digitalized symbolic content designed through a combination of art and science
Source of legitimacy	Credentials, reputation, research eminence	Community engagement	Governing board, policies, and procedures	Market ranking, brand, revenue	Democratic participation	Social citizenship engagement	Association with established higher education organizations
Basis of norms	Shared governance, academic freedom, employment tenure	Shared learning experience	Management practices and principles	Revenue-focus, customer-orientation	Compliance with government policies	Well-rounded education	Computerized, massively scalable, data-driven
Basis of attention	Changing faculty role, content ownership, student engagement	University culture	Faculty resistance to online, teaching quality, online quality	Competition, return on investment, cost	Focus on student-learning outcomes	Access, diversity, social engagement	Quality, interactive learning experience, privacy
Basis of strategy	Scholarship, teacher-student interaction	Student social integration	Data-driven decision making	Expand, diversify, innovate	Measuring quality in education	Service learning, technology to enable access	Innovate, engage, track, measure, and adapt
Economic system	State support	Cooperative	Governing board, investors, government	Market	Welfare capitalism	State support	Part of or partnering with universities

education. Education that focuses on workforce development is geared toward the corporate-market orientations because it fulfills market demand whereas the education for citizenship development prioritizes the community-social orientations.

Amidst all this push and pull, the emerging cyber-cultural logic needs to find its orientations that aligns with the prevailing logics more than it conflicts with them. And this is where the parallels from other cultural institutions can offer some guidance. I discuss some of these ideas in my next chapter.

7   Looking Ahead

Although the emerging information technologies offer solutions or pathways to the problems facing the higher education sector, their use is mired with conflicts among multiple constituencies, perspectives, and missions. Or in other words, ensuring that the field of higher education applies online education to the practice of teaching in a manner that can address the cost, quality, and access issues without losing its eminence and reputation is a complex endeavor because of the "contested terrain" characterization of the field (Scott 2010, 5). My study reveals the landscape of this contested terrain in a way that allows deeper analysis and exploration of a possible pathway. It exposes the misalignment among institutional logics across multiple levels—field, organizations, and individuals, as well as multiple types of entities across the for/non-profit and online/resident spectrum. Engaging the two societal-level theories reveals a new emerging institutional logic that not only explains the contemporary phenomenon but also provides a fresh perspective to look for solutions. Following sections provide further details on how this new framework contributes to the research in this field.

Research Contributions

Two field-level theoretical analyses that provided the inspiration and informed this research are Gumport (2000) and Scott (2010) who identified institutional logics in the field and applied the theory to analyze their influences. In my research, I built upon their findings by applying the meta-theoretical architecture of institutional logics developed by Thornton, Ocasio, and Lounsbury (2012) and focused on two specific aspects of contemporary higher education field—teaching practice and online education. This allowed me to arrive at a comprehensive picture that included not only the field level but also organizational- and individual-level patterns in the phenomenon of interest.

Applying the theory of mediatization aided the analysis of the impact of technology mediation on teaching practice. As mediatization is about change in institutional logics due to the mediation of communication processes, two theories were engaged to examine the entire phenomenon at multiple levels. Although there has been a conceptual exploration of the mediatization of teaching practice (Friesen and Hug 2009), this research furthers the inquiry by establishing theoretical explication as well as empirical exploration. Thus, this study makes three key contributions in the field of higher education that are discussed ahead.

Empirical Identification of 'Institutional Logics'

This study empirically substantiates the existence of institutional pluralism in higher education organizations, showing how it manifests and how it influences the actions of the participants in different roles within the organizations. Five logics—academic, community, corporation, market, and state—guided by the framework in Thornton, Ocasio, and Lounsbury (2012), two logics—social and market—guided by the analysis in Gumport (2000) and Scott (2010), and one logic—cyber-cultural—identified empirically using grounded research techniques in this study give a comprehensive view of the entire field in general, and teaching practice in particular. Each logic was identified through a combination of bottom-up and top-down approach. The field study demonstrates their emergence through top-down structures imposed by higher societal logics, and case studies reveal their bottom-up emergence from the micro-level individual and organizational agency. This modular explication provides a foundation for conducting further quantitative as well as qualitative research to continue this stream of inquiry.

Theoretical Integration of Mediatization With Institutional Logics

This study also demonstrates the integration of the theory of mediatization with the theory of institutional logics, which currently stand as two independent theories. This integration allows deeper analysis of the mediatization phenomenon and benefits from the well-developed theoretical foundation of institutional logics. A second, related contribution is that the theory of mediatization has been applied in many domains, such as politics, performing arts, and culture (Mazzoleni and Schulz 1999; Auslander 2008; Hjarvard 2013). But its explication as well as empirical exploration in higher education teaching, to the best of my knowledge, has not been done before this research. This introduction of a new theory into the domain of higher education can inform future research in this field.

Practical Implications

The findings from this research study show that the challenges faced by higher education field require a much broader perspective to come up with a sustainable solution. It also emphasizes how, despite the rapid pace of online adoption and the emergence of new educational models, answers to the basic questions about accountability and quality remain elusive. The case studies show contemporary challenges of teaching practice across a variety of higher education organizations. And the field study shows how many of these challenges have been recognized and many attempts have been made to address them in the past. The archival analysis of agencies that influence policy at the state and national levels reveal how the phenomenon of the mediatization of higher education in general, and teaching practice in particular, has evolved through phases. These findings have practical implications that are discussed ahead in this chapter.

Complexity of Disruption

Higher education has been viewed as glacial when it comes to innovating itself in the age of information highways and e-commerce (Anderson, Boyles, and Rainie 2012). This research explains the reason behind this perceived inertia: a complex inter-institutional system of logics that create multiple conflicts at every step. Unlike business organizations that are governed mostly by the market and corporation logics, the higher education sector is almost a microcosm of our societal logics that needs to bring along all its members together to make a sustainable change. It explains why the projections of disruption made by scholars have not yet come to fruition. They compared the field of higher education to commodity product or service markets that do not encounter such complex forces resisting change, and therefore do not capture all of its institutional dynamics.

While many emerging elements in the contemporary landscape, such as alternative-education providers and credit recommendation services, seem ready to bring change, they still need to leverage the credibility and reputation of the traditional education establishment to be considered legitimate. MOOCs bring professors from the elite universities and ACE requires faculty members in the established universities to conduct credit recommendation evaluations. But without the traditional establishment backing them, their sustenance may be untenable. The market logic of supply and demand and the corporate logic of command and control can see how technology can quickly meet what they seek. But they need to augment their agility with a thoughtful alignment with the academic, community, social, state, and now cyber-cultural logics. In the absence of such an alignment, all projections of disruption may either fail to materialize or may take a lot longer than expected.

Needs for Disruption

It is important to note that while technology provided the means for online education, the real forces that accelerated its adoption were the unmet needs that the higher education field was trying to address for a long time. These needs can be grouped into three categories: flexibility, scalability, and measurability.

- Flexibility: The emergence of distance education in the 1890s was a manifestation of the need for flexibility, and higher education constituents have tried to address it to some extent through channels such as correspondence, radio, television, and now the Internet. The urgency to break learning out of structural rigidities imposed by traditional colleges and universities can be heard in the report from the Commission on Non-traditional Study that was formed in 1971 (Gould 1973). Also, as the data shows, a large percentage of growth in online adoption comes from non-traditional student groups who need the flexibility to get an education anywhere anytime. The emergence of alternative-education providers (e.g., MOOCs) and alternative credit recommendation services (e.g., ACE and NCCRS) provide yet another material evidence of this need.
- Scalability: While face-to-face education has its merits, it fails to scale without compromising the quality of the learning experience. The attempt to measure this experience as the student-to-faculty ratio is an indicator that the traditional classroom model cannot scale. NCES started posting this metric on its college navigator website as a quality indicator of undergraduate programs in 2007–8 (Borden 2011). But the simplicity of this metric fails to capture what is intended. Although online education started as an even poorer version of the traditional model where instead of a classroom the lecture was recorded on a video, the new technologies hold the promise to make learning personalized, interactive, and adaptive.
- Measurability: The greater the urgency to make higher education accountable, the more severe the need to measure its quality. Student-learning outcome as a metric has gained acceptance but needs effective means to institutionalize. This metric requires technology to track learning at a very granular level, such as provided by the emerging adaptive courseware and learning analytics tools.

The traditional model of face-to-face education cannot address this urgency to be flexible, scalable, and measurable. However, it doesn't mean that the new must replace the old, for such projections have not only misguided the policymakers, they have also created unnecessary divisions among academicians because a majority of them still believe in the value of tradition. The right mindset to bring sustainable change in higher education was articulated by Gould (1973), whose guidance can be applicable even today:

> In summary, I am saying that traditionalist and non-traditionalist are not adversaries; that one cannot supplant or supersede the other; and

that they are partners in the single grand enterprise to promote learning. The rigor and discipline of the traditional approach should commend it to the attention of the non-traditionalist; opportunities for individualistic and independent study, for flexible patterns and new techniques, or for lifelong enrichment are equally worthy of notice by the traditionalist.

This assertion is neither empty rhetoric nor a retreat to consensus; it is a realistic affirmation of the total possibility awaiting the public, who voice their rising educational needs and expectations more clearly every day. If these needs and expectations are to be met, we require more institutions of higher learning, more diversity among them, more understanding of individual students and more capacity to guide them, more rapid response to change and more ability to cope with it, more willingness to put students squarely in the center of the undergraduate learning process, more money and better stewardship of it, more enthusiastic and wholehearted commitment to the future.

(xvii–xviii)

The Emergence of Cyber-Cultural Institution

The emergence of a cyber-cultural institution holds promise to address the needs discussed earlier if it aligns with other prevailing logics in the field. Specific to teaching practice, it promises to preserve its art as well as science by using technology not only to create content designed around pedagogic principles but also to make it aesthetically appealing that captures attention. While the market, corporation, state, and social logics favor this logic in some ways, the academic logic conflicts with it the most. The reasons behind this resistance are complex and several, such as the fear of exclusion, devaluation of traditional teaching and learning practices, deep concerns about its effectiveness, misrepresentation of the academic content, digital surveillance, or privacy concerns that always come with all things digital. Therefore, to bring sustainable change, all these apprehensions will have to be addressed through a carefully designed policy framework that considers the microcosm of higher education in its entirety. The findings from this research provide some guidance toward how this could be done. Two of these suggestions are proposed next.

First, the teaching role can be redefined by aligning it with the phenomenon of content stratification. Guru, coach, and artist are deepseated schemas that individuals—both teachers and students—use to form their expectations around teaching and learning behaviors. Integrating the phenomenon of content stratification with three teaching schemas can guide as to how teachers play their roles most effectively in the online world.

Guru seeks opportunities to create and share knowledge and enjoys the recognition that it begets. Therefore, more opportunities can be created for subject matter experts who can focus on creating content where they are duly recognized. The coach can be equipped with resources to engage with students through advanced technologies and tools instead of having to laboriously write e-mails and create videos from one's home office. And the artist can create engaging content with the help from media specialists by injecting humor, interesting stories, and compelling visuals that align with the subject matter and drive the point home.

Second, taking the lessons from the music and theater industries, the actors in the educational, content-development lifecycle, including the teachers, instruction designers and technology support teams, need to be recognized and acknowledged to the audience (i.e., students) and to the larger world—similar to performing arts—thereby increasing incentives for quality, creativity, and innovation. The content should be viewed as a work of art that requires not only pedagogy, technology, and subject matter expertise but also the best practices of media packaging and presentation, thereby learning how to engage audience's attention from the entertainment sector.

Conclusion

The extant research viewed higher education mostly as a combination of a social institution and an industry. I adopted this perspective and proposed to conduct a qualitative field study to apply the theory of mediatization of higher education. My research has uncovered several other logics prevailing in the field and has also introduced the new perspective of a cyber-cultural institution that offers critical insights to comprehend its dynamics. Further, I examined how these institutional logics are being mediatized, influencing the practice of teaching with increasing adoption of online models. Therefore, building upon two existing theoretical foundations—the institutional logics theory and the theory of mediatization—my research contributes to the extant research by identifying institutional logics that influence teaching practice and analyzing the phenomenon of their mediatization.

Results

This section provides a summary of answers to the research questions pursued in this study. The study reveals six prevailing institutional logics and one new, emerging logic that influence the practice of teaching in the context of higher education in the US. The prevailing logics are—academic, community, social, state, corporation, and market.

Each of these logics was explicated as per the theoretical constructs at the field, organizational, and individual level. The new emerging logic is a combination of the cultural elements of teaching as an art and the cyber element of teaching as a science and technology. The indicator that points to the emergence of a new institutional logic is the fact that teaching practice is being redefined into the new cyber world where content is getting stratified, and the schemas of teaching are accordingly getting realigned. Teachers are acquiring pedagogical as well as technical skills over and above the subject matter expertise that they always needed to have.

The content is not only becoming digitalized and stratified into the core and the supplemental but is also being designed to engage and "edutain" students while also tracking their learning behaviors and their interactions with their teachers. The new resource environment of interaction over the Internet and learning through adaptive courseware are enabling the emergence of this new logic.

This new logic showed some similarities to what the cultural institutions underwent when their processes were mediatized. For example, the rise of copyright concerns, the unbundling of the teaching role, the emergence of new specialized roles who develop instructional material, the increased variety, granulized content, and the rise of new organizational forms providing instructional products or services. However, this new logic has many new elements that are unique to education because of the nature of the communication between a teacher and a student being interactive rather than one way as in the case of performing arts. This interactive element has added the cyber element to it by not only being scalable but also adaptable and measurable.

The emergence of cyber-cultural logic contradicts academic logic because it seems to threaten its core values while also trying to change its role in the higher education landscape. The role of a scholar specializing in disciplinary knowledge is being displaced by a virtual teacher who not only has the knowledge but also focuses on coaching and pedagogy using technology. It supports social logic by removing access barriers but poses challenges for the community logic as online learners find it difficult to build communities of learners. It supports state logic by offering new technologies to measure quality and improve access, which is being reciprocated by the government investing in research into new learning models using cyber-cultural approaches. It also supports the market logic by offering flexible approaches to extend online education, thereby expanding enrollments, and it supports the corporation logic by helping standardize the content, providing measurement and tracking tools and metrics, and creating opportunities to proactively manage student retention and graduation by using learning and predictive analytics.

Future Directions

Several potential future research directions can be pursued based on the contributions and the impact of the research presented earlier. From the theoretical standpoint, the explication of institutional logics can be further enriched by replicating this across other types of organizations, especially the newly emerging forms such as MOOCs as they are setting the future directions for the field of higher education and evolving at a very fast pace. A deeper study of such organizations can give more insight into the cyber-cultural logic that surfaced in this study.

Another direction that can be pursued from this stream of inquiry is a historical comparison of other cultural institutions with higher education to identify parallels, especially in terms of the challenges faced and the solutions found that could potentially guide policy development in higher education. The findings from such a comparison can contribute toward redefining the role of a teacher in the cyber-cultural world who are reshaping the instructional content into its new digital forms.

The cyber-cultural characteristics of higher education identified in this research are undergoing changes as technology is making inroads. Each of these characteristics, identified under theoretical constructs such as the root metaphor or the source of identity (see Table 6.7) offers a starting point to redefine higher education. Should the field derive its identity from the content it creates? How does this new identity impact students and teachers within the educational ecosystem? Should the relationship between the traditional and the alternate education be considered as adversarial or as an interdependence that requires some fine-tuning to make it into a sustainable partnership? Such a line of questioning can help us rethink the future of higher education.

Appendix A
Theory Selection

The decision to adopt the theoretical framework that integrates the theory of institutional logics with the theory of mediatization was not swift. It took several rounds of iterative consideration and exploration of various potential alternatives. The following discussion summarizes the deliberations undertaken in the theory selection process:

1. Technology vs. human agency dualism: The phenomenon of interest in this research is institutional changes brought about by mediated teaching, whose higher abstraction can be viewed as mediated communication which in turn point toward media theories. However, media theories such as media effects and uses and gratification take a micro-level, technology-deterministic or media-deterministic view. Similarly, theories of social construction or shaping of technology (SCOT/SST) focus on the role of humans in the design and use of technological artifacts (Williams 1996). Both approaches focus more on technology design and use, and less on their larger long-term social impact on the practice and the field. Taking an "integrativism" approach that explains how society and technology mutually shape each other can help transcend such dualism between technology determinism vs. social constructivism (Hofkirchner 2010).

2. Structure vs. individual agency dualism and media logic vs. practice conflict: The theory that analyzes how institutions shape individual action is the structuration theory, of which the theory of mediatization is a variant (Hjarvard 2013). This genre of theories accords higher agency to structure over individuals, thereby creating a dualism. Also, the use of the theory of mediatization has generated some debate over the use of media logic vs. practice to capture the phenomenon (Couldry 2004). Engaging the institutional logics perspective helps overcome the two issues of structure versus agency dualism and logic versus practice debate. It also explains the constraining and enabling role of structure and transforming and innovating role of the individual agency. It links the higher institutional logic with lower-level practice (Thornton, Ocasio, and Lounsbury 2012),

thereby overcoming the media logic vs. practice gap in the theory of mediatization as well.

3.   Historical dimension: As the changes at field level occur over a long period, the theory needs to engage temporal dimension to afford historical analysis. Focusing strictly on technology adoption and use, the theory of diffusion of innovations (Rogers 1995) could be a likely candidate as it engages macro as well as temporal dimensions. However, its interest lies in diffusion and not on the long-term institutional changes at the field level. The institutional logic perspective as well as the theory of mediatization engage historical dimension as they analyze long-term structural changes at the societal or field level.

4.   Multiple levels of analysis: Although the phenomenon of interest is at the field level, the focus is on teaching practice that manifests at the micro level of transactions. Capturing the dynamics at these two levels requires a theory that engages multiple levels of analysis, which is offered by the meta-theoretical architecture of institutional logics proposed by Thornton, Ocasio, and Lounsbury (2012) discussed earlier.

5.   Critical vs. analytical lens: Researchers have used mediatization predominantly as a concept that is "instrumental in critical assessments of social change with the latent function of expressing a certain attitudinal or political position" (Schulz 2004, 87–88). Such a critical perspective limits the value of the theory for scientific analysis, motivating researchers to seek a non-normative definition of the concept (Schulz 2004; Strömbäck 2008; Hjarvard 2013). I, therefore, integrate the theory of mediatization with the meta-theoretical framework proposed by Thornton, Ocasio, and Lounsbury (2012) to overcome this limitation and allow an analytical interpretation of mediatization.

In summary, although the broad range of theories in the field of organizational sociology, media studies, and information systems offer useful perspectives that could potentially inform this research, they lack the specific features required to fulfill the needs of this study. The selection of the institutional logics' perspective and the theory of mediatization provides a comprehensive framework to circumscribe the phenomenon of interest along all the dimensions discussed earlier.

Appendix B
Research Methodology

The strategy adopted in this research used retroduction and abduction that transcends the inductive and deductive divide. I used interpretive epistemology and qualitative methods to gather and interpret the data. Following the established guidelines, I carried out a multi-level multi-unit case study to arrive at the findings. In the following sections, I provide more details on each of these aspects of my research.

Retroduction and Abduction

As was suggested in the first chapter, the motivation behind my research was the recognition that the perspectives being adopted to comprehend contemporary dynamics in the higher education field are proving to be deficient in some ways. I argued that by shifting our focus from economic factors such as cost to an alternate factor that is instructional content may uncover additional points of view. But such a shift changes the onto-logical positioning of higher education sector from being an economic or a social entity to a cultural entity because entities that engage in cre-ation and dissemination of symbolic content are inherently cultural in their makeup. My personal observations and professional interactions followed by a literature review that compared the transformations that other cultural industries underwent with those currently witnessed in higher education further strengthened my starting premise. So I started this research with a priori understanding that one of the lenses missing from the toolbox that scholars use to analyze higher education could potentially be that of a cultural institution.

Such a priori perspective makes my research neither deductive nor inductive (Alvesson and Sköldberg 2009). It is instead a retroductive approach in which hypothetical models are built from imagination, intui-tion, guesswork, or free creation of our minds that can potentially explain the patterns observed in the phenomenon of interest (Blaikie 2007). It involves "imagining a model of a mechanism, which if it were real, would account for the phenomenon in question" (Bhaskar 2014, vii). Intro-duced as a research strategy to overcome the deficiencies of induction or deduction by Charles S. Pierce, who described it as "an instinctive mode of inference" (Ayim 1974, 34), retroduction is yet to gain wide acceptance in social science research in general (Blaikie 2003b). However, its application has been significant in research using critical realism as its philosophical paradigm (Bhaskar 2013). It starts with an observed pattern, in this case, the similarities between higher education and other cultural institutions, based on which a researcher develops an explanatory model. Then the existence of this model is established through empirical study and experiment (Blaikie 2007).

Some scholars use a related term "abduction" interchangeably with retroduction (Richardson and Kramer 2006; Alvesson and Sköldberg 2009; Niiniluoto 1999), perhaps because the difference between them is only relative (Bhaskar 2014) (Bhaskar 2014). However, drawing from Blaikie (2003a, 2003b, 2007) and Ackroyd and Karlsson (2014), I consider them as two distinct research strategies, with retroductive logic based on the researchers' hypothesized model that potentially explains the observed patterns, and abductive logic relying on people's account of why they do what they do to explain the phenomenon.

The transformations in higher education are similar to changes experienced by cultural institutions when their communication processes were mediated. This premise is used here to develop the retroductive logic to explain how changing institutional logics are influencing the practice of teaching. This retroductive logic is substantiated and further developed by the findings of a qualitative field study that captures the accounts of institutional actors—i.e., field-level agencies, organizations, and individuals— therefore adopting abductive strategy as defined earlier. In this manner, I have adopted a combination of retroductive and abductive strategies with the former proposing higher education as a cultural institution and the latter empirically substantiating it by analyzing its actors' narratives on the practice of teaching.

Evaluation

With interpretive epistemology, qualitative methodology, and retroductive/abductive research strategy guiding the research design, there are several threats to the trustworthiness of the research that needed to be acknowledged and proactively addressed. To address these issues, I adopted the following key techniques:

•   Conducted a pilot study to test the instruments and interpretation strategy to expose any biases or predispositions. This pilot comprised three interviews in three different organizations followed by a preliminary round of analysis to assess the effectiveness of my interview protocol. One of the insights uncovered in this exercise was the difference between asking a question about 'what is' versus 'what should be.' For example, asking the question 'What is the role of higher education in our society?' generated more substantive and analyzable responses than the question 'What should be the role of higher education in our society?' While the former allowed participants to share their real experiences, the latter often took them to a hypothetical realm not relevant for my study.

- Adopted seven principles of conducting and evaluating interpretative research (Klein and Myers 1999):

1. The fundamental principle of the hermeneutic circle: This principle requires iterating between individual parts and the whole to arrive at a complete contextual understanding. I incorporated this principle by designing several iterations at all three levels of analysis. The next section explains these iterations in more detail.

2. The principle of contextualization: This principle requires bringing out the social and historical context that helps to develop a more accurate interpretation of the current situation. The temporal analysis of higher education in the US partially fulfilled this principle because it helped to understand the historical origins of some of the contemporary dynamics. Similarly, the individual interview data was also interpreted in light of each organization's history and its current position in the field of higher education, thereby providing a rich context.

3. The principle of interaction between the researchers and the subjects: This principle played a significant role as I was a peer or a teacher to some of the participants interviewed in this study. Throughout the data collection and interpretation activities, I had to reflexively question my own assumptions about the phenomenon I was asking my participants about. I also had to weigh their responses against my relationship with them to check if my presence influenced their responses in any way. This approach helped me look for patterns that otherwise I would have missed, and arrive at interpretations that went deeper than just the first impressions.

4. The principle of abstraction and generalization: This principle pertains to relating the idiographic details in data to abstract theoretical concepts. The two theories chosen for this study greatly aided the adherence to this principle. Both have a rich set of constructs explicated in sufficient detail and applied in many empirical studies that helped significantly in systematic coding and analysis of my data.

5. The principle of dialogical reasoning: This principle requires the researcher to recognize and confront one's preconceptions if they have contributed to research design, and to acknowledge

transparently if these preconceived notions are countered by actual findings. I started my research with the notion that higher education could also be a cultural institution, as I have argued in the first chapter of this book. But soon enough my findings started deviating from this idea as technology-influences on teaching practice started emerging almost as often, if not more, as teaching's cultural attributes. I had to alter my analytical lens then to accommodate new findings.

6. The principle of multiple interpretations: This principle requires the researcher to be sensitive to different interpretations among the participants. This principle articulates the very essence of the theory that is premised on how individuals draw different interpretations based on the institutional logics they subscribe to. Hence his principle formed the foundational approach of my research.

7. The principle of suspicion: This principle requires the researcher to be sensitive to individual biases and distortions in their narratives. Although this principle is more relevant to studies that adopt critical epistemology, it helped me in my research in a slightly different way. Having worked for several years as a teacher in the higher education field, I could understand many unstated dynamics between teachers, students, and administrators that would be inaccessible to an outsider. So while being an 'insider' posed come challenges adhering to the principle of interaction between the research and the subjects as discussed earlier, it aided in interpreting the interaction with sufficient contextual knowledge.

• Employed the criteria of credibility, transferability, dependability, and confirmability to ensure trustworthiness (Lincoln and Guba 1985; Shenton 2004)

1. The technique of prolonged engagement was applicable at the field level and to some extent in some of the organizations where I conducted case studies as I had been associated with them in the past. This association with higher education helped me understand the prevailing culture in the field in general and in some of the organizations in particular. For organizations other than these, I ensured that I developed an "early familiarity" through consultation of appropriate documents before the actual interview sessions (Shenton 2004, 65).

2. The second technique to develop credibility that I used was triangulation. I arrived at the findings by analyzing data from multiple sources and levels—i.e., individual interviews, organizational-document analysis, and field-level archival analysis.

3. I used the technique of member-checking—"a trustworthiness technique to improve credibility" (Lincoln and Guba 1985, 11) in two ways. First, my research committee members themselves being academicians served as sources for member-checking. Second, I shared a smaller set of findings from this research in a research panel at the ASHE-2016 Conference. Acceptance in this conference followed by panel members' endorsements helped strengthen my research design and findings' credibility.

4. My research offers transferability through thick descriptions of the sources, observations, and data excerpts through which I have derived my findings. Some efforts in purposeful sampling that are elaborated further in the next section also strengthen transferability.

5. I have elaborated all the findings of this research by explaining how I arrived at those findings, thereby making them auditable and confirmable.

The Analysis Approach

Using an iterative approach to capture and refine the findings systematically, I divided the analysis into three parts. The first part focused on field-level secondary data to arrive at a macro-level big picture. The second part contained unit-level analysis based on primary data gathered in six case studies, which provided individual- and organizational-level themes. As both parts neared completion, I started a comprehensive analysis to arrive at the third and final set of integrated findings and conclusions. The entire analysis was conducted using a computer-based qualitative analysis tool called NVivo from QSR International. This tool provides features to capture data into 'nodes' which are containers that can then be collectively analyzed for emerging themes. These nodes are then mapped to various 'classification' tables. The following sections provide further details.

Field-Level Analysis

Institutional logics manifest symbolically as theories and frames and materially as structures and practice at a field level. These manifestations were captured using archival analysis that also helped identify lower-level categorical elements of different institutional logics. This means identifying the root metaphor, the source of identity, the source of legitimacy, the basis of attention, the basis of norms, the basis of strategy, and the economic system that undergird a specific logic. I based the selection of a document for analysis on whether it directly or indirectly referred to teaching practice. To manage the large volume of documents available from various sources, I followed a three-step approach for document selection—skimming for superficial examination, reading for a thorough examination, and finally interpreting for thematic analysis—as proposed by (Bowen 2009). While the first step helped in ensuring appropriate selection, the next two steps helped in comprehending and interpreting the meaning.

Each document was read to capture excerpts that pointed to either a concept relevant to the theory of institutional logics or the theory of mediatization. The emerging patterns could then be mapped toward theoretical constructs of institutional logics or to material events reflecting mediatization signifying long-term structural changes in the institutions of higher education. The following example illustrates how I mapped a data excerpt to an ideal type and its categorical element using theory-driven selective coding approach. This excerpt is from an article published by AAUP in 2000 about how distance education constrains academic freedom in teaching:

> Distance education creates special concerns with academic freedom and educational quality to the extent that the creation, use, and revision of course materials may not necessarily be handled by the same faculty member(s)—or even by faculty members at all. In some for-profit institutions, for example, the individuals who create original course materials are not involved at all in the use of those materials and do not interact with students. Thus, their ideas are left in the hands of others to interpret and revise. The individuals who are responsible for the "delivery" of the course content may not have the same expertise or training as the creators. The institution might also ask for courses to be structured and packaged in very specific ways to meet its own needs, thus placing other constraints on traditional academic freedom in teaching.
>
> (Euben 2000)

I captured this excerpt in a node titled "Distance Education Constrains Academic Freedom," and then classified by assigning two codes: logic as an "academic" and categorical element as "basis of attention," as it represents the challenge of adopting online education as perceived by academic ideal type that captures its attention. This process is depicted in Figure B.1.

At this point, it is important to note that the initial set of ideal types were either drawn from the theoretical framework or prior research for selective coding. The strategy was to identify nodes that represent something about online education or teaching practice. In instances where such nodes could not be mapped to any of the predefined ideal types thereby indicating a coding "breakdown," which "occurs during interpretive analysis when a new theme is emerging" (Trauth, Quesenberry, and Huang 2009, 484), the analysis moved to open coding followed by

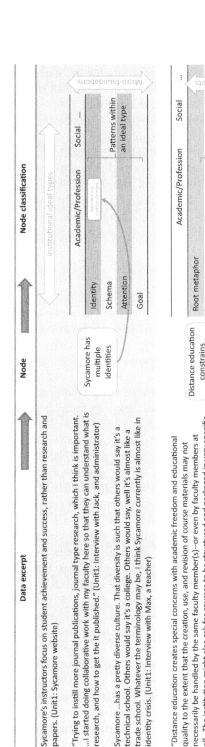

Data excerpt | **Node** | **Node classification**

Sycamore's instructors focus on student achievement and success, rather than research and papers. (Unit1: Sycamore website)

"Trying to instill more journal publications, journal type research, which I think is important. ...I started doing collaborative work with my faculty here so that they can understand what is research, and how to get the it published." (Unit1: Interview with Jack, and administrator)

Sycamore ...has a pretty diverse culture. That diversity is such that others would say it's a technical school. Others would say it's a college. Others would say, well it's almost like a trade school. Whatever the terminology may be, I think Sycamore currently is almost like in identity crisis. (Unit1: Interview with Max, a teacher)

→ Sycamore has multiple identities

Institutional ideal types

	Academic/Profession	Social	...
Identity			
Schema		Sycamore has multiple identities	
Attention			
Goal			

{ Patterns within an ideal type }

Micro-foundations

"Distance education creates special concerns with academic freedom and educational quality to the extent that the creation, use, and revision of course materials may not necessarily be handled by the same faculty member(s)--or even by faculty members at all...The institution might also ask for courses to be structured and packaged in very specific ways to meet its own needs, thus placing other constraints on traditional academic freedom in teaching." (Euben, 2000)

→ Distance education constrains academic freedom in teaching

	Academic/Profession	Social
Root metaphor		
Source of identity		
Basis of attention		Distance education constrains academic freedom in teaching
Basis of norms		
.... Etc.		

{ Patterns within an ideal type }

Category elements

"The preparation of materials has morphed over the recent years. Many moons ago when I was teaching, I could rely on students to focus and concentrate for almost an entire hour and a half session. That's not the case today, at least in my experience. So I have to had to evolve the materials in sufficiently modular lumps, interruptible lumps, and changed something, put a video up there that is related, ask a question for discussion, have to do something approximately every 7 to 10 minutes. Otherwise I lose them to some other semi-innocent distraction, typically smartphone." (Unit3: Caleb, a teacher)

"I think they are easily distracted. ....You can't lecture like in old days for 75 minutes. That doesn't work for students....So students get distracted - how do you deal with that. I think you have to break up your content. Make it interactive. You have to constantly ask them questions." (Unit3: Teresa, a teacher)

→ Students' attention span getting shorter

Teaching practice

Content — Teacher — Student

{ Patterns within core-entities of teaching practice }

Figure B.1 Data coding approach

axial coding, which then fed back into the coding scheme for selective coding. In this way, I adopted the approach applicable for the elaboration of existing theories, as has been recommended by Strauss and Corbin (1994) and applied by Trauth, Quesenberry, and Huang (2009). These were collected following the process shown earlier in an 'unnamed' ideal type that potentially represented the emerging logic.

Following the principle of theoretical saturation (Patton 2015), new nodes were created until no new nodes could be formed that contributed any new information to the analysis. This process resulted in 141 nodes from 110 source documents, capturing 426 data excerpts. Finally, having captured all logics and their categorical elements, I conducted a detailed analysis to surface any themes to answer the research questions pursued in this study.

Unit-Level Analysis

The interviews and organizational data were transcribed and classified in three iterations, each iteration comprising four steps. In the first iteration, I primarily focused on setting up the coding scheme in NVivo and refining my analysis approach using data from two units. I then applied the learnings from this iteration into the second iteration and coded all six units. Finally, the third iteration allowed me to revise the final set of themes and patterns in the context of overall research findings that emerged from the first two rounds.

Within each unit, I first coded data into nodes, generating about 600 nodes from 1,100 data excerpts. Some of these nodes were then classified into first-order constructs based on theory-driven selective coding. The selective coding started with theoretical constructs derived from two sources. The first set of theoretical constructs came from micro-foundations of institutional logics at the individual and organizational levels. These constructs are identity, goal, schema, and attention of the constituents. The second set came from the three core entities in the model of teaching practice—student, teacher, and content. As this part of the analysis was not based on theory, the analysis approach required open and axial coding based on Strauss and Corbin (1994).

The first round of selective coding required extracting first-level constructs that are the "understandings held by the observed people themselves" (Lee and Baskerville 2003, 230). Therefore, this step focused on extracting individual and organizational identity, goal, schema, and attention. For example, the identity construct revealed a pattern of multiple identities held by different individuals. An example from Unit 1 in Sycamore Institute is illustrated in Figure B.1. As shown in the data excerpt, three different sources expressed their organization's identity differently. An organizational document as the first source stated that the faculty members at Sycamore focus on teaching and not on research.

An individual as the second source talked about how he is encouraging faculty members to conduct more research and get published. And another individual as the third source expressed that Sycamore in general and the program, in particular, are being perceived as multiple things and, hence, having an identity crisis. These three excerpts from three sources were captured into one node named "Sycamore has multiple identities." As this node maps to identity construct and reflects internal conflicts in the organization's academic identity, the node was classified as "identity."

While identity, schema, attention, and goal are first-order constructs, the institutional ideal types are second-level constructs that "explain the patterning of the first-order data" and articulate "interpretation of interpretations" (Maanen 1979, 541). These second-order constructs are the researcher's understanding resulting from the analysis of first-order constructs and relationships among them (Lee and Baskerville 2003). Therefore I made the leap from first-order constructs to institutional ideal types based on my interpretation of data and emerging themes.

Similarly, I captured the patterns for core entities of teaching practice by looking at those nodes that reflect how teaching and learning get done within a unit. Another example from Unit 3 (Redwood University), as shown in Figure B.1, reflects this approach. In this example, two teachers talked about how they find students' attention span to be shortening over the years and how that makes them come up with content that is more granular so that they can keep switching from one to the next, thereby keeping students engaged. I coded this excerpt in a node named "student attention span getting shorter," and then classified it under "student" as it reflects how students' learning style is changing teaching practice.

The nodes that could not be mapped to a theory-driven code indicated a "breakdown," thereby once again necessitating open and axial coding. After completing coding for each case study, I looked for within-case patterns, and then cross-case patterns (Patton 2015; Eisenhardt 1989). The last step involved a comparison analysis across six units in terms of the patterns found in their ideal types, categories, and values. This then resulted in the first cut of micro-foundational patterns, their influence on teaching practice, and how they are changing with increasing adoption of online education.

Integration

Bringing all the elements of analysis together, the entire research approach was integrated into seven steps, as depicted in Figure B.2:

1. Retroduction
2. Conceptual framework development
3. Data source identification
4. Data collection

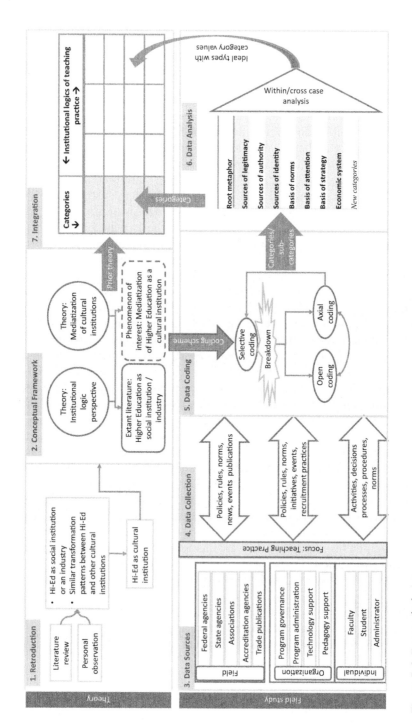

Figure B.2 Research design

5. Data coding
6. Data analysis and abduction
7. Integration

Integration of organizational-level findings with field-level findings helped articulate field-level institutional logics. It involved revisiting the conceptualized institutional logics of higher education identified in extant research and literature—i.e., academic, industry, and social institutional logics. As stated before, extant literature does discuss prevailing institutional logics in the field of higher education. However, they focus on the general field and not on any specific practice.

While integrating the field- and unit-level findings were integrated, patterns reflecting material and symbolic changes triggered by the mediation of teaching practice were also traced. To trace mediatization occurring over long periods of time, I captured all events on a timeline that signified either mediation, adoption, reciprocation, or domination phases, as defined earlier. These events were captured from within the document corpus collected for data and coded in NVivo for traceability. All these findings were synthesized with the extant literature to come up with a comprehensive set of institutional logics as the outcome of this study.

Limitations

Like all research, mine is not free of limitations. First is the relatively small size of the unit-level and field-level data for a study of such a complex topic. The findings of this study, though triangulated by using multiple levels, sources, and types of data, may need further refinement through an expanded and more in-depth study of the field. The access to some of the organizations in the case studies was fairly limited because of their for-profit nature and, therefore, the interpretation of the data collected from those sources lacks sufficient depth in the description.

The history of higher education in the US is rooted in colonial colleges that had deep religious foundations (Geiger 2011), but this research did not find any presence of religion as an institutional logic in the field of higher education. It is likely that expanding data collection to other types of organizations such as Jesuit colleges and universities may reveal the presence of religion also as one of the institutional logics in the sector. I acknowledge that this is another limitation of the findings from this study.

Appendix C
Interview Protocol

Research Question 1

What are the prevailing institutional logics that influence the practice of teaching in the context of higher education in the US?

Mini-Research Questions:

1. What are the different identities, goals, and schemas that individuals draw from?
2. To what is their attention, decision, and action often directed?

Interview Questions:

1. According to you, what is the role of higher education in our society? What is the role of your organization? What is your role?
2. Are there any specific organizational, personal, or professional goals that currently you are working toward? How does your role help in achieving these goals?
3. Can you compare the teaching profession to any other profession or activity that is similar in some ways? Can you give a metaphor or an analogy for teaching or for a teacher that comes to your mind?
4. What have been the most important or urgent challenges or concerns that you have dealt with during your career in this field? What takes most of your mindshare nowadays? What decisions have you taken to overcome these challenges? Why did you take them and what was their impact?

Research Question 2

How is the adoption of online education mediatizing these prevailing institutional logics?

Mini-Research Questions:

1. Teacher: Change in teaching tools, techniques, and skills. Preference between resident vs. online teaching. Criteria to assess the quality of teaching. Change in technologies used in content creation and dissemination. Organizational policy changes related to teachers or teaching
2. Student: Change in student-learning behaviors. Organizational policy changes related to students or learning
3. Content: Change in types of content. Organizational policy changes related to content

Interview Questions:

1. What different teaching techniques are used by faculty members? How are these changing?
2. Why do/don't you teach/learn online?
3. Are there some teaching techniques defined/recommended at your organization level? Do you follow them? Why/why not?
4. What new skills have faculty members had to learn to teach in this organization? How are these skills changing?
5. What key criteria do you look for when hiring or promoting faculty? Is it same across different delivery models? Is your hiring criteria for teachers changing? How and why?
6. What other roles help teachers in teaching activities? Is there any change over the years?
7. Is the program accredited? Is teaching influenced by accreditation criteria?
8. In your experience, how do students learn? Do they work in teams? How? Why?
9. How do you think teachers create their presence in different delivery model settings?
10. How do you assess the quality of teaching? How is it different across different settings?
11. What different content types/formats are used by teachers?
12. What content platforms do you use to deliver content?
13. Who creates these contents?
14. How often is the content changed, why, and by who?
15. Is there a copyright associated with them? Who owns the copyright?
16. Are there any policy changes related to teaching, hiring, content development in your organization in recent past that have resulted from online adoption?

Appendix D
Inter-institutional System Ideal Types

Table D.1 Inter-institutional system ideal types (Thornton, Ocasio, and Lounsbury 2012, 73)

Y-Axis	X-Axis: Institutional Orders						
Categories	Family 1	Community 2	Religion 3	State 4	Market 5	Profession 6	Corporation 7
Root Metaphor 1	Family as firm	Common boundary	Temple as bank	State as redistribution mechanism	Transaction	Profession as relational network	Corporation as hierarchy
Sources of Legitimacy 2	Unconditional loyalty	Unity of will Belief in trust and reciprocity	Importance of faith and sacredness in economy and society	Democratic participation	Share price	Personal expertise	Market position of firm
Sources of Authority 3	Patriarchal domination	Commitment to community values and ideology	Priesthood charisma	Bureaucratic domination	Shareholder activism	Professional association	Board of directors Top management
Sources of Identity 4	Family reputation	Emotional connection Ego-satisfaction and reputation	Association with deities	Social and economic class	Faceless	Association with quality of craft Personal reputation	Bureaucratic roles
Basis of Norms 5	Membership in household	Group membership	Membership in congregation	Citizenship in nation	Self-interest	Membership in guild and association	Employment in firm
Basis of Attention 6	Status in household	Personal investment in group	Relation to supernatural	Status of interest group	Status in market	Status in profession	Status in hierarchy
Basis of Strategy 7	Increase family honor	Increase status & honor of members & practices	Increase religious symbolism of natural events	Increase community good	Increase efficiency profit	Increase personal reputation	Increase size & diversification of firm
Informal Control Mechanism 8	Family politics	Visibility of actions	Worship of calling	Backroom politics	Industry analysts	Celebrity professionals	Organization culture
Economic System 9	Family capitalism	Cooperative capitalism	Occidental capitalism	Welfare capitalism	Market capitalism	Personal capitalism	Managerial capitalism

Appendix E
A Sample of Field-Level Agencies

Agencies Representing the Faculty

American Association of University Professors (AAUP: www.aaup.org)

AAUP was founded in the year 1915 as a non-profit membership association of faculty and academic professionals. The agency focuses on academic freedom, shared governance, and issues related to faculty salaries, careers, and their employment conditions. At an overall level, key issues raised by AAUP are related to de-professionalization of academic role by increasing contingent teachers in the universities, increasing vocationalization of higher education, administrators' focus on increasing enrollment and revenues, corporatization of universities, increasing consumerism of students, setting up measurements such as learner outcomes based on material factors, such as jobs, adoption of online education, and using technology for student and teacher surveillance with increasing online adoption. Specific to this research, AAUP has raised several concerns regarding the increasing adoption of online education.

1. Faculty's role in terms of course design and content creation and selection
2. Intellectual property of the content created for teaching
3. Quality of teaching and learning
4. Teacher-preparation, time, and effort, required to teach online
5. Academic freedom for the content to be used for teaching

American Educational Research Association (AERA: www.aera.net)

AERA, founded in 1916 is a national research society to promote the use of research to improve education and serve the public good. It has over 25,000 members as faculty, researchers, graduate students, and other professionals with expertise in education research. This agency has a wide focus covering K–12 as well as higher education. In the higher education areas, it focuses on the following aspects:

1. Federal funding for education research and related policies
2. Diversity and equity in higher education
3. Faculty employment conditions such as tenure
4. Academic freedom
5. Faculty evaluation
6. Research on teaching and learning, especially in K–12

It strongly supports the principles of tenure and academic freedom, and faculty evaluations based on learning outcomes instead of student-evaluation ratings (AERA 2013b). While it has a Special Interest Group (SIG)—Online Teaching and Learning, there was no further data available related to this aspect of higher education at the time this study was conducted. However, there were several articles about the ineffectiveness of online education in community colleges in its monthly newsletter that referred to the research published in its journals. This suggests that the agency doesn't promote online education.

Agencies Representing the Administration

The two agencies discussed next belong to the "group of six"[1] most important presidentially based higher education associations in the US.

American Association of Community Colleges (AACC: www.aacc.nche.edu)

AACC, founded in 1920, calls itself as the national voice for community colleges. It represents 1,200 two-year, associate degree-granting institutions and more than 13 million students, enrolling 45% of undergrad students in the country. More than one-third of public four-year college students have prior community college experience. Its focus areas are federal policy for student financial aid and community college enrollments and completion rates. In its strategic plan, one of its top goals is to help community colleges reduce the number of unprepared students by half by 2020, indicating student unpreparedness to be one if its topmost concerns. In its tenth Annual Distance Education Survey (Finkel 2015), the following was reported:

- Online education has entered the mainstream, reaching the point of maturation. The online growth represents the entire growth of community colleges during the past decade.
- Nearly all administrators say that the quality of their online courses is equivalent or superior to traditional courses.
- Almost all community colleges have faculty training and instructional design support for online education.

- Student retention in online has improved but still 8% lower than resident teaching.
- Nearly 80% of campuses require faculty members to participate in online course training.

American Council on Education (ACE: www.acenet.edu)

ACE, founded in 1918, represents 1,800 higher education organization presidents and executives of related associations. It influences federal policies related to issues such as Pell grant funding, research, and tax proposals. It uses data gathered by USDE for further analysis and policy recommendations. ACE represents the structural changes emerging in the field of higher education, especially in the context of teachers and teaching practice. Some of these changes are listed next.

- **Alternative credit recommendations:** It focuses on expanding access for adult learners and military veterans through alternative/non-traditional education providers. It offers College Credit Recommendation Service (CREDIT) for helping students gain academic credit for formal courses and examinations taken outside traditional degree programs. It has reviewed over 35,000 courses across the nation that are offered in an extra-institutional setting. In this context, it is also evaluating MOOCs as the potential alternative-education provider for credit recommendations. It makes credit recommendations for learning at the workplace through employer organizations such as Microsoft, Starbucks, Pearson, and McDonald's, as well as government agencies such as NASA and the FAA. It employs faculty members from traditional colleges and universities to review courses for credit recommendations.
- **Teachers professional development:** It launched a professional development services program for college instructors (Association of College and University Educators—ACUE) in 2014 to expand the effective teaching practices.
- **Internationalization of higher education:** It emphasizes teachers' roles in the internationalization of higher education in two ways: infusing internationalization knowledge and expertise into faculty hiring and career development, as well as incorporating international subject matter and pedagogy into the curriculum.

Agencies Representing Accreditation

US Department of Education (USDE: www.ed.gov)

USDE, a federal agency created in 1980 whose mission in the context of higher education, is to increase access, affordability, quality, and completion (USDE 2016). The department establishes policies relating to federal financial aid for students, collects data and publishes reports on most aspects of education, makes recommendations for education reform, and enforces federal statutes to ensure equal access. It also provides oversight to ensure appropriate standards are being met by the accreditation agencies as they qualify the higher education organizations to participate in Title IV program.

The central database for the data collected by USDoE-NCES is IPEDS The Integrated Postsecondary Education Data System (IPEDS). The higher education organizations participating in federal student aid programs report data on enrollments, degree completions, graduation rates, faculty and staff, finances, institutional prices, and student financial aid. All information collected through IPEDS is publicly available. The IPEDS system dates back to 1986. Most of the data collected for this research is from the Institute of Education Sciences (IES), which is the statistics, research, and evaluation arm of the USDE (www.ies.ed.gov). It encompasses four centers: the National Center for Education Research (NCER), the National Center for Education Statistics (NCES), the National Center for Education Evaluation and Regional Assistance (NCEE), and the National Center for Special Education Research (NCSER). Key themes relevant to this research that emerges from the USDoE data:

1. **Student success**: The focus is to improve student success in terms of student outcomes and completion of the degree. Graduation rates and cohort default rates are key metrics followed closely. Student engagement is the central focus area around which all other efforts are being aligned. Along with the economic and the social theories, many theories from other fields are employed to understand and explain various issues facing the contemporary higher education field, such as organizational, cultural, and psychological theories. All these theories and perspectives focus on understanding student learning and performance in a higher education setting. Three initiatives to achieve the aforementioned are—reduce cost and debt, shift focus toward student outcomes and make institutions accountable, and drive innovation.

2. **Teaching practice**: While teaching is recognized as key to student success, most of the statistical data on teachers is about factors such as their demographic, education, and employment conditions. There are some publications that explore and recommend teaching practices to make students successful, and there is significant emphasis on teachers needing to learn about how to engage students in their learning. Key recommendations are around using active and collaborative learning and improving student-teacher interaction.

3. **Online adoption**: The agency acknowledges online education's scope to make an impact in terms of cost and access, and tracks its adoption across the higher education field at the institution, teacher, and student levels. In 1997–98, some reports noted the increase in online adoption and pointed out the need to address the emerging policy

issues related to faculty employment, faculty role, accreditation, and quality of DE programs, copyright and intellectual property rights, and organizational structures and arrangements. However, no further reports addressed these issues. The reports on online education identify the institutions' key motivations as an increase in access, increase in enrollments, reform education, reduce cost, offer flexibility to students, and ease capacity constraints. The barriers are concerns about quality, student experience, faculty workload, program development costs, and technology infrastructure.

Council of Higher Education Accreditation (CHEA: www.chea.org)

CHEA, founded in 1996, is a private non-profit national organization that represents over 3,000 higher education organizations and 60 national, regional, and specialized accreditors. Its mission is articulated as to

> serve students and their families, colleges and universities, sponsoring bodies, governments, and employers by promoting academic quality through formal recognition of higher education accrediting bodies and will coordinate and work to advance self-regulation through accreditation.
>
> (Eaton 2015)

CHEA is governed by a 20-person board of higher education organization's presidents, institutional representatives, and public members, and funded through annual fees paid by its institutional members. It works in close coordination with USDE to develop accreditation standards for quality as well as to award or deny recognition status. It works through a hierarchy of 18 institutional accrediting organizations that accredit higher education organizations. Of these 18, 7 of them cover the higher education organizations offering two- to four-year degree programs:

1. Middle States Association of Colleges and Schools, Middle States Commission on Higher Education
2. New England Association of Schools and Colleges, Commission on Institutions of Higher Education
3. North Central Association of Colleges and Schools, The Higher Learning Commission
4. Northwest Commission on Colleges and Universities
5. Southern Association of Colleges and Schools, Commission on Colleges
6. Western Association of Schools and Colleges, Accrediting Commission for Senior Colleges and Universities
7. Western Association of Schools and Colleges, Accrediting Commission for Community and Junior Colleges

There are seven key areas that the accrediting organizations examine when assessing the quality of distance education: institutional mission; institutional organization structure; institutional resources, curriculum, and instruction; faculty support; student support; and student-learning outcomes. These seven areas are then further elaborated by the individual accrediting agencies.

Note

1. ACE, AACC, NASULGC, AASCU, AAU, and NAICU.

Bibliography

Archival Data Sources

AAUP. 2015a. *Policy Documents & Reports*. Vol. 11. Washington, DC: American Association of University Professors.

AAUP. 2015b. "Statement on Copyright." In *AAUP Policy Documents and Reports*, edited by AAUP, 264–266. Washington, DC: The John Hopkins University Press.

AAUP. 2015c. "Statement on Online and Distance Education." In *AAUP Policy Documents and Reports*, edited by AAUP, 254–256. Washington, DC, Baltimore, MD: The John Hopkins University Press.

AAUP. 2016. "Higher Education at a Crossroads: The Economic Value of Tenure and the Security of the Profession." *Academe* 102 (March–April):9–23.

ACE. 2016. *ACE and ACUE Announce Landmark Collaboration to Advance Student Success Through Effective College Instruction*. Washington, DC: American Council on Education.

ACE-CEAI. 2014. "The Students of the Future." In *Presidential Innovation Lab (White paper series)*, edited by Cathy A. Sandeen. American Council on Education. Washington, DC.

AERA. 2013a. *Non-Tenure-Track Faculty in U.S. Universities: AERA Statement and Background Report*. Washington, DC: The American Educational Research Association.

AERA. 2013b. *Rethinking Faculty Evaluation*. Washington, DC: AERA.

AFT. 2011. *Student Success in Higher Education*. American Federation of Teachers. https://www.aft.org/position/student-success

Aldridge, Susan C., David L. Clinefelter, and Andrew Magda. 2013. *AASCU Members at Forefront on Providing Online Education*. American Association of State Colleges and Universities (AASCU). http://www.aascu.org/WorkArea/DownloadAsset.aspx?id=7445

Allen, I. Elaine, and Jeff Seaman. 2015. *Grade Level: Tracking Online Education in the United States*, 10. Babson Park, MA: Babson Survey Research Group.

Anderson, Janna Quitney, Jan Lauren Boyles, and Lee Rainie. 2012. *The Future of Higher Education*. Washington, DC: Pew Research Center's Internet & American Life Project.

Andrews, James G. 2006. *How We Can Resist Corporatization*. Washington, DC: American Association of University Professors.

APLU. 2016. *Personalizing Learning with Adaptive Courseware.* APLU. www.aplu.org/projects-and-initiatives/personalized-learning-consortium/plc-projects/plc-adaptive-courseware/

Bailey, T., J. Bashford, A. Boatman, J. Squires, M. Weiss, William R. Doyle, J. C. Valentine, R. LaSota, J. R. Plolanin, E. Spinney, W. Wilson, and S. H. Younh. 2016. *Strategies for Postsecondary Students in Developmental Education—A Practice Guide for College and University Administrators, Advisors, and Faculty*, edited by What Works Clearinghouse. Washington, DC: U.S. Department of Education.

Bienkowski, Marie, Mingyu Feng, and Barbara Means. 2014. *Enhancing Teaching and Learning Through Educational Data Mining and Learning Analytics: An Issue Brief.* Washington, DC: US Department of Education.

Blumenstyk, Goldie. 2016. "Experiment with New Education Providers Also Tests New Ways to Measure Quality." *The Chronicle of Higher Education*, August 17.

Borden, Victor M. H. 2011. *Suggestions for Improvements to the Student-To-Faculty Ratio in IPEDS.* Washington, DC: National Postsecondary Education Cooperative.

Bossaller, Jenny S., and Jenna Kammer. 2014. "On the Pros and Cons of Being a Faculty Member at an E-text University." *AAUP Journal of Academic Freedom 5.*

Boyte, Harry C., and Nancy N. Kari. 2000. "Renewing the Democratic Spirit in American Colleges and Universities." In *Civic Responsibility and Higher Education*, edited by Thomas Ehrlich, 37–60. Westport, CT: American Council on Education and Onyx Press.

Braxton, John M. 2006. "Faculty Professional Choices in Teaching That Foster Student Success." *National Postsecondary Education Cooperative.*

Buller, Jeffrey L. 2014. "The Two Cultures of Higher Education in the Twenty-First Century and Their Impact on Academic Freedom." *AAUP Journal of Academic Freedom* 5:1–8.

Carnevale, Dan. 2000. "Faculty Union Opposes Undergraduate Degrees Earned Entirely Through Distance Learning." *The Chronicle of Higher Education*, July 21.

Carver, Leland, and Laura M. Harrison. 2013. "MOOCs and Democratic Education." *Liberal Education* 99 (4).

Champagne, John. 2011. "Teaching in the Corporate University: Assessment as a Labor Issue." *AAUP Journal of Academic Freedom* 2 (1):1–26.

CHEA. 2002. "Accreditation and Assuring Quality in Distance Learning." In *CHEA Monograph Series 2002*, edited by CHEA. Washington, DC: CHEA Institute for Research and Study of Accreditation and Quality Assurance.

CHEA, New Leadership Alliance. 2012. *Assuring Quality: An Institutional Self-Assessment Tool for Excellent Practice in Student Learning Outcomes Assessment.* Washington, DC: New Leadership Alliance for Student Learning and Accountability.

Crotty, James Marshall. 2012. *The Coming Age of The Teaching Megastar.* Forbes.

CUSU, and APLU. 2016. "Revolutionizing the Role of the University: Collaboration to Advance Innovation in Higher Education." *Coalition of Urban Serving*

Universities, Association of Public Landgrant Universities. http://www.aplu. org/library/revolutionizing-the-role-of-the-university/File

Dehaye, Paul-Olivier. 2016. *MOOC Platforms, Surveillance, and Control.* Washington, DC: American Association of University Professors.

de Vise, Daniel. 2011. "U.S. News College Rankings Are Denounced But Not Ignored." *The Washington Post,* September 3, Education.

Dougherty, Kevin J., Sosanya M. Jones, Hana Lahr, Lara Pheatt, Rebecca S. Natow, and Vikash Reddy. 2016. *Performance Funding for Higher Education.* Baltimore, MD: The John Hopkins University Press.

Eaton, Judith S. 2002. "Maintaining the Delicate Balance: Distance Learning, Higher Education Accreditation, and the Politics of Self-Regulation." In *Distributed Education: Challenges, Choices, and a New Environment.* Washington, DC: American Council on Education, EDUCAUSE.

Eaton, Judith S. 2015. *An Overview of US Accreditation.* Washington, DC: Council for Higher Education Accreditation.

Economist, The. 2014. "Higher education: Creative destruction." *The Economist,* June.

Economist, The. 2015. "Our First-ever College Rankings." *The Economist,* October 29.

Ehrenberg, Ronald, and Liang Zhang. 2004. *Do Tenured and Tenure-Track Faculty Matter?* National Bureau of Economic Research.

Elias, Adam. 2016. "It's Not Just About Teaching Online. It's About Teaching, Period." *The Chronicle of Higher Education* 62 (31):B24.

Euben, Donna R. 2000. "Faculty Rights and Responsibilities." Distance Learning 14: 2008.

Ewell, Peter T. 2001. "Accreditation and Student Learning Outcomes: A Proposed Point of Departure. CHEA Occasional Paper."

Figlio, David N., Morton O. Schapiro, and Kevin B. Soter. 2015. "Are Tenure Track Professors Better Teachers?" *The Review of Economics and Statistics* 97 (4):715–724. doi: 10.1162/REST_a_00529.

Finkel, Ed. 2015. "Online Education Enters the Mainstream." *Community College Journal* 86 (1):26.

Freeland, Richard M. 2017. "Stop Looking at Rankings. Use Academe's Own Measures Instead." *The Chronicle of Higher Education,* September 08.

GAO, U. S. 2014. *Higher Education: State Funding Trends and Policies on Affordability. Report to the Chairman, Committee on Health, Education, Labor, and Pensions, United States Senate.* Washington, DC: United States Government Accountability Office.

GatesFoundation.org. 2012. *Gates Foundation Announces $9 Million in Grants to Support Breakthrough Learning Models in Postsecondary Education | Bill & Melinda Gates Foundation.* Gates Foundation. www.gatesfoundation. org/Media-Center/Press-Releases/2012/06/Gates-Foundation-Announces-Grants-to-Support-Learning-Models

Gerber, Larry. 2010. "Professionalization as the Basis for Academic Freedom and Faculty Governance." *AAUP Journal of Academic Freedom* 1:1–26.

Grapevine. 2018. *Annual Grapevine Compilation of State Fiscal Support for Higher Education: Results for Fiscal Year 2017–2018,* edited by Jim Palmer. IL: Center for the Study of Education Policy, Illinois State University. Normal, Illinois.

Green, Kenneth C. 2013. *Mission, MOOCs, & Money: In Trusteeship Magazine.* Washington, DC: AGB.

Green, Kenneth C., and Ellen Wagner. 2011. "Online Education: Where Is It Going? What Should Boards Know." *Trusteeship* 19 (1):24–29.

Gross, Daniel A. 2015. "To Attract Students, Professors Produce Hollywood-Style Previews." *The Chronicle of Higher Education.*

Hegji, Alexander. 2016. "An Overview of Accreditation of Higher Education in the United States." *Congressional Research Service.* https://fas.org/sgp/crs/misc/R43826.pdf

Hill, Phil. 2016a. "Amazon's Quiet Dominance of Higher-Ed Learning Platforms." *The Chronicle of Higher Education.*

Hill, Phil. 2016b. "Distance Ed's Second Act." *The Chronicle of Higher Education.*

Hill, Phil. 2016c. "A 'Netflix for Education'? Why LinkedIn's New Product Should Give Us Pause." *The Chronicle of Higher Education.*

Hitt, John C., and Joel L. Hartman. 2002. *Distributed Learning: New Challenges and Opportunities for Institutional Leadership.* American Council on Education. Washington, D.C.

Hobbs, Frank, and Nicole Stoops. 2002. "Demographic Trends in the 20th Century." In *Census 2000 Special Reports.* Washington, DC: U.S. Department of Commerce.

Hollander, Elizabeth L., and Matthew Hartley. 2000. "Civic Renewal in Higher Education." In *Civic Responsibility and Higher Education*, edited by Thomas Ehrlich, 345–366. Westport, CT: American Council on Education and Onyx Press.

Hollander, Elizabeth L., and John Saltmarsh. 2000. *The Engaged University.* Washington, DC: American Association of University Professors.

Humes, Karen R., Nicholas A. Jones, and Roberto R. Ramirez. 2011. "Overview of Race and Hispanic Origin: 2010." In *2010 Census Briefs.* Washington, DC.: U.S. Department of Commerce, Economics and Statistics Administration.

IES-NCES. 1991. "Digest of Education Statistics." In *Digest of Education Statistics*, edited by IES-NCES. Washington, DC: National Center for Education Statistics, Institute of Education Sciences, U.S. Department of Education.

IES-NCES. 1998. *Distance Education in Higher Education Institutions: Incidence, Audiences, and Plans to Expand*, edited by IES-NCES. Washington, DC: National Center for Education Statistics, Institute of Education Sciences, U.S. Department of Education.

IES-NCES. 2014. "Table 311.22. Number and Percentage of Undergraduate Students Taking Distance Education or Online Classes and Degree Programs, by Selected Characteristics: Selected Years, 2003–04 Through 2011–12." In *Digest of Education Statistics*, edited by IES-NCES. Washington, DC: National Center for Education Statistics, Institute of Education Sciences, U.S. Department of Education.

IES-NCES. 2016a. "Table 306.10: Total Fall Enrollment in Degree-Granting Postsecondary Institutions, by Control and Classification of Institution, Level of Enrollment, and Race/Ethnicity of Student: 2015." In *Digest of Education Statistics*, edited by IES-NCES. Washington, DC: National Center for Education Statistics, Institute of Education Sciences, U.S. Department of Education.

IES-NCES. 2016b. "Table 315.10. Number of Faculty in Degree-Granting Post-secondary Institutions, by Employment Status, Sex, Control, and Level of Institution: Selected Years, Fall 1970 Through Fall 2015." In *Digest of Education Statistics*, edited by IES-NCES. Washington, DC: National Center for Education Statistics, Institute of Education Sciences, U.S. Department of Education.

IES-NCES. 2016c. "Table 317.10. Degree-granting Postsecondary Institutions, by Control and Level of Institution: Selected Years, 1949–50 Through 2015–16." In *Digest of Education Statistics*, edited by IES-NCES. Washington, DC: National Center for Education Statistics, Institute of Education Sciences, U.S. Department of Education.

IES-NCES. 2016d. "Table 326.10. Graduation Rate from First Institution Attended for First-Time, Full-Time Bachelor's Degree-Seeking Students at 4-Year Postsecondary Institutions, by Race/Ethnicity, Time to Completion, Sex, Control of Institution, and Acceptance Rate: Selected Cohort Entry Years, 1996 Through 2009." In *Digest of Education Statistics*, edited by IES-NCES. Washington, DC: National Center for Education Statistics, Institute of Education Sciences, U.S. Department of Education.

IES-NCES. 2016e. "Table 326.30. Retention of First-Time Degree-Seeking Undergraduates at Degree-Granting Postsecondary Institutions, by Attendance Status, Level and Control of Institution, and Percentage of Applications Accepted: Selected Years, 2006 to 2015." In *Digest of Education Statistics*, edited by IES-NCES. Washington, DC: National Center for Education Statistics, Institute of Education Sciences, U.S. Department of Education.

IES-NCES. 2017a. "Change in Number and Types of Postsecondary Institutions: 2000 to 2014." In *Data Point*, edited by IES-NCES. Washington, DC.: IES-NCES.

IES-NCES. 2017b. *Projections of Education Statistics to 2025*, edited by IES-NCES. Washington, DC.: IES-NCES.

IES-NCES. 2017c. "Table 303.10. Total Fall Enrollment in Degree-Granting Postsecondary Institutions, by Attendance Status, Sex of Student, and Control of Institution: Selected Years, 1947 Through 2026." In *Digest of Education Statistics*, edited by IES-NCES. Washington, DC: National Center for Education Statistics, Institute of Education Sciences, U.S. Department of Education.

IES-NCES. 2017d. "Table 316.81. Percentage of Full-Time Faculty (instruction, research, and public service) with Tenure at Degree-Granting Postsecondary Institutions with a Tenure System, by Control, Level, and State: 2015–16." In *Digest of Education Statistics*, edited by IES-NCES. Washington, DC: National Center for Education Statistics, Institute of Education Sciences, U.S. Department of Education.

IES-NCES. 2017e. "Table 322.10. Bachelor's Degrees Conferred by Postsecondary Institutions, by Field of Study: Selected Years, 1970–71 Through 2015–16." In *Digest of Education Statistics*, edited by IES-NCES. Washington, DC: National Center for Education Statistics, Institute of Education Sciences, U.S. Department of Education.

Immerwahr, John, Jean Johnson, and Paul Gasbarra. 2008. "The Iron Triangle: College Presidents Talk about Costs, Access, and Quality. National Center Report# 08–2." *National Center for Public Policy and Higher Education and Public Agenda*. https://files.eric.ed.gov/fulltext/ED503203.pdf

Jaschik, Scott. 2015. "Online Penalty." *Inside Higher Ed*, April 20.

Kellogg Commission. 1998. "Returning to Our Roots: Student Access." *National Association of State Universities and Land-Grant Colleges.* http://www.aplu. org/library/returning-to-our-roots-student-access-1998/file

Kellogg Commission. 1999. "Returning to Our Roots: A Learning Society." *National Association of State Universities and Land-Grant Colleges.* http:// www.aplu.org/library/returning-to-our-roots-a-learning-society/file

Kellogg Commission. 2000. "Returning to Our Roots: Toward a Coherent Campus Culture." *National Association of State Universities and Land-Grant Colleges.* http://www.aplu.org/library/returning-to-our-roots-toward-a-coherent-campus-culture/file

Kena, G, William Hussar, Joel McFarland, Cristobal de Brey, Lauren Musu-Gillette, Xiaolei Wang, Jijun Zhang, Amy Rathbun, Sidney Wilkinson-Flicker, and Melissa Diliberti. 2016. "The Condition of Education 2016. NCES 2016–144." *National Center for Education Statistics.*

Kuh, George D., Jillian Kinzie, J. Buckley, Brian K. Bridges, and John C. Hayek. 2006. "What Matters to Student Success: A Review of the Literature, Commissioned Report for the National Symposium of Postsecondary Student Success: Spearheading a Dialog on Student Success." National Postsecondary Education Commission []. https://nces.ed.gov/npec/pdf/Kuh_Team_Report.pdf

Lambert, Lance. 2015. "Performance-Based Funding Can Be Fickle, One University's Close Call Shows." *The Chronicle of Higher Education.*

Lane, Jason, and Kevin Kinser. 2012. "MOOCs and the McDonaldization of Global Higher Education." *The Chronicle of Higher Education* 30536: 1.

Lee, John Michael Jr., and Samaad Wes Keys. 2013. "High Tech, High Touch: Campus-Based Strategies for Student Success." *Association of Public Land-grant Universities.* http://www.aplu.org/library/high-tech-high-touch-campus-based-strategies-for-student-success/file

Lerman, Steven R., and Shigeru Miyagawa. 2002. "Open Course Ware and the Mission of MIT" In *Academe.* American Association of University Professors. http://www.jstor.org/stable/40252217

Levesque, Karen, Jennifer Laird, Elisabeth Hensley, Susan P. Choy, Emily Forrest Cataldi, and Lisa Hudson. 2008. *Career and Technical Education in the United States: 1990 to 2005.* Washington, DC: National Center for Education Statistics, Institute of Education Sciences, U.S. Department of Education.

Levine, Arthur, and Jeffrey C. Sun. 2002. "Barriers to Distance Education." *American Council on Education.* https://www.acenet.edu/news-room/Documents/Barriers-to-Distance-Education-2003.pdf

Lewis, Laurie, Kyle Snow, Elizabeth Farris, and Douglas Levin. 2000. "Distance Education at Postsecondary Education Institutions: 1997–98." *National Center for Education Statistics* 13.

Mackay, RF. 2013. "Learning Analytics at Stanford Takes Huge Leap Forward with MOOCs." *Stanford Report.*

Mangan, Katherine. 2016. "The Personal Lecture: How to Make Big Classes Feel Small." *The Chronicle of Higher Education*, December 4.

McFarland, Joel, William Hussar, Cristobal de Brey, Tom Snyder, Xiaolei Wang, Jijun Zhang, Amy Rathbun, Sidney Wilkinson-Flicker, Semhar Gebrekristos, Amy Barmer, Farrah Bullock Mann, Serena Hinz, Thomas Nachazel, Wyatt Smith, and Mark Ossolinski. 2017. "The Condition of Education 2017, NCES 2017–144." *National Center for Education Statistics.*

McKenna, Barbara. 2013. "Rutgers Faculty Say No to Pearson eCollege." *News.*

Mortenson, Thomas G. 2012. "State Funding: A Race to the Bottom." *The Presidency* 15 (1):26–29.

NCSES. 2014. *STEM Education Data and Trends 2014: What Percentage of Postsecondary Institutions Offer Distance Education?* National Science Foundation. www.nsf.gov/nsb/sei/edTool/data/college-03.html

NCSL. 2015. "Performance-based Funding for Higher Education." NCSL. www.ncsl.org/research/education/performance-funding.aspx

Newstok, Scott L. 2013. "A Plea for 'close learning.'" In *Liberal Education.* Washington, DC: AACU.

Oblinger, Diana, Carole A. Barone, and Brian L. Hawkins. 2001. *Distributed Education and Its Challenges: An Overview.* Washington, DC: American Council on Education.

Oremus, Will. 2012. "The New Public Ivies: Will Online Education Startups like Coursera End the Era of Expensive Higher Education?" *Slate,* July 17, http://www.slate.com/articles/technology/future_tense/2012/07/coursera_udacity_edx_will_free_online_ ivy_league_courses_end_the_era_of_expensive_ higher_ ed_.html.

Pappano, Laura. 2013. "The Value in a Free Degree: Where Are the Graduates of University of the People?" *The New York Times.* www.nytimes.com/2013/11/03/education/edlife/where-are-the-graduates-of-university-of-the-people.html?pagewanted=all

Payne, Mario D. 1993. *Distance Learning and Adults with Disabilities.* Washington, DC: American Council on Education.

Rees, Jonathan. 2014. "More Than MOOCs: What Are the Risks for Academic Freedom?" *Academe* 100 (3):13.

Rubiales, David, Melvin T. Steely, Craig E. Wollner, James T. Richardson, and Mark F. Smith. 1998. "Distance Learning." *Academe* 84 (3):30–38. doi: 10.2307/40251264.

Saba, Farhad. 2011. "Distance Education in the United States: Past, Present, Future." *Educational Technology* 51 (6):11.

Sax, Linda J. 2000. "Citizenship Development and the American College Student." In *Civic Responsibility and Higher Education,* edited by Thomas Ehrlich, 3–18. Westport, CT: American Council on Education and The Onyx Press.

Selingo, Jeffrey J. 2016. *2026, the Decade Ahead: The Seismic Shifts Transforming the Future of Higher Education.* Washington, DC: The Chronicle of Higher Education.

Shallard, Shari. 2016. "The Data-Driven Campus—Using Learning Analytics to Optimize Teaching, Learning, and Student Persistence." *AcroBatiq.* https://sf-asset-manager.s3.amazonaws.com/96945/2/90.pdf

SHEEO. 2018. "SHEF: FY 2017" State Higher Education Executive Officers Association. http://www.sheeo.org/projects/shef-%E2%80%94-state-higher-education-finance

Siemens, George. 2012. "Learning Analytics: Envisioning a Research Discipline and a Domain of Practice." Proceedings of the 2nd International Conference on Learning Analytics and Knowledge, Vancouver, British Columbia, Canada.

Sparks, Dinah, and Nat Malkus. 2013. "First-Year Undergraduate Remedial Coursetaking: 1999–2000, 2003–04, 2007–08. Statistics in Brief. NCES 2013–013." In *National Center for Education Statistics.* Washington, DC: U.S. Department of Education.

Spellings, Margaret. 2006. *A Test of Leadership: Charting the Future of US Higher Education*. US Department of Education. Washington, DC.

Stein, Michael, Christopher Scribner, and David Brown. 2013. "Market Forces in the College Classroom: Losing Sovereignty." *Journal of Academic Freedom* 4 (9):10.

Supiano, Beckie. 2016. "When States Tie Money to Colleges' Performance, Low-Income Students May Suffer." *The Chronicle of Higher Education*.

Syed, Mahbubur Rahman. 2009. Technologies Shaping Instruction and Distance Education: New Studies and Utilizations. IGI Global.

Trower, Cathy. 2012. "Academic Tenure and the Traditional Assumptions Boards Should Question." *Trusteeship Magazine*, December.

USDE. 2006. *Changes made by the Higher Education Reconciliation Act of 2005 (HERA) to Student and Institutional Eligibility, and Student Assistance General Provisions, under the Federal Student Aid Programs*. Washington, DC: U.S. Department of Education.

USDE. 2016. *US Department of Education FY2016 Agency Financial Report*. Washington, DC: U.S. Department of Education.

Vedder, Richard. 2016. "Saylor Academy Sidesteps the Evil Duo." *Forbes—Education*, January 13.

Washburn, Jennifer. 2011. "Academic Freedom and the Corporate University." *Academe* 97 (1):8.

Wexler, Ellen. 2016. "State Support on the Rise." *Inside HigherEd*. www.insidehighered.com/news/2016/01/25/state-support-higher-education-rises-41-percent-2016

References

Ackroyd, Stephen, and Jan C. Karlsson. 2014. "Critical Realism, Research techniques, and Research Design." In *Studying Organizations Using Critical Realism: A Practical Guide*, edited by Paul Edwards and Joe O'Mahoney. Oxford, UK: Oxford University Press.

Adorno, Theodor W., and Anson G. Rabinbach. 1975. "Culture Industry Reconsidered." *New German Critique*:12–19.

Ally, Mohamed. 2004. "Foundations of Educational Theory for Online Learning." *Theory and Practice of Online Learning* 2:15–44.

Altbach, Philip G. 1999. "Private Higher Education: Themes and Variations in Comparative Perspective." *Prospects* 29 (3):310–323. doi: 10.1007/BF02736957.

Altbach, Philip G. 2011. "Patterns of Higher Education Development." In *American Higher Education in the Twenty-First Century*, edited by Philip G. Altbach, Patricia J. Gumport and Robert O. Berdahl. Baltimore, MD: The Johns Hopkins University Press.

Altbach, Philip G., Patricia J. Gumport, and Robert O. Berdahl. 2011. *American Higher Education in the Twenty-First Century: Social, Political, and Economic Challenges*. Baltimore, MD: The Johns Hopkins University Press.

Altheide, David L., and Robert P. Snow. 1979. *Media Logic*. Beverly Hills, CA: Sage Publications, Inc.

Alvesson, Mats, and Kaj Sköldberg. 2009. *Reflexive Methodology: New Vistas for Qualitative Research*. London, Los Angeles, CA: Sage Publications, Inc.

Amundsen, Cheryl. 1993. "The Evolution of Theory in Distance Education." In *Theoretical Principles of Distance Education*, edited by Desmond Keegan, 61–79. London and New York: Routledge.

Anderson, Terry. 2003. "Modes of Interaction in Distance Education: Recent Developments and Research Questions." In *Handbook of Distance Education*, edited by Michael G. Moore and William G. Anderson. Vol. 1, 129–144. Mahwah, NJ: Lawrence Erlbaum Associates.

Anderson, Terry. 2008. "Towards a Theory of Online Learning" In *The Theory and Practice of Online Learning*, edited by Terry Anderson, 45–74. Edbonton, AB: Athabasca University Press.

Anderson, Terry D., and D. R. Garrison. 1995. "Critical Thinking in Distance Education: Developing Critical Communities in an Audio Teleconference Context." *Higher Education* 29 (2):183–199. doi: 10.1007/BF01383838.

Anson, Seers. 2007. "Management Education in the Emerging Knowledge Economy: Going Beyond 'Those Who Can, Do: Those Who Can't, Teach.'" *Academy of Management Learning & Education* 6 (4):558–567. doi: 10.2307/40214484.

Archibald, Robert B., and David H. Feldman. 2011. *Why Does College Cost So Much?* New York: Oxford University Press.

Augoustinos, Martha, Iain Walker, and Ngaire Donaghue. 2014. *Social Cognition: An Integrated Introduction*. Los Angeles, London, New Delhi, Singapore, Washington DC: Sage Publications, Inc.

Auslander, Philip. 2008. *Liveness: Performance in a Mediatized Culture*. Abingdon, Oxon: Routledge.

Ayim, Maryann. 1974. "Retroduction: The Rational Instinct." *Transactions of the Charles S. Peirce Society* 10 (1):34–43. doi: 10.2307/40319699.

Baumol, William J., and William G. Bowen. 1967. *Performing Arts, the Economic Dilemma: A Study of Problems Common to Theater, Opera, Music, and Dance*. New York: Twentieth Century Fund.

Beldarrain, Yoany. 2006. "Distance Education Trends: Integrating New Technologies to Foster Student Interaction and Collaboration." *Distance Education* 27 (2):139–153.

Benjamin, Walter. 2006. "The Work of Art in the Age of Mechanical Reproduction." In *Media and Cultural Studies: Keyworks*, edited by Meenakshi Gigi Durham and Douglas M. Kellner, 18–40. MA, USA; Oxford, UK; Victoria, Australia: Blackwell Publishing.

Bhaskar, Roy. 2013. *A Realist Theory of Science*. Routledge. London and New York.

Bhaskar, Roy. 2014. "Foreword." In *Studying Organizations Using Critical Realism*, edited by Paul Edwards, Joe O'Mahoney and Steve Vincent. Oxford, UK: Oxford University Press.

Blaikie, Norman. 2003a. *Abduction: The SAGE Encyclopedia of Social Science Research Methods*. Thousand Oaks, CA: Sage Publications, Inc.

Blaikie, Norman. 2003b. *Retroduction: The SAGE Encyclopedia of Social Science Research Methods*. Thousand Oaks, CA: Sage Publications, Inc.

Blaikie, Norman. 2007. *Approaches to Social Enquiry*. England, UK. Polity Press.

Blumler, Jay G., and Dennis Kavanagh. 1999. "The Third Age of Political Communication: Influence and Features." *Political Communication* 16 (3):209.

Boldt, Arnold. 1998. "The Transmission Perspective: Effective Delivery of Content." *Five Perspectives on Teaching in Adult and Higher Education*:57–82.

Bowen, Glenn A. 2009. "Document Analysis as a Research Method." *Qualitative Research Journal* (2):27–40.

Bowen, Howard Rothmann. 1980. *The Costs of Higher Education: How Much Do Colleges and Universities Spend per Student and How Much Should They Spend?* Vol. 1. San Francisco: Jossey-Bass Publishers.

Bramwell, Gillian, Rosemary C. Reilly, Frank R. Lilly, Neomi Kronish, and Revathi Chennabathni. 2011. "Creative Teachers." *Roeper Review* 33 (4):228–238.

Brandtzæg, Petter Bae. 2010. "Towards a Unified Media-User Typology (MUT): A Meta-Analysis and Review of the Research Literature on Media-User Typologies." *Computers in Human Behavior* 26 (5):940–956. doi: http://dx.doi.org/10.1016/j.chb.2010.02.008.

Braun, Hans-Joachim. 2000. "Introduction: Technology and the Production and Reproduction of Music in the 20th Century." In *Music and Technology in the Twentieth Century*, edited by Hans-Joachim Braun. Baltimore, MD: The John Hopkins University Press.

Chanan, Michael. 1995. *Repeated Takes: A Short History of Recording and Its Effects on Music*. London and New York: Verso.

Christensen, Clayton M., and Henry J. Eyring. 2011. *The Innovative University: Changing the DNA of Higher Education from the Inside Out*. San Francisco, CA: Jossey-Bass.

Clark, Burton R. 1987. *The Academic Profession: National, Disciplinary, and Institutional Settings*. Berkeley: University of California Press.

Clark, Burton R., and Martin Trow. 1966. "The Organizational Context." In *College Peer Groups: Problems and Prospects for Research*, edited by Theodore M. Newcomb and Everett K. Wilson, 17–70. Chicago: Aldine Publishing Company.

Clark, Richard E. 1983. "Reconsidering Research on Learning from Media." *Review of Educational Research* 53 (4):445–459. doi: 10.2307/1170217.

Couldry, Nick. 2004. "Theorising Media as Practice." *Social Semiotics* 14 (2):115–132. doi: 10.1080/1035033042000238295.

Couldry, Nick. 2008. "Mediatization or Mediation? Alternative Understandings of the Emergent Space of Digital Storytelling." *New Media & Society* 10 (3):373–391. doi: 10.1177/1461444808089414.

Curtin, Michael. 2009. "Thinking Globally: From Media Imperialism to Media Capital." *Media Industries: History, Theory, and Method*, edited by Jennifer Holt and Alisa Perren: 108–119. West Sussex, UK: Wiley-Blackwell Publishing.

DiMaggio, Paul J. 1991. "Constructing an Organizational Field as a Professional Project: U.S. Art Museums, 1920–1940." In *The New Institutionalism in Organizational Analysis*, edited by Paul J. DiMaggio and Walter W. Powell. Chicago, IL: University of Chicago Press.

DiMaggio, Paul J., and Walter W. Powell. 1991. "Introduction." In *The New Institutionalism in Organizational Analysis*, edited by Paul J. DiMaggio and Walter W. Powell. Chicago, IL, London: University of Chicago Press.

Diwanji, P., B. P. Simon, M. Märki, S. Korkut, and R. Dornberger. 2014. "Success Factors of Online Learning Videos." 2014 International Conference on

Interactive Mobile Communication Technologies and Learning (IMCL2014), Thessaloniki, Greece. 13–14 Nov. 2014.

Doty, D. Harold, and William H. Glick. 1994. "Typologies as a Unique Form of Theory Building: Toward Improved Understanding and Modeling." *The Academy of Management Review* 19 (2):230–251. doi: 10.2307/258704.

Driessens, Olivier, Karin Raeymaeckers, Hans Verstraeten, and Sarah Vandenbussche. 2010. "Personalization According to Politicians: A Practice Theoretical Analysis of Mediatization." *Communications: The European Journal of Communication Research* 35 (3):309–326. doi: 10.1515/COMM.2010.017.

Dunn, Mary B., and Candace Jones. 2010. "Institutional Logics and Institutional Pluralism: The Contestation of Care and Science Logics in Medical Education, 1967–2005." *Administrative Science Quarterly* 55 (1):114–149. doi: 10.2307/27856090.

Durham, Meenakshi Gigi, and Douglas M. Kellner. 2009. *Media and Cultural Studies: Keyworks.* Vol. 2. Victoria, Australia: John Wiley & Sons.

Egenfeldt-Nielsen, Simon. 2011. "What Makes a Good Learning Game? Going Beyond Edutainment." *Elearn* (2):2. doi: 10.1145/1943208.1943210.

Ehrlich, Thomas. 2003. "The Credit Hour as a Potential Barrier to Innovation: Lessons from Innovative Institutions." *New Directions for Higher Education* (122):31–43. doi: 10.1002/he.108.

Eisenhardt, Kathleen M. 1989. "Building Theories from Case Study Research." *The Academy of Management Review* 14 (4):532–550.

Feldman, Martha S., and Wanda J. Orlikowski. 2011. "Theorizing Practice and Practicing Theory." *Organization Science* 22 (5):1240–1253. doi: 10.1287/orsc.1100.0612.

Ferguson, Rebecca. 2012. "Learning Analytics: Drivers, Developments and Challenges." *International Journal of Technology Enhanced Learning* 4 (5–6):304–317.

Fiske, Susan T., and Shelley E. Taylor. 2013. *Social Cognition: From Brains to Culture.* Vol. 2. London: Sage Publications, Inc.

Fitzgerald, Hiram E., Karen Bruns, Steven T. Sonka, Andrew Furco, and Louis Swanson. 2012. "The Centrality of Engagement in Higher Education." *Journal of Higher Education Outreach and Engagement* 16 (3).

Frank, Robert H. 2004. *Are Arms Races in Higher Education a Problem. Publications from the Forum for the Future of Higher Education.* Cambridge: Forum for the Future of Higher Education.

Freidson, Eliot. 1989. "Theory and the Professions." *Indiana Law Journal* 64 (3):423.

Friedland, Roger, and Robert R. Alford. 1991. "Bringing Society Back in: Symbols, Practices and Institutional Contradictions." In *In the New Institutionalism in Organizational Analysis,* edited by Walter W. Powell and Paul J. DiMaggio, 232–263. Chicago, IL: University of Chicago Press.

Friesen, Norm, and Theo Hug. 2009. "The Mediatic Turn: Exploring Concepts for Media Pedagogy." *Mediatization: Concept, Changes, Consequences,* 63–83. Frankfurt a. M.: Lang.

Fuchs, Christian. 2011. *Foundations of Critical Media and Information Studies.* Abingdon, Oxon: Taylor & Francis.

Galloway, Scott. 2017. *The Four: The Hidden DNA of Amazon, Apple, Facebook, and Google.* New York: Portfolio, Penguin.

Garrison, D. Randy. 1993. "Quality and Access in Distance Education: Theoretical Considerations." In *Theoretical Principles of Distance Education*, edited by Desmond Keegan, 9–21. London, New York: Routledge.

Garrison, D. Randy, and Terry Anderson. 2003. *E-learning in the 21st Century: A Framework for Research and Practice*. New York, London: RoutledgeFalmer.

Garrison, D. Randy, Terry Anderson, and Walter Archer. 2003. "A Theory of Critical Inquiry in Online Distance Education." In *Handbook of Distance Education*, edited by Michael G. Moore and William G. Anderson. Vol. 1, 113–127. Mahwah, NJ: Lawrence Erlbaum Associates.

Gehrke, Sean, and Adrianna Kezar. 2015. "Unbundling the Faculty Role in Higher Education: Utilizing Historical, Theoretical, and Empirical Frameworks to Inform Future Research." In *Higher Education: Handbook of Theory and Research: Volume 30*, edited by B. Michael Paulsen, 93–150. Cham: Springer International Publishing.

Geiger, R. L. 2011. "The Ten Generations of American Higher Education." In *American Higher Education in the Twenty-First Century*, edited by Philip G. Altbach, Patricia J. Gumport and Robert O. Berdahl, 37–68. Baltimore, MA: The Johns Hopkins University Press.

Gibson, Chris, and Natascha Klocker. 2004. "Academic Publishing as 'Creative' Industry, and Recent Discourses of 'Creative Economies': Some Critical Reflections." *Area* 36 (4):423–434. doi: 10.2307/20004416.

Gleick, James. 2011. *The Information*. New York: Pantheon Books.

Gonzales, Leslie D., and David F. Ayers. 2018. "The Convergence of Institutional Logics on the Community College Sector and the Normalization of Emotional Labor: A New Theoretical Approach for Considering the Community College Faculty Labor Expectations." *The Review of Higher Education* 41 (3):455–478.

Gould, Samuel B. 1973. *Diversity by Design*. Vol. 1. San Francisco: Jossey-Bass Publishers.

Gumport, Patricia J. 2000. "Academic Restructuring: Organizational Change and Institutional Imperatives." *Higher Education* 39 (1):67–91. doi: 10.1023/A:1003859026301.

Guri-Rozenblit, Sarah. 1990. "The Potential Contribution of Distance Teaching Universities to Improving the Learning/Teaching Practices in Conventional Universities." *Higher Education* 19 (1):73–80. doi: 10.1007/BF00142024.

Hanna, Donald E. 2003. "Organizational Models in Higher Education, Past and Future." In *The Handbook of Distance Education*, edited by Michael G. Moore and William G. Anderson. Vol. 1, 67–78. Mahwah, NJ: Lawrence Erlbaum Associates.

Harcleroad, Fred F., and Judith S. Eaton. 2005. "The Hidden Hand: External Constituencies and Their Impact." In *American Higher Education in the Twentieth Century: Social, Political, and Economic Challenges*, edited by Philip G. Altbach, Patricia J. Gumport and Robert O. Berdahl, 253–283. Baltimore, MA: The Johns Hopkins University Press.

Hartley, John. 2009. "From the Consciousness Industry to the Creative Industries: Consumer-Created Content, Social Network Markets, & the Growth of Knowledge." In *Media Industries: History, Theory & Method*, edited by Jennifer Holt and Alisa Perren. 231–244. West Sussex, UK: John Wiley & Sons.

Hendrickson, Robert M., Jason E. Lane, James T. Harris, and Richard H. Dorman. 2013. *Academic Leadership and Governance of Higher Education: A Guide for Trustees, Leaders, and Aspiring Leaders of Two-and Four-Year Institutions*. Sterling, VA: Stylus.

Hesmondhalgh, David. 2007. *The Cultural Industries*. Los Angeles, CA: Sage Publications, Inc.

Hibbert, Melanie C. 2014. "What Makes an Online Instructional Video Compelling?" *Educause Review Online*.

Highet, Gilbert. 1954. *The Art of Teaching*. Vol. K-1. New York: Vintage Books.

Hjarvard, Stig. 2008. "The Mediatization of Religion: A Theory of the Media as Agents of Religious Change." *Northern Lights: Film & Media Studies Yearbook* 6 (1):9–26.

Hjarvard, Stig. 2013. *The Mediatization of Culture and Society*. Hoboken: Taylor & Francis. http://pensu.eblib.com/patron/FullRecord.aspx?p=1154284

Hofkirchner, Wolfgang. 2010. "A Taxonomy of Theories about ICTs and Society." *tripleC: Communication, Capitalism & Critique. Open Access Journal for a Global Sustainable Information Society* 8 (2):171–176.

Holmberg, Borje. 2003. "A Theory of Distance Education Based on Empathy." In *Handbook of Distance Education*, edited by Michael G. Moore and William G. Anderson. Vol. 1, 79–86. Mahwah, NJ: Lawrence Erlbaum Associates.

Holmberg, Borje. 2005. *Theory and Practice of Distance Education*. New York, London: Routledge.

Holt, Jennifer, and Alisa Perren. 2011. *Media Industries: History, Theory, and Method*. West Sussex, UK: Wiley-Blackwell Publishing.

Horne, Herman Harrell. 1917. *The Teacher as Artist: An Essay in Education as an Aesthetic Process*. New York, Boston: Houghton Mifflin company.

Horng, Jeou-Shyan, Jon-Chao Hong, Lih-Juan ChanLin, Shih-Hui Chang, and Hui-Chuan Chu. 2005. "Creative Teachers and Creative Teaching Strategies." *International Journal of Consumer Studies* 29 (4):352–358. doi: 10.1111/j.1470-6431.2005.00445.x.

James, William. 1899. *Talks to Teachers on Psychology: And to Students on Some of Life's Ideals*. Mineola, New York: Dover Publications, Inc.

Jarvis, Peter. 1993. "The Education of Adults and Distance Education in Late Modernity." In *Theoretical Principles of Distance Education*, edited by Desmond Keegan, 165–174. London, New York: Routledge.

Johnson, Janice, and Daniel D. Pratt. 1998. "The Apprenticeship Perspective: Modelling Ways of Being." In *Five Perspectives on Teaching in Adult and Higher Education*, 83–103. Malabar, FL: Krieger Publishing Company.

Kamens, David H. 1977. "Legitimating Myths and Educational Organization: The Relationship Between Organizational Ideology and Formal Structure." *American Sociological Review* 42 (2):208–219. doi: 10.2307/2094601.

Kanuka, Heather, Kam Jugdev, Robert Heller, and Dan West. 2008. "The Rise of the Teleworker: False Promises and Responsive Solutions." *Higher Education* 56 (2):149–165. doi: 10.1007/s10734-007-9095-z.

Katz, Mark. 2010. *Capturing Sound: How Technology Has Changed Music*. Berkley and Los Angeles, CA: University of California Press.

Kessler, Ian, and Stephen Bach. 2014. "Comparing Cases." In *Studying Organizations Using Critical Realism: A Practical Guide*, edited by Paul Edwards and Joe O'Mahoney. Oxford, UK: Oxford University Press.

Kezar, Adrianna, and Elizabeth Holcombe. 2015. "The Professoriate Reconsidered." *Academe* 101 (6):13.

Kibby, Marjorie D. 2000. "Home on the Page: A Virtual Place of Music Community." *Popular Music* 19 (1):91–100.

King, Alison. 1993. "From Sage on the Stage to Guide on the Side." *College Teaching* 41 (1):30–35.

Klein, Heinz K., and Michael D. Myers. 1999. "A Set of Principles for Conducting and Evaluating Interpretive Field Studies in Information Systems." *MIS Quarterly* 23 (1):67–93.

Knopf, Robert. 2005. *Theater and Film: A comparative anthology*. New Haven, CT: Yale University Press.

Kolb, David A. 1984. *Experiential Learning: Experience as the Source of Learning and Development*. Vol. 1. Englewood Cliffs, NJ: Prentice-Hall.

Kracauer, Siegfried. 2005. "Remarks on the Actor." In *Theater and Film: A Comparative Anthology*, edited by Robert Knopf. New York: Yale University Press.

Krotz, Friedrich, and Andreas Hepp. 2012. "A Concretization of Mediatization: How 'Mediatization Works' and Why Mediatized Worlds Are a Helpful Concept for Empirical Mediatization Research." *Empedocles: European Journal for the Philosophy of Communication* 3 (2):137–152. doi: 10.1386/ejpc.3.2.137_1.

Lash, Scott, and Celia Lury. 2007. "Global Culture Industry: The Mediation of Things." *Historian*:403.

Lasswell, Harold D. 1948. "The Structure and Function of Communication in Society." *The Communication of Ideas*:37.

Layder, Derek. 1993. *New Strategies in Social Research: An Introduction and Guide*. Cambridge: Polity Press.

Lee, Alison, and Roger Dunston. 2011. "Practice, Learning and Change: Towards a Re-theorisation of Professional Education." *Teaching in Higher Education* 16 (5):483–494. doi: 10.1080/13562517.2011.580840.

Lee, Allen S., and Richard L. Baskerville. 2003. "Generalizing Generalizability in Information Systems Research." *Information Systems Research* 14 (3):221–243.

Lengnick-Hall, Cynthia A., and Martha M. Sanders. 1997. "Designing Effective Learning Systems for Management Education: Student Roles, Requisite Variety, and Practicing What We Teach." *Academy of Management Journal* 40 (6):1334–1368.

Lenzner, Robert, and Stephen S. Johnson. 1997. "Seeing Things as They Really Are." *Forbes* 159 (5):122–128.

Levine, Arthur. 1997. "How the Academic Profession is Changing." *The American Academic Profession* 126 (4):1–20.

Lincoln, Yvonna S., and Egon G. Guba. 1985. *Naturalistic Inquiry*. Beverly Hills, CA: Sage Publications, Inc.

Lipinski, Tomas A. 2003. "Legal Issues in the Development and Use of Copyrighted Material in Web-based Distance Education." In *Handbook of Distance Education*, edited by Michael G. Moore and William G. Anderson, 481–505. Mahwah, NJ: Lawrence Erlbaum Associates.

Ljoså, Erling. 1993. "Understanding Distance Education." In *Theoretical Principles of Distance Education*, edited by Desmond Keegan. London, New York: Routledge.

Lloyd, Steven A., Michelle M. Byrne, and Tami S. McCoy. 2012. "Faculty-Perceived Barriers of Online Education." *Journal of Online Learning and Teaching* 8 (1):1.

Lounsbury, Michael, and Seth Pollack. 2001. "Institutionalizing Civic Engagement: Shifting Logics and the Cultural Repackaging of Service-Learning in US Higher Education." *Organization* 8 (2):319–339. doi: 10.1177/1350508401082016.

Lull, James. 2000. *Media, Communication, Culture: A Global Approach.* New York: Columbia University Press.

Lundby, Knut. 2009. "Introduction: 'Mediatization' as Key." Mediatization: Concept, Changes, Consequences:1–18.

Maanen, John Van. 1979. "The Fact of Fiction in Organizational Ethnography." *Administrative Science Quarterly* 24 (4):539–550. doi: 10.2307/2392360.

Macfarlane, Bruce. 2011. "The Morphing of Academic Practice: Unbundling and the Rise of the Para-academic." *Higher Education Quarterly* 65 (1):59–73. doi: 10.1111/j.1468-2273.2010.00467.x.

Marshall, Philip D. 2009. "New Media as Transformed Media Industry." In *Media Industries: History, Theory, and Method*, edited by Jennifer Holt and Alisa Perren, 81–90. West Sussex, UK: Wiley-Blackwell Publishing.

Martin, Robert E. 2011. *The College Cost Disease: Higher Cost and Lower Quality.* Northampton, MA, Cheltenham, UK: Edward Elgar.

Mason, Jennifer. 2002. *Qualitative Researching.* Los Angeles: Sage Publications, Inc.

Mazzoleni, Gianpietro, and Winfried Schulz. 1999. ""Mediatization" of Politics: A Challenge for Democracy?" *Political Communication* 16 (3):247–261. doi: 10.1080/105846099198613.

Metzger, Walter P. 1987. "The Academic Profession in the United States." *The Academic Profession: National, Disciplinary, and Institutional Settings*:123–208.

Meyer, John W., and Brian Rowan. 1977. "Institutionalized Organizations: Formal Structure as Myth and Ceremony." *American Journal of Sociology* 83 (2):340–363.

Meyer, Katrina A. 2002. *Quality in Distance Education: Focus on On-Line Learning. ASHE-ERIC Higher Education Report. Jossey-Bass Higher and Adult Education Series.* Washington, DC: ERIC.

Miège, Bernard. 2008. "For a Communications Approach to the Use of ICT in Education." In *Convergence and Fragmentation: Media Technology and the Information Society*, edited by Peter Ludes, 117–130. Bristol, UK: Intellect Books.

Moore, Helen. 2012. "Passing on Faculty Roles, Cui Bono?" *Contexts* 11 (4):76–79. doi: 10.1177/1536504212466346.

Moore, Michael G. 1993. "Theory of Transactional Distance." In *Theoretical Principles of Distance Education*, edited by Desmond Keegan, 22. London, New York: Routledge.

Moore, Michael G., and William G. Anderson. 2003. *Handbook of Distance Education.* Mahwah, NJ: Lawrence Erlbaum Associates.

Moore, Michael G., and Greg Kearsley. 2011. *Distance Education: A Systems View of Online Learning.* Belmont, CA: Cengage Learning.

Moore, Michael G., and Greg Kearsley. 2012. *Distance Education: A Systems View of Online Learning.* Belmont, CA: Wadsworth Cengage Learning.

Narula, Uma. 2006. *Dynamics of Mass Communication Theory and Practice.* New Delhi: Atlantic Publishers & Distributors (P) Ltd.

Newcomb, Theodore M. 1966. "The General Nature of Peer Group Influence." In *College Peer Groups: Problems and Prospects for Research*, edited by Theodore M. Newcomb and Everett K. Wilson, 2–16. Chicago, IL: Aldine Publishing Company.

Nicolini, Davide. 2012. *Practice Theory, Work, and Organization: An Introduction.* Oxford, UK: Oxford University Press.

Niiniluoto, Ilkka. 1999. "Defending Abduction." *Philosophy of Science* 66 (3):S436.

Novak, Richard J. 2002. "Benchmarking Distance Education." *New Directions for Higher Education* (118):79–92. doi: 10.1002/he.57.

Nugent, Gwen C. 1982. "Pictures, Audio, and Print: Symbolic Representation and Effect on Learning." *Educational Communication and Technology* 30 (3):163–174. doi: 10.2307/30219835.

O'Connor, Kate. 2014. "MOOCs, Institutional Policy and Change Dynamics in Higher Education." *Higher Education* 68 (5):623–635. doi: 10.1007/s10734-014-9735-z.

Patton, Michael Quinn. 2015. *Qualitative Research & Evaluation Methods: Integrating Theory and Practice.* Vol. 4. Thousand Oaks, CA: Sage Publications, Inc.

Paulson, Karen. 2002. "Reconfiguring Faculty Roles for Virtual Settings." *The Journal of Higher Education* 73 (1):123–140. doi: 10.1353/jhe.2002.0010.

Pavlik, John Vernon. 2013. *Media in the Digital Age.* New York: Columbia University Press.

Peters, Otto. 1967; 1994. "Distance Education and Industrial Production: A Comparative Interpretation in Outline (1973)." www.c3l.uni-oldenburg.de/cde/found/peters67.htm

Peters, Otto. 1993. "Distance Education in a Postindustrial Society." In *Theoretical Principles of Distance Education*, edited by Desmond Keegan, 39–58. London, New York: Routledge.

Peters, Otto. 1998. *Learning and Teaching in Distance Education: Analyses and Interpretations from an International Perspective.* London: Kogan Page.

Peters, Otto. 2003. "Learning with New Media in Distance Education." In *Handbook of Distance Education*, edited by Michael G. Moore and William G. Anderson, 87–112. Mahwah, NJ: Lawrence Erlbaum Associates.

Picciano, Anthony G. 2002. "Beyond Student Perceptions: Issues of Interaction, Presence, and Performance in an Online Course." *Journal of Asynchronous Learning Networks* 6 (1):21–40.

Picciano, Anthony G. 2017. "Theories and Frameworks for Online Education: Seeking an Integrated Model." *Online Learning* 21 (3).

Powell, Richard J, and Clive Keen. 2006. "The Axiomatic Trap: Stultifying Myths in Distance Education." *Higher Education* 52 (2):283–301. doi: 10.1007/s10734-004-4501-2.

Pratt, Daniel D. 1998. *Five Perspectives on Teaching in Adult and Higher Education.* Malabar, FL: Krieger.

Qvortrup, Lars. 2008. "E-Learning—a Knowledge Theoretical Approach." In *Convergence and Fragmentation: Media Technology and the Information Society*, edited by Peter Ludes, 131–50. Bristol, UK: Intellect Books.

Rawolle, Shaun, and Bob Lingard. 2014. "Mediatization and Education: A Sociological Account." In *Mediatization of Communication*, edited by Knut Lundby, 595–614. Berlin, Boston: De Gruyter, Inc.

Rawolle, Shaun. 2010. "Understanding the mediatisation of educational policy as practice." *Critical Studies in Education*, 51 (1) 21–39.

Rayner, Philip, Peter Wall, and Stephen Kruger. 2004. *AS Media Studies: The Essential Introduction*. London: Routledge.

Reunanen, E. S. A., Risto Kunelius, and Elina Noppari. 2010. "Mediatization in Context: Consensus Culture, Media and Decision Making in the 21st Century, the Case of Finland." *Communications: The European Journal of Communication Research* 35 (3):287–307. doi: 10.1515/COMM.2010.016.

Richardson, Rudy, and Eric Hans Kramer. 2006. "Abduction as the Type of Inference that Characterizes the Development of a Grounded Theory." *Qualitative Research* 6 (4):497–513. doi: 10.1177/1468794106068019.

Rödder, Simone, and Mike S. Schäfer. 2010. "Repercussion and Resistance. An Empirical Study on the Interrelation Between Science and Mass Media." *Communications: The European Journal of Communication Research* 35 (3):249–267. doi: 10.1515/COMM.2010.014.

Rogers, Everett. 1995. *Diffusion of Innovation*. New York: The Free Press.

Rowland, Stephen, Catherine Byron, Frank Furedi, Nicky Padfield, and Terry Smyth. 1998. "Turning Academics into Teachers?" *Teaching in Higher Education* 3 (2):133–141. doi: 10.1080/1356215980030201.

Rudolph, Frederick. 1962. *The American College and University: A History*. Athens, Georgia: University of Georgia Press.

Rungtusanatham, Manus, Lisa M. Ellram, Sue P. Siferd, and Steven Salik. 2004. "Toward a Typology of Business Education in the Internet Age*." *Decision Sciences Journal of Innovative Education* 2 (2):101–120. doi: 10.1111/j.1540-4609.2004.00040.x.

Ryan, Bill. 1992. *Making Capital from Culture: The Corporate form of Capitalist Cultural Production*. Vol. 35. Berlin, Germany: Walter de Gruyter.

Salmon, Gilly. 2005. "Flying Not Flapping: A Strategic Framework for E-learning and Pedagogical Innovation in Higher Education Institutions." *Research in Learning Technology* 13 (3).

Sawyer, R. Keith. 2004. "Creative Teaching: Collaborative Discussion as Disciplined Improvisation." *Educational Researcher [H.W.Wilson—EDUC]* 33 (2):12.

Schatzki, Theodore R. 2001. "Introduction: Practice Theory." In *The Practice Turn in Contemporary Theory*, edited by Theodore R. Schatzki, Karin Knorr Cetina and Eike von Savigny. London, New York: Routledge.

Schatzki, Theodore R., Karin Knorr-Cetina, and Eike von Savigny. 2001. *The Practice Turn in Contemporary Theory*. Abingdon, Oxon: Routledge.

Schulte, Aileen. 2003. "Discussions in Cyberspace: Promoting Interactivity in an Asynchronous Sociology Course." *Innovative Higher Education* 28 (2):107–118. doi: 10.1023/B:IHIE.0000006286.31570.92.

Schulz, Winfried. 2004. "Reconstructing Mediatization as an Analytical Concept." *European Journal of Communication* 19 (1):87–101. doi: 10.1177/0267323104040696.

Scott, W. Richard. 2005. "Institutional Theory: Contributing to a Theoretical Research Program." In *Great Minds in Management: The Process of Theory*

Development, edited by Ken G. Smith and Michael A. Hitt, 460–484. Oxford, UK: Oxford University Press.

Scott, W. Richard. 2008. *Institutions and Organizations: Ideas and Interests.* Thousand Oaks, CA: Sage Publications, Inc.

Scott, W. Richard. 2010. "Higher Education in America: An Institutional Field Approach." *Reform and Innovation in the Changing Ecology of US Higher Education: Inaugural Strategy Session*, December:2–3.

Shenton, Andrew K. 2004. "Strategies for Ensuring Trustworthiness in Qualitative Research Projects." *Education for Information* 22 (2):63–75.

Shirky, Clay. 2012. "Napster, Udacity, and the Academy." www.shirky.com/weblog/2012/11/napster-udacity-and-the-academy/

Slaughter, Sheila, and Gary Rhoades. 2004. *Academic Capitalism and the New Economy: Markets, State, and Higher Education.* Baltimore, MD: The Johns Hopkins University Press.

Slaughter, Sheila, and Gary Rhoades. 2011. "Markets in Higher Education: Trends in Academic Capitalism." In *American Higher Education in the Twenty-First Century: Social, Political, and Economic Challenges*, edited by Philip G. Altbach, Patricia J. Gumport and Robert O. Berdahl. Baltimore, MD: The Johns Hopkins University Press.

Šlaus, Ivo, Winston P. Nagan, Garry Jacobs, Janani Harish, Souza Heitor Gurgulino de, and Alberto Zucconi. 2013. "Reflections on the Future of Global Higher Education—WAAS Conference Report." *Cadmus* 2:62–84.

Song, Liyan, Ernise S. Singleton, Janette R. Hill, and Myung Hwa Koh. 2004. "Improving Online Learning: Student Perceptions of Useful and Challenging Characteristics." *The Internet and Higher Education* 7 (1):59–70. doi: http://dx.doi.org/10.1016/j.iheduc.2003.11.003.

Strauss, Anselm, and Juliet Corbin. 1994. "Grounded Theory Methodology. An Overview." In *Handbook of Qualitative Research*, edited by Norman K. Denzin and Yvonna S. Lincoln. Thousand Oaks, CA: Sage Publications, Inc.

Strömbäck, Jesper. 2008. "Four Phases of Mediatization: An Analysis of the Mediatization of Politics." *The International Journal of Press/Politics* 13 (3):228–246.

Strömbäck, Jesper. 2011. "Mediatization of Politics." In *Sourcebook for Political Communication Research*, 367–382. London, New York: Routledge.

Strömbäck, Jesper, and Frank Esser. 2009. "Shaping Politics: Mediatization and Media Interventionism." In *Mediatization: Concepts, Changes, Consequences*, edited by Knut Lundby, 205–223. New York: Peter Lang.

Swail, Watson Scott, and Eva Kampits. 2001. "Distance Education and Accreditation." *New Directions for Higher Education* (113):35–48. doi: 10.1002/he.3.

Tabata, LynnN, and LindaK Johnsrud. 2008. "The Impact of Faculty Attitudes Toward Technology, Distance Education, and Innovation." *Research in Higher Education* 49 (7):625–646. doi: 10.1007/s11162-008-9094-7.

Tagg, Philip. 1982. "Analysing Popular Music: Theory, Method and Practice." *Popular Music* 2:37–67. doi: 10.2307/852975.

Thelin, John R. 2006. "Small by Design: Resilience in an Era of Mass Higher Education." Meeting the Challenge: America's Independent Colleges and Universities Since 1956.

Thelin, John R. 2013. *The Rising Costs of Higher Education: A Reference Handbook.* Santa Barbara, CA: ABC-CLIO.

Thompson, John B. 1995. *Media and Modernity: A Social Theory of the Media.* Stanford, CA: Stanford University Press.

Thornton, Patricia H. 2004. *Markets from Culture: Institutional Logics and Organizational Decisions in Higher Education Publishing.* Stanford, CA: Stanford University Press.

Thornton, Patricia H., and William Ocasio. 1999. "Institutional Logics and the Historical Contingency of Power in Organizations: Executive Succession in the Higher Education Publishing Industry, 1958-1990." *The American Journal of Sociology* 105 (3):801–843. doi: 10.1086/210361.

Thornton, Patricia H., and William Ocasio. 2008. "Institutional Logics." In *The Sage Handbook of Organizational Institutionalism,* edited by Royston Greenwood and Christine Oliver. 99–128. London: Sage Publications.

Thornton, Patricia H., William Ocasio, and Michael Lounsbury. 2012. *The Institutional Logics Perspective: A New Approach to Culture, Structure and Process.* Oxford, UK: Oxford University Press.

Throsby, C. D. 2001. *Economics and Culture.* Cambridge, UK, New York: Cambridge University Press.

Tinto, Vincent. 1987. *Leaving College: Rethinking the Causes and Cures of Student Attrition.* Chicago, IL: University of Chicago Press.

T'Kenye, C. 1998. "The Nurturing Perspective: Facilitating Self-Efficacy." *Five Perspectives on Teaching in Adult and Higher Education:*151–172.

Townley, Barbara. 1997. "The Institutional Logic of Performance Appraisal." *Organization Studies* 18 (2):261–285. doi: 10.1177/017084069701800204.

Trauth, Eileen M. 2001. "The Choice of Qualitative Methods in IS Research." *Qualitative Research in IS: Issues and Trends:*1–19.

Trauth, Eileen M., Jeria L. Quesenberry, and Haiyan Huang. 2009. "Retaining Women in the U.S. IT Workforce: Theorizing the Influence of Organizational Factors." *European Journal of Information Systems* 18 (5):476–497. doi: 10.1057/ejis.2009.31.

Tsai, Chin-Chung. 2000. "A Typology of the Use of Educational Media, with Implications for Internet-Based Instruction." *Educational Media International* 37 (3):157–160. doi: 10.1080/09523980050184718.

Tunstall, Jeremy. 1983. *The Media in Britain.* New York: Columbia University Press.

Twigg, Carol A. 2003. "Models for Online Learning." *Educause Review:*28–38.

Villegas-Reimers, Eleonora. 2003. *Teacher Professional Development: An International Review of the Literature.* Paris: International Institute for Educational Planning.

Walsh, James P. 1995. "Managerial and Organizational Cognition: Notes from a Trip Down Memory Lane." *Organization Science* 6 (3):280–321.

Wedemeyer, Charles A. 1981. *Learning at the Back Door Reflections on Nontraditional Learning in the Lifespan.* Madison, WI: University of Wisconsin.

Weick, Karl E. 1976. "Educational Organizations as Loosely Coupled Systems." *Administrative Science Quarterly:*1–19.

Wellman, Jane V. 2003a. "Accreditation and the Credit Hour." *New Directions for Higher Education* 2003 (122):57–69. doi: 10.1002/he.110.

Wellman, Jane V. 2003b. "Of Time and the Feds: The Federal Interest in Enforcing the Credit Hour." *New Directions for Higher Education* 2003 (122):71–81. doi: 10.1002/he.111.

Werry, Chris. 2002. "The Rhetoric of Commercial Online Education." *The Radical Teacher* (63):7–13. doi: 10.2307/20710136.

Williams, Raymond. 1981. *The Sociology of Culture*. Chicago, IL: University of Chicago Press.

Williams, Raymond. 1991. "Base and Superstructure in Marxist Cultural Theory." *Rethinking Popular Culture: Contemporary Perspectives in Cultural Studies* 407:423.

Williams, Robin. 1996. "The Social Shaping of Technology." *Research policy* 25 (6):865–899. doi: 10.1016/0048-7333(96)00885-2.

Willinsky, J., G. Fischman, and A. S. Metcalfe. 2011. *The Digital Technologies of Learning and Research, American Higher Education in the Twenty-First Century: Social, Political, and Economic Challenges*. 3rd ed. Baltimore, MD: The Johns Hopkins University Press.

Wisher, Robert A., and Christina K. Curnow. 2003. "Video-based Instruction in Distance Learning: From Motion Pictures to the Internet." In *Handbook of Distance Education*, edited by Michael G. Moore and William G. Anderson, 315–330. Mahwah, NJ: Lawrence Erlbaum Associates

Witkin, H. A., C. A. Moore, D. R. Goodenough, and P. W. Cox. 1977. "Field-Dependent and Field-Independent Cognitive Styles and Their Educational Implications." *Review of Educational Research* 47 (1):1–64. doi: 10.2307/1169967.

Wurtzler, Steve. 1992. "She Sang Live, but the Microphone Was Turned Off: The Live, the Recorded, and the Subject of Representation." In *Sound Theory Sound Practice*, 87–103. New York, NY: Routledge

Yin, Robert K. 2009. "Designing Case Studies." In *Case Study Research: Design and Methods*. Thousand Oaks, CA: Sage Publications, Inc.

Zawacki-Richter, Olaf, Eva Maria Bäcker, and Sebastian Vogt. 2009. "Review of Distance Education Research (2000 to 2008): Analysis of Research Areas, Methods, and Authorship Patterns." *The International Review of Research in Open and Distance Learning* 10 (6):21–50.

Zemsky, Robert, Gregory R. Wegner, and William F. Massy. 2005. *Remaking the American University: Market-smart and Mission-centered*. Piscataway, NJ: Rutgers University Press.

Index

Note: page numbers in *italics* and **bold** denote references to Figures and Tables, respectively.